Trauma-Informed Restorative Dialogues

This book combines trauma-informed practice with restorative justice to explore how restorative dialogues can support those affected by trauma. Trauma-informed practice involves understanding the impact of trauma and creating an environment that is sensitive to its effects, which is essential for fostering meaningful dialogue between victims and offenders. Conversely, restorative justice focuses on addressing harm through inclusive processes involving victims, offenders and the community, and aims to respond to the needs of all parties affected by the harm.

By integrating these perspectives, the book illustrates how trauma-informed restorative dialogues – an approach that expands access to restorative justice when direct encounters between victims and offenders are not possible – can improve access to justice, promote recovery and facilitate transformation. It provides practical guidance based on insights from victims and facilitators in five European countries and offenders in Swiss prisons, and addresses secondary trauma among practitioners, offering strategies for their self-care and organisational care.

Aimed at practitioners, academics, policy makers and service providers, this in-depth research fills a gap in the restorative justice literature by demonstrating how trauma-informed principles can strengthen communities and support those affected by serious harm.

Claudia Christen-Schneider is a criminologist and restorative justice practitioner, president of the Swiss RJ Forum and board member of the EFRJ. She leads restorative justice projects in Swiss prisons and is a guest lecturer at the Swiss Competence Centre in Corrections and some universities.

Contemporary Issues in Restorative Practice

Contemporary Issues in Restorative Practice explores the processes and techniques used to resolve and/or prevent crime and conflict using restorative principles. Each book in the series addresses a theme within a specific setting and contains a range of pedagogical features on 'how to' achieve effective practice. Whilst incorporating a wide range of real-life examples, authors will also ground practice within the established conceptual and theoretical literature and, where appropriate, develop this further. In this way, the series will support both academic and professional development through a synthesis of experiential and evidential knowledge.

The series will appeal to practitioners, researchers, scholars, and organisations with an interest in restorative justice and restorative practices.

Setting Relations Right in Restorative Practice
Broadening Mindsets and Skill-sets
David B. Moore and Alikki Vernon

Trauma-Informed Restorative Dialogues
The Power of Community
Claudia Christen-Schneider

"*Trauma-Informed Restorative Dialogues* offers an excellent basis to understand the deep dynamics and power when a small group of people meet to share their plural narratives on harm and suffering. Claudia Christen-Schneider has been able to explore in a remarkable way the lived experience of all involved, combining theoretical insights, research and practice. A safe and sustainable guide for all who want to enrich the field of restorative justice through transformative encounters of victims and offenders of unrelated crimes."

Ivo Aertsen, Emeritus Professor of Criminology at KU Leuven, Co-Editor of the *International Journal of Restorative Justice* and General Co-Editor of *The International Encyclopaedia of Restorative Justice*

"*Trauma-Informed Restorative Dialogues* is a book that beautifully blends theory and practice, something that few books achieve. It is also innovative in that it approaches a restorative practice that has been poorly described in the literature from a particular angle, shedding light on the foundations of restorative justice."

Daniela Bolívar, Associate Professor, Pontificia Universidad Católica de Chile

"This book on the relatively unexamined process of restorative dialogues will, indeed, contribute to increasing the access of victims and perpetrators of harm to safe and healing spaces in which they can address what needs to be restored in their lives. Claudia Christen-Schneider presents a clear explanation of a complex restorative practice model which integrates contextualisation, the pluralistic nature of narratives, and trauma-informed practice. Combining theory, her own practice experience and the narratives of practitioners and participants of restorative justice, her style of writing is accessible and very useful to practitioners, students and scholars. She elevates restorative dialogues from a pragmatic, second best alternative to face-to-face meetings to a process which stands as a valuable process in its own right."

Tim Chapman, Visiting Professor at the University of Strathclyde

"Claudia Christen-Schneider's book *Trauma-Informed Restorative Dialogues* offers a clear and comprehensive analysis of the conceptual foundation and practical dimensions of this form of restorative justice. The widespread potential of restorative dialogues to fill unmet needs for victims and offenders makes this work a welcome resource for practitioners."

Kay Pranis, Author, Trainer, Peacemaking Circles and Restorative Justice

Trauma-Informed Restorative Dialogues

The Power of Community

Claudia Christen-Schneider

Routledge
Taylor & Francis Group
LONDON AND NEW YORK

Designed cover image: © Shutterstock

First published 2025
by Routledge
4 Park Square, Milton Park, Abingdon, Oxon OX14 4RN

and by Routledge
605 Third Avenue, New York, NY 10158

Routledge is an imprint of the Taylor & Francis Group, an informa business

British Library Cataloguing-in-Publication Data
A catalogue record for this book is available from the British Library

Library of Congress Cataloging-in-Publication Data
Names: Christen-Schneider, Claudia, author.
Title: Trauma-informed restorative dialogues : the power of community / Claudia Christen-Schneider.
Description: Abingdon, Oxon ; New York, NY : Routledge, 2025. |
Series: Contemporary issues in restorative practice | Includes bibliographical references and index.
Identifiers: LCCN 2024045403 (print) | LCCN 2024045404 (ebook) |
ISBN 9781032222165 (hardback) | ISBN 9781032222134 (paperback) |
ISBN 9781003271611 (ebook)
Subjects: LCSH: Restorative justice.
Classification: LCC HV8688 .C527 2025 (print) | LCC HV8688 (ebook) |
DDC 364.6/8–dc23/eng/20250130
LC record available at https://lccn.loc.gov/2024045403
LC ebook record available at https://lccn.loc.gov/2024045404

ISBN: 978-1-032-22216-5 (hbk)
ISBN: 978-1-032-22213-4 (pbk)
ISBN: 978-1-003-27161-1 (ebk)

DOI: 10.4324/9781003271611

Typeset in Sabon
by Taylor & Francis Books

Contents

Illustrations

Figures

Tables

Case studies

Acknowledgements

I would like to express my deepest gratitude to everyone who has supported me in the writing of this book.

To my beloved family – my husband Ralph and our sons Noë and Yosia – thank you for your endless patience, care and understanding. Your unwavering support and encouragement at moments when I felt overwhelmed made all the difference. I am deeply grateful for your presence by my side every step of the way.

To my dear friend Megan Thomas, whose faithful companionship and encouragement have been a constant source of strength. Our weekly writing retreats have been a lifeline; I truly don't know what I would have done without you. Thank you for lifting me up when I was down and celebrating every milestone with me.

To my dear friends and fellow board members of the Swiss RJ Forum, Aurélie Stoll and Claudia Campistol, your friendship and support have meant the world to me. Thank you for believing in me and for the many encouragements and valuable tips you have given me along the way.

To my incredible colleagues and friends from the Swiss RJ Forum – Mina Rauschenbach, for your invaluable insights and support; Valérie Kernen, Janique Porchet, Karine Richard, Werner Burkhard, Kenny Chengalaran, Bruno Graber, Marco Mona, and all those who have co-facilitated and shaped the Swiss programme over the years – thank you for your dedication, creativity and collaboration.

To all our participants, including former 'victims' and 'offenders', thank you for your invaluable input and ideas that have helped us to adapt and improve the programme. I have learned so much from each and every one of you, and your courage and willingness to engage has been truly inspiring.

To all the interviewees who have contributed so much to this book with their experiences, insights and recommendations – thank you for sharing your stories and expertise. Your contributions have been invaluable in shaping this work.

To the heads of correctional services, prison directors and prison staff who have supported us over the years, thank you for making it possible to implement restorative dialogues in Switzerland. Your commitment to this work was essential.

To my EFRJ family, especially the staff and fellow board members, thank you for your friendship, encouragement and unwavering support over the past two years.

Last but not least, to Kerry Clamp, whose prompt inspired this book in the first place – thank you for believing in me and for your valuable input and support. Without you, this book would not exist.

With heartfelt thanks,

Claudia Christen-Schneider

1 Laying the foundations

Introduction

The room is silent, except for the sound of a single voice. A group of 12 people sit in a circle, listening intently as Nita recounts the moment she found out her parents had been killed and the profound effect it had on her life. She speaks without interruption for 45 minutes, and the silence is so deep you could hear a pin drop. Many in the room have tears in their eyes. Although this is only their fourth meeting, the respect and empathy among the group is palpable.

This is the essence of restorative dialogues – a practice in which victims and offenders of serious crime come together, often in prisons, to share their stories, work through their emotions and pain, and support each other in their paths of recovery. In these dialogues, they are not on opposing sides, as one might expect, but have begun to form a supportive community where labels fade and they meet eye to eye, person to person.

Unlike other restorative justice practices, restorative dialogues uniquely bring together people who are not directly connected by a single offence, with the aim of fostering mutually beneficial conversations. This book explores this distinctive approach and shows how these dialogues create a space for shared understanding, healing and support among participants.

This introductory chapter sets the scene for the rest of the book by contextualising the approach and distinguishing it from other restorative justice practices. It introduces the framework of trauma-informed practice and prepares the reader for the detailed exploration that follows. The chapter concludes with an overview of the structure of the book, providing a roadmap for the chapters that follow. These include practical strategies for implementing restorative dialogues, insights into the experiences of participants and experts, and considerations for the well-being of facilitators.

Before delving deeper into the topic, it is important to clarify what is meant by 'restorative dialogues'. Understanding this term will help to frame the discussions and applications that follow.

DOI: 10.4324/9781003271611-1

What is the meaning behind the term 'restorative dialogues'?

I first used the term 'restorative dialogues' in Switzerland while implementing this approach in which victims and offenders,[1] who do not know each other and are not connected by a direct offence, meet to share their experiences and listen to each other. I chose this term because it effectively captures the essence of these group discussions, focusing on the concepts of both 'dialogue' and 'restoration'. The term 'dialogue' comes from the Greek word '*dialogos*'. '*Dia*' means 'through' and '*logos*' means 'word' or 'conversation'. Therefore, a dialogue is a process that occurs through conversation between multiple parties. In contrast to debates and discussions, which are confrontational in nature, dialogue focuses on empathy and understanding.[2] As Patricia Romney eloquently explains:[3]

> Dialogue is focused conversation, engaged in intentionally with the goal of increasing understanding, addressing problems, and questioning thoughts or actions. It engages the heart as well as the mind. It is different from ordinary, everyday conversation, in that dialogue has a focus and a purpose. Dialogue is different from debate, which offers two points of view with the goal of proving the legitimacy or correctness of one of the viewpoints over the other. Dialogue, unlike debate or even discussion, is as interested in the relationship(s) between the participants as it is in the topic or theme being explored. Ultimately, real dialogue presupposes an openness to modify deeply held convictions.

This description highlights the purpose and aims of restorative dialogues:

1 *Clear focus and purpose*: Restorative dialogues focus on addressing the harm and consequences of crime in the lives of those present. They aim to promote empathy and understanding between participating victims and offenders and to encourage a deep exploration of participants' thoughts and actions. Through this process, participants gain insight and understanding of each other's perspectives and experiences.
2 *Engagement of both mind and heart*: Restorative dialogues engage not only the intellect but also emotions, facilitating a more profound connection and empathy between participants.
3 *Openness*: Effective restorative dialogues require participants to be open to modifying their deeply held convictions, which is crucial for having meaningful conversations.

The concept of 'restoration' in restorative dialogues has its roots in the late fourteenth century, when it was defined as "a means of healing or restoring health; renewing something that has been lost".[4] This original meaning is relevant to the aims of restorative dialogues, as they play a crucial role in promoting healing and recovery, particularly in helping both victims and offenders deal with the complex emotions and losses that follow a crime.

Victims may lose their sense of safety and, on occasion, even their sense of self-worth or dignity. They may blame themselves for what happened or feel blemished or unworthy after the crime. Victims may also lose their connection with others, feeling misunderstood or even blamed.[5] Similarly, offenders may lose their sense of self-worth and dignity, and experience profound shame and guilt for their actions. They may lose social connections and respect within their communities, leading to stigma and isolation. In addition, offenders may lose their freedom through incarceration or social rejection, reinforcing their loss of a positive self-identity.[6]

Restorative dialogues cannot completely 'restore' all harms and losses experienced by participants, but they create a path for dialogue that can address some of these issues in a healing way. Thus, restorative dialogues aim to foster deep conversations that promote understanding, connection, and healing or transformation.

While restorative dialogues cannot fully undo the harm or loss experienced by participants, they do provide an opportunity for meaningful conversations that promote healing. As Peter Block notes, the essence of restoration lies in the quality of our interactions,[7] which in this context means fostering understanding and transformation through dialogue.

Having established the meaning behind the term 'restorative dialogues', it is time to explore the aims of this book and understand the methodology that underpins it.

Aims of this book and methodology used

What this book aims for

Recognising the potential of restorative dialogues to facilitate meaningful change, this book aims to provide an in-depth understanding of this restorative approach by sharing insights from victims, offenders, experts and extensive field experience. Each chapter, with the exception of Chapter 7, provides theoretical insights, considers the experiences and needs of participants, examines the impact of offending, and offers suggestions for safe and effective facilitation. Chapter 7 is different in that it looks at the impact of facilitating restorative dialogues on practitioners, thus shifting the focus away from the participants involved in the process.

As the title suggests, this book is particularly concerned with the trauma-informed implementation of restorative dialogues. The emphasis on a trauma-informed approach has developed through years of experience in Switzerland working with victims and offenders of serious harm. It became clear early on, through observation and feedback from both victims and practitioners, that those struggling with the aftermath of traumatic experiences needed a trauma-informed approach to support their recovery. Victims often exhibited symptoms such as heightened anxiety, distrust or even emotional numbness, which needed to be addressed appropriately. However, listening to the stories of offenders, it also became clear that many had experienced significant trauma themselves, often stemming from complex childhood trauma. Recognising this dual need underlined the importance of a trauma-informed approach for both victims and offenders.

However, trauma-informed practice does not only consider the safety of clients but also that of professionals. This is also a crucial element in the implementation of restorative dialogues, as facilitators are constantly exposed to the sometimes very traumatic accounts of participants, creating a risk for the development of secondary trauma, which will be addressed in Chapter 7. It is therefore essential that the implementation of restorative dialogue programmes considers not only the well-being and safety of participants but also that of facilitators.

For this reason, this book aims to demonstrate how restorative dialogues can be implemented from a trauma-informed perspective to create a safe and supportive space for all participants, including facilitators. In doing so, the book seeks to address a gap in the current literature. There is presently little literature on the need for a trauma-informed approach to restorative justice, and even less on how it can be applied in practice. This book aims to fill this gap by providing both theoretical insights and practical examples, specifically through the lens of restorative dialogues.

The book also seeks to fill a second gap in the literature. While there are studies of specific programmes – such as research on Prison Fellowship International's Sycamore Tree Project®[8] and annual reports such as the *Enquête nationale sur la justice restaurative* published by the French Institute for Restorative Justice (IFJR)[9] – there is a noticeable lack of comprehensive publications that examine restorative dialogues in depth. Most of the existing literature tends to focus on individual programmes or outcomes without thoroughly examining the broader dynamics, functioning and wider implications of the approach.

This book aims to address this shortcoming by providing a detailed analysis that not only focuses on the implementation of restorative dialogues in Switzerland but also provides an overview of different implementations across Europe. By including the perspectives of victims, offenders and experts from different programmes, the book broadens the understanding of restorative dialogues. These diverse voices help to shed light on the complexities and nuances of the approach. The methods used to gather these insights are detailed in the following section.

Methodology and use of real-life case studies

To complement the theoretical insights and provide a comprehensive practical perspective, this book includes real-life case studies in each chapter. These case studies, based on actual experiences, provide tangible examples of the significance and impact of restorative dialogues on participants. They serve to deepen the reader's understanding of the processes and outcomes of these dialogues by presenting authentic accounts from victims, offenders and facilitators, and demonstrate the transformative power of these conversations in addressing trauma and the complexities of the aftermath of crime. In addition, direct quotations are included throughout the book. These insights were gathered while conducting semi-structured interviews with nine victims and nine facilitators from five European countries.

Interviews with victims

The semi-structured interviews with victims were conducted between November 2023 and January 2024, using a trauma-informed approach to ensure the ethical and sensitive treatment of participants' experiences. This approach goes beyond standard ethical research practice by ensuring that researchers understand trauma and involve participants in planning and decision-making. Specific measures included allowing participants to choose the format of their interviews, avoiding pressure to recall painful memories, and having protocols in place to address any trauma that might emerge during the interviews.[10]

Semi-structured interviews are a qualitative research method that involves a dynamic dialogue between the researcher and the participants. Some questions are pre-determined, but can be adapted and expanded to explore specific topics in depth.[11] This method allows for the collection of open-ended data, delving deeply into personal and sometimes sensitive issues.[12]

The primary purpose of these interviews was to understand the needs of victims within their communities, their motivations for participating in restorative group processes, and how these processes could support their trauma recovery. The interview guide was developed with input from victims who had previously participated in restorative dialogues to ensure that the questions were respectful, meaningful and trauma-informed. Potential interviewees were identified through colleagues involved in restorative dialogues across Europe. Detailed information about the study was provided to all participants, emphasising voluntary participation, anonymity, confidentiality and the sensitivity of the issues discussed. Participants signed informed consent forms prior to the interviews, and support was offered during or after the sessions if needed. To build trust and ensure comfort, each interview began with an informal discussion. All interviews were audio-recorded with consent, transcribed and checked for accuracy by the participants

Interviews with facilitators

The semi-structured interviews with facilitators experienced in running restorative dialogues were conducted between December 2023 and January 2024. Before agreeing to take part, they received detailed information about the study, emphasising the voluntary nature of participation, anonymity and confidentiality of the data provided. The purpose of these interviews was to explore the facilitators' experiences in developing and implementing restorative dialogues, including the techniques and approaches they find effective when working with trauma survivors, the challenges they face during the programmes, and how they address these. The issues they raised are addressed throughout the book, with their insights and direct quotes woven into the narrative to enrich the reader's understanding of the complexities involved in restorative dialogues.

Content analysis

The data collected from both sets of interviews – those with victims and those with facilitators – were systematically analysed using content analysis.[13] This method involved applying descriptive codes to the transcribed interviews to identify patterns and themes. These themes were then categorised into major themes, which are reflected in the findings presented in this book. Direct quotations were selected to highlight the participants' insights and experiences, particularly in Chapters 2 to 6, and to add depth and authenticity to the discussion.

Additional data sources

Offenders' experiences were collected through anonymous evaluation forms and feedback from group evaluations conducted by the Swiss RJ Forum between 2017 and 2024. These insights are also reflected in Chapters 2 to 6, contributing to a comprehensive understanding of restorative dialogues from multiple perspectives.

As such, the book is grounded in the lived experiences of victims and offenders, as well as the expert insights of facilitators from across Europe, ensuring that their voices are authentically represented through direct quotes and real-life case studies.

In addition to the methodology used, understanding how restorative justice is conceptualised in this book and how restorative dialogues fit into the wider practice of restorative justice is another crucial aspect of understanding the overall approach of this work.

Situating restorative dialogues within the wider field of restorative justice

How restorative justice is understood in this book

This book adopts a broad understanding of restorative justice as a philosophy that aims to involve those affected by crime in a voluntary, needs-based and flexible process. Central to the process is a dialogue that seeks to address and work through the harm suffered and caused, and to find meaningful ways to redress that harm.

The process aims to promote healing and restoration for victims, accountability and transformation for offenders, and encourages the active participation of all involved. Crucial to this process are trained practitioners who can adapt the process to the nature and seriousness of the offence, the backgrounds of the participants, and the specific legal and social framework within which the process takes place.

Key aspects to this view of restorative justice practice include:

Aims: The primary aim of any restorative process is to create a safe space for dialogue where all parties can openly share their experiences, feelings and the impact of the offence. This space should encourage genuine communication and allow participants to express themselves without fear. Parties must be free to explore and identify ways of dealing with the consequences of the offence that are meaningful to them. The process should empower them to make choices based on their personal experiences and needs, and promote healing, restoration, accountability and transformation.[14]

Stakeholders: Restorative processes should involve those directly affected by the offence, including victims and offenders, as well as others who may be affected, such as family members, close friends or other supporters. The aim is to identify who can benefit from the restorative process and how they can be meaningfully involved. While those directly affected are at the centre of the process, it may be beneficial for them to be accompanied by their circle of support. People close to the victim and offender may also be deeply affected by the crime and may need a safe space to process their experiences and the impact on their lives. In addition, the community of care surrounding both parties can also play a crucial role in supporting those directly affected in their journey of recovery and transformation, and in fostering mutual understanding.[15]

Process: All restorative justice processes must be voluntary, as affirmed in many official documents, such as the *UNODC Handbook on Restorative Justice Programmes* and the Council of Europe Recommendation on Restorative Justice in Criminal Matters.[16] If a restorative process is not voluntary, it risks doing more harm than good. If a victim is confronted with an offender who does not acknowledge the harm or even blames the victim, the process cannot be restorative. There are also victims who do not want to participate in such a process, and they should never be forced to do so. Voluntariness must therefore be a core value.[17]

Flexibility is essential, allowing for tailored approaches that take into account the unique circumstances and challenges of each case.[18] Meetings may take place face to face, via videoconferencing, or through facilitators where direct interaction is unsafe or inappropriate. By emphasising a needs-based approach, restorative justice can better balance support for both victims and offenders, countering the tendency of the criminal justice system to focus primarily on offenders.

Facilitators: Trained facilitators play a crucial role in ensuring the safety and effectiveness of restorative processes. They need to have a sound knowledge of the philosophy, values and standards of restorative justice. Regardless of whether they are professional or volunteer facilitators, they should have training in a range of restorative practices to adapt the process to the specific context and needs of participants.[19] This training must include a thorough understanding of trauma and its impact, as well as cultural competence to conduct restorative processes respectfully and inclusively. In addition, facilitators need specialised training in dealing with different types of harm, particularly in sensitive cases such as gender-based violence, hate crimes, homicide or politically motivated harm.[20] Comprehensive training enables facilitators to deal with the complexity and emotional intensity of these cases and to ensure that all parties feel heard, respected and safe.

Situating restorative dialogues within the broader framework of restorative justice

Restorative justice processes typically bring together the victims and offenders directly involved. However, this is not always possible, and yet, the Council of Europe states that restorative justice should be a generally available service.[21] While direct meetings between related victims and offenders have been the most implemented form of restorative processes in recent decades, it is also true that such meetings are only possible if both parties agree and have been identified. There are many crimes where neither the victim nor the offender is known, so even considering only these two constraints, it becomes evident that there may be a large percentage of individuals affected by crime who would be interested in a restorative process but are unable to participate if the other party is unwilling or unidentified. Other reasons may increase the difficulty of such a meeting, as discussed in Chapter 2.

This means that although the service may be generally available, it may not be accessible to all who are interested. Broadening access to restorative justice, therefore, requires an even wider range of approaches to serve those who cannot engage in direct dialogue with their counterpart. One effective option is found in restorative dialogues, which provide an alternative by facilitating interactions between victims and offenders who are not directly related. This approach increases access to restorative justice by providing a meaningful process for individuals who are unable to participate in encounters with their direct counterpart. In a supportive environment, participants can still address their needs and experiences, promoting healing and transformation. However, the successful implementation of this approach requires careful planning and consideration.

Considerations for the implementation of restorative dialogues

As restorative dialogues become an alternative to direct victim–offender interaction, particularly in cases of serious harm, their implementation must be approached with careful consideration to ensure the safety of these processes for all involved.

To successfully implement restorative dialogues, several key considerations need to be addressed:

- *Victim-centred approach*: It is essential that the process is centred on the needs and experiences of victims.[22] This approach ensures that victims' voices are heard and their needs are addressed in a safe and supportive environment. The dialogue should empower victims to express their experiences and needs without fear of retribution or re-traumatisation.

- *Balanced sensitivity*: While prioritising the needs of victims is critical, it is also important to remain sensitive to the needs and circumstances of offenders. A balanced approach ensures that the restorative process does not inadvertently neglect or stigmatise offenders. By addressing the needs of both parties, restorative dialogues can foster a more just and inclusive process of healing and transformation.
- *Facilitator expertise*: The success of restorative dialogues depends heavily on the skills and expertise of the facilitators. Facilitators should be able to manage complex emotional dynamics and ensure that the process remains constructive and respectful. Their ability to create a safe and neutral space for dialogue is fundamental to achieving meaningful outcomes.
- *Contextual adaptation*: Each restorative dialogue process should be adapted to the specific legal, social and cultural context in which it takes place. This includes understanding the unique circumstances of the participants and the nature of the harm. Flexibility and adaptability in the implementation process will help to meet diverse needs and promote effective outcomes.
- *Trauma-informed practices*: Given the potential for ongoing trauma, it is essential that restorative dialogues incorporate a trauma-informed perspective. Facilitators should be trained to recognise and respond to the impact of trauma on all of the participants, creating an environment that respects their emotional well-being and minimises the risk of further harm. This approach helps to ensure that the dialogue process is both supportive and sensitive to the complexities of trauma.

By addressing these considerations, restorative dialogues can effectively serve individuals who are unable to participate in direct encounters, ensuring that restorative justice remains accessible and effective for a wider range of participants. Due to the pervasiveness of trauma and its impact on participants, the next section explores the prevalence of trauma and how trauma-informed approaches are integral to the success of restorative dialogues.

The pervasiveness of trauma and its intersection with restorative justice

Understanding trauma is crucial in the context of restorative justice as it affects many of those who use these services.[23] Trauma can affect anyone, regardless of age, culture, religion, socio-economic status or sexual orientation. Its prevalence has made it a public health concern, often referred to as the world's largest invisible epidemic.[24] According to the World Health Organization, 70% of the world's population will experience at least one traumatic event in their lifetime, and 30.5% will be exposed to four or more such events.[25]

Trauma can have long-lasting effects on individuals, changing the way they perceive themselves, others and the world. It can also affect family members, communities and service providers who have not experienced trauma directly, but who have witnessed trauma or support those who have.[26] Not only individuals but also entire communities can suffer from trauma. This can be the result of a variety of factors, including experiences of oppression, discrimination, poverty, war and genocide of racial, cultural and ethnic groups.[27]

Interpersonal trauma is considered to be the type of trauma most likely to cause profound and lasting traumatic effects.[28] Many individuals seeking restorative justice services have experienced interpersonal violence, meaning that practitioners often work with clients who have experienced trauma. However, practitioners may lack specialist training to deal effectively with these issues, which can raise concerns among victim services and advocates about the provision of adequate protection and support for trauma survivors.

This is why a trauma-informed approach to restorative justice is essential. It helps practitioners respond to the specific needs of trauma survivors and create a safe and empowering environment, without requiring expertise in trauma therapy. Such an approach ensures that restorative justice can truly serve as a healing and supportive process for those affected by trauma. Before exploring in more detail why restorative justice needs to be trauma-informed, it is necessary to clarify what the term 'trauma-informed practice' refers to.

What is trauma-informed practice?

Trauma-informed practice is a comprehensive framework that recognises the pervasive impact of trauma on an individual's neurobiological, biological, psychosocial and social development and well-being. Furthermore, it considers how trauma affects a person's worldview and relationships.[29] Originally proposed by Harris and Fallot in response to the growing recognition of trauma in public service delivery, this framework prioritises trauma-sensitive service delivery and emphasises the need for collaborative relationships between service providers and its recipients.[30] Thus, the aim is to involve clients as much as possible in the provision of services and to empower them to have their voices heard and to have a say in what they need and how they need it. Empowerment is therefore a key aspect of trauma-informed practice.[31]

The primary aim of trauma-informed practice is to equip service providers, such as restorative justice facilitators, with trauma-specific knowledge and skills. This enables them to tailor their services sensitively to the needs of trauma survivors, thereby increasing the safety and effectiveness of restorative processes. Central to this approach is the prevention of re-traumatisation, which occurs when inadvertent reminders of trauma reignite feelings of powerlessness and helplessness.[32]

Trauma-informed practice is underpinned by the '5 R's', as illustrated in Figure 1.1.[33]

Figure 1.1 The 5 R's of trauma-informed practice

Expert organisations such as SAMHSA, the Scottish Government and NHS Education for Scotland explain the 5 R's as follows:[34]

- *Realise the pervasiveness of trauma and its widespread impact, understand potential paths for recovery*: Recognise that trauma is common and can affect people from different backgrounds and that recovery from trauma is possible and may involve different pathways such as therapy, support groups and self-care practices. It is also important to understand that trauma manifests itself differently in each individual and that each person's recovery journey is unique.
- *Recognise the signs and symptoms of trauma in individuals*: Identify common signs and symptoms of trauma, which can include hypervigilance, avoidance behaviour, flashbacks and mood swings. By recognising these subtle signs of trauma, professionals can better support and respond to the needs of trauma survivors with sensitivity and empathy, understanding that their behaviours may be coping mechanisms for past trauma.
- *Respond to the effects of trauma by fully integrating knowledge about trauma into policies, procedures, practices and settings*: Integrate trauma-informed approaches into all aspects of service delivery, including organisational policies, procedural guidelines, daily practices and the physical environment. This will ensure that interactions and environments are sensitive to and supportive of the needs of trauma survivors.
- *Resist re-traumatisation proactively*: Take proactive measures to avoid inadvertently triggering or re-traumatising people who have experienced trauma. This can be achieved by creating a safe and predictable environment, using trauma-sensitive language, and respecting survivors' boundaries and autonomy.
- *Recognise the essential role of relationships in recovery from trauma*: Emphasise the importance of building trusting and supportive relationships with trauma survivors. Such relationships serve as a foundation for healing and resilience, providing individuals with the safety and support they need on their journey to recovery.

Trauma-informed practice does not require becoming a trauma specialist, but involves understanding the pervasive effects of trauma and using this knowledge to protect individuals from further harm and re-traumatisation. It also aims to promote safe and supportive relationships. Thus, trauma-informed practice is about understanding how each professional can contribute to facilitating both individual and collective healing from trauma.[35] It is a person-centred and strengths-based approach that aims to address the emotional impact of traumatic events by empowering survivors to regain control over their lives.[36]

Guided by six core principles – safety, trust, choice, collaboration, empowerment and cultural humility – trauma-informed practice is both proactive and reactive.[37] It anticipates and addresses trauma-related needs before they manifest, ensuring that services are sensitive to survivors' experiences.

Furthermore, a trauma-informed approach prioritises the individual's strengths and avoids focusing on the person's supposed 'weaknesses'. Instead, it emphasises the creation of quality relationships between facilitators and the individual, focuses on recognising and identifying the person's personal resources, and aims to support and empower them to use these resources.[38] Central to this approach is the recognition that during a traumatic event individuals may feel a profound lack of control, agency, voice and power, leaving them vulnerable.[39] The six principles of trauma-informed practice are therefore specifically designed to counteract such feelings and give the person back a sense of agency and control over their lives.

Furthermore, a trauma-informed approach recognises that trauma can manifest itself in behaviours that may be perplexing to others. These behaviours are often consequences of the traumatic experience. As a result, there is a paradigm shift in how individuals are perceived. The focus shifts from 'what is wrong with a person' to 'what has happened to them', recognising the profound influence of trauma on perceptions and behaviours.[40]

Trauma-informed practice is therefore not a specific therapeutic technique but rather a framework that emphasises the importance of building quality relationships. This is underlined by research that highlights the central role of safe and supportive relationships in trauma recovery and building resilience.[41] As will be seen in Chapter 3, research participants too have reiterated the importance of safe relationships in which they feel heard and taken seriously. Therefore, the quality of relationships that trauma survivors have with others, including in restorative justice settings, is crucial and can serve as a cornerstone in their journey of recovery from trauma. Restorative justice facilitators therefore have an important role to play in fostering such supportive relationships by engaging with clients and colleagues in a compassionate and understanding way – as colleagues may also be affected by trauma and will benefit from a trauma-informed approach. Despite this understanding, the question may still arise: why should restorative justice be trauma-informed? This question needs to be explored further.

Why should restorative justice be trauma-informed?

A common question I have been asked is whether restorative justice is not inherently trauma-informed. The answer becomes evident when considering the key goals of trauma-informed practice, which require service providers to *be knowledgeable about trauma*, to *recognise its signs*, to *understand the impact* of trauma on survivors, and to *adapt services* in ways that support recovery and resilience.[42] These goals cannot be achieved without specific trauma education and training. Thus, to be truly trauma-informed, restorative justice must be underpinned by a conscious commitment to understanding and addressing trauma.

Restorative justice therefore should be trauma-informed for a number of reasons. Firstly, while restorative justice aims to create safe spaces for all participants, trauma and trauma-informed practices are not typically included as core topics in restorative justice training. This lack of focus on trauma risks inadvertently re-traumatising people who have experienced trauma. To ensure the creation of safe spaces, restorative justice facilitators need to understand the profound impact of trauma and how to effectively support trauma survivors.[43]

Secondly, as the field of restorative justice expands to encompass all types of crime, including the most serious offences, an increasing number of people who have experienced trauma are accessing these services. This includes not only victims but also family members, supporters and even offenders themselves, as anyone can be affected by trauma. Therefore, facilitators need to be trained to work in a trauma-informed manner in order to prevent further harm to all participants involved in a restorative justice process.[44]

Thirdly, a trauma-informed approach offers significant benefits for all participants by fostering a safe and trusting environment, which is crucial for effective restorative justice processes. By adopting a trauma-informed approach, restorative justice services can better understand and respond to the needs of those affected by trauma while creating a safe and healthy environment for all involved, including clients and practitioners. Given the emotionally demanding nature of restorative justice work, it is also crucial to prioritise the holistic well-being of practitioners. They are constantly exposed to traumatic material, which may also have a negative impact on them. Caring for practitioners in this way not only promotes their well-being but also the safe and professional delivery of services. After all, to deliver safe and efficient services, staff need to feel at their best.

While restorative justice and trauma-informed practices are distinct approaches, they are compatible and complementary. Both seek to create safe environments that facilitate the recovery from harm and foster trust. This safe and trusting environment is particularly important to support the honest and vulnerable dialogue that underpins restorative justice processes. Integrating trauma-informed principles into restorative justice thus requires concrete and practical implementation, with facilitators understanding the impact of trauma and how to work effectively and supportively with trauma survivors.

Failure to adopt a trauma-informed approach to restorative justice can, as noted above, lead to criticism and opposition, particularly from victims and women's advocates concerned about the safety of those who have been harmed. Restorative justice is not immune to the risk of re-traumatisation. While the incidence of re-traumatisation may be relatively low, it remains a significant concern, particularly with the current expansion and inclusion of the most serious crimes, which may increase this risk. There is therefore an urgent need for restorative justice to be implemented in a trauma- and victim-sensitive way, and to be recognised as such by other professions.

However, restorative justice does not only need to be trauma-informed with regard to the individuals labelled as 'victims' within its processes. Due to the pervasiveness of trauma, offenders may also have experienced serious harm and also need a trauma-informed approach to be safe during restorative justice processes. Consider this real-life example of the risks when restorative justice services are not trauma-informed:

Case study 1.1: Allan and the need for a trauma-informed approach with offenders

Allan was accused of causing sexual harm to another person when he was a child. He agreed to participate in a restorative justice process. However, when he first met the facilitators, he found that they labelled him as the 'offender' and were not interested in hearing his own story. He had been the victim of complex childhood trauma and had suffered various forms of abuse over many years, but the facilitators were not interested in hearing this. He was there as 'the offender' and was treated as such. Their approach was deeply hurtful and humiliating for him and both he and the victim decided to seek another service. The victim also felt that the services were not safe for her and that she was in fact re-traumatised by the way she was treated by the facilitators. They both later shared their experiences and explained what a difference it made when they found a service that treated them with the care they needed and a trauma-informed approach. While it was a beneficial and healing journey for both of them, Allan said that he in particular, as the 'offender', had never imagined that this challenging process of facing his own victim could be so healing for him. However, because of the trauma-sensitive approach of the new facilitators, he too made significant steps in his trauma recovery, and the insights he gained into his own pain and healing journey helped him to empathise with his victim on a much deeper level. This in turn was a very meaningful experience for his own victim. Thus, not working in a trauma-informed way in restorative justice runs the risk of causing more harm rather than alleviating pain.

Ultimately, a trauma-informed approach to restorative justice recognises the significant impact of trauma, addresses the specific needs of survivors, and promotes safe, healing and empowering spaces for all participants. By prioritising the creation of safe and trusting relationships, restorative justice facilitators can better understand and address the individual needs of their clients, regardless of whether they are 'victims' or 'offenders'. This needs-based approach ensures that all participants receive the support they need based on their unique experiences.

This book, therefore, places significant emphasis on promoting 'trauma-informed restorative justice' into all aspects of practice, including restorative dialogues. Given that most restorative dialogue programmes, such as the one in Switzerland, focus on addressing serious harm, there is a significant likelihood that some participants will have experienced trauma. Consequently, the risk of re-traumatisation is as high in these dialogues as in direct victim–offender processes. For this reason, this book offers detailed strategies for implementing a trauma-informed approach to restorative dialogues.

Structure of the book

The structure of the book is designed so that each chapter builds on the previous one to enhance the understanding and application of trauma-informed restorative dialogues. Chapter 2 begins by outlining the basic principles and dynamics of restorative dialogues, highlighting different programmes that have been implemented across Europe. This chapter sets the stage by defining key concepts and illustrating how these dialogues operate in different cultural and legal contexts.

Chapter 3 shifts to a deeper exploration of the experiences of participants who have actively engaged in restorative dialogues. The chapter draws on findings from interviews with victims, anonymous feedback from offenders and group feedback at the end of each programme. This approach provides a comprehensive understanding of participants' perspectives and experiences and highlights common themes, challenges and outcomes observed across different restorative dialogue programmes.

Chapter 4 provides an insight into the first experiences of implementing restorative dialogues, first in Chile and then in Switzerland. It highlights the importance of collaboration with prison staff, the need for thorough individual preparation of participants, and the methodological changes influenced by an understanding of the trauma of victims and offenders. It discusses the practical challenges and successes encountered, underlining the need for in-depth training of facilitators.

Chapter 5 explores in more detail what a trauma-informed approach to restorative justice might look like. It examines the integration of trauma awareness into restorative practices, emphasising the importance of understanding the impact of trauma on individuals. This chapter outlines essential principles for creating safe and supportive environments that facilitate meaningful engagement for trauma survivors.

Chapter 6 applies the trauma-informed approach specifically to restorative dialogues. It explains how these principles are operationalised in practice, particularly in the Swiss context. The chapter describes in detail the strategies used to ensure that restorative dialogues are conducted in a manner that is sensitive to the needs of trauma survivors and promotes safety and empowerment. It also discusses challenges that experienced facilitators have encountered and how these might be addressed.

Chapter 7 shifts the focus from participants to facilitators, examining the implications of working with trauma survivors for restorative justice practitioners. It highlights the risk of secondary trauma and outlines individual and organisational strategies to address this risk. The chapter emphasises the importance of self-care, supervision and support systems to maintain facilitators' well-being and ensure that they can continue to provide an effective and empathetic service.

Chapter 8 concludes the book by offering some 'food for thought' and exploring questions and considerations that have emerged throughout the text. This chapter invites the reader to reflect further on the implementation of restorative dialogues, considering future directions, potential challenges and the ongoing development of the practice.

Finally, the appendix provides a basic understanding of trauma and its effects. This section is intended for readers who may not be very familiar with trauma and who wish to gain some preliminary knowledge before engaging with the main content of the book. It serves as a basic resource, providing essential insights into the impact of trauma on individuals and the importance of trauma-informed care in restorative justice settings.

Conclusion

This first chapter has explored the meaning of the term 'restorative dialogues' and explained how this approach fits into the broader framework of restorative justice processes. It has outlined the foundational understanding of restorative justice that underpins this book and highlighted its essential relationship with trauma-informed practice. Furthermore, an initial introduction to trauma-informed practice has been provided and its intersection with restorative justice has been explored, emphasising the need for restorative dialogues to be conducted in a trauma-informed manner.

Subsequent chapters will delve deeper into these concepts, highlighting how restorative dialogues can be a powerful tool for widening access to restorative justice. Practical strategies for conducting these dialogues in a trauma-informed way are explored, ensuring that the process is safe and supportive for all participants. In addition, the crucial aspect of facilitator well-being will be addressed, recognising that the well-being and resilience of those facilitating restorative processes is critical to their success.

Ultimately, this book aims to provide a comprehensive understanding of how restorative dialogues can be effectively implemented to promote healing, accountability and transformation for all involved.

Notes

1 A note about language: The terms 'victim', 'trauma survivor' and 'offender' are used throughout the book. Their use is not intended to label individuals, but rather to avoid confusion and facilitate reader comprehension. Nevertheless, the author refrains from labelling participants in restorative processes and endorses the view that labels should be avoided whenever possible, as they can be stigmatising and cause further harm.
2 New World Encyclopedia (n.d.).
3 Romney (n.d.).
4 Online Etymology Dictionary (2023).
5 Herman (1997); Keenan (2014).
6 See Clear (2007); Gilligan (2003); Liebling and Maruna (2005).
7 Block (2008).
8 See, for example: Feasy and Williams (2009).
9 See, for example: IFJR (2021).
10 Kim et al. (2022).

11 Barclay (2018).
12 De Jonckheere and Vaughn (2019).
13 Zhang and Wildemuth (2005).
14 EFRJ (2021).
15 EFRJ (2021).
16 UNODC (2020); Council of Europe (2018).
17 EFRJ (2021).
18 EFRJ (2021).
19 Council of Europe (2018); EFRJ (2021).
20 See Council of Europe (2018).
21 Council of Europe (2018).
22 Wilson (2005).
23 UNODC (2020).
24 See Anda et al. (2006); Klinic Community Health Centre (2013); ITTIC (2021).
25 Benjet et al. (2016).
26 Klinic Community Health Centre (2013).
27 ITTIC (2021).
28 Benjet et al. (2016); Charuvastra and Cloitre (2008); Johansen et al. (2022).
29 NHS Education for Scotland (2022).
30 Harris and Fallot (2001).
31 Scottish Government (2021).
32 CPI (2017); SAMHSA (2014); Wilson et al. (2015).
33 NHS Education for Scotland (2022); SAMHSA (2014).
34 SAMHSA (2014); Scottish Government (2021); NHS Education for Scotland (2022).
35 CTRI (2019).
36 CPI (2023); SAMHSA (2014).
37 SAMHSA (2014); Scottish Government (2021).
38 SAMHSA (2014); Scottish Government (2021).
39 Herman (1997).
40 SAMHSA (2014).
41 NHS Education for Scotland and Scottish Government (2019).
42 SAMHSA (2014).
43 APPG on Restorative Justice (2023); Bargen et al. (2018); Chapman et al. (2022); Keenan (2018).
44 UNODC (2020).

References

Anda, R. F., Felitti, V. J., Bremner, J. D., Walker, J. D., Whitfield, C., Perry, B. D., Dube, S. R., & Giles, W. H. (2006). The enduring effects of abuse and related adverse experiences in childhood: A convergence of evidence from neurobiology and epidemiology. *European Archives of Psychiatry and Clinical Neuroscience*, 256(3), 174–186.

APPG on Restorative Justice. (2023, September 13). *Restorative justice briefing papers – Workstream* 1. https://rjappg.co.uk/briefing-papers/

Barclay, C. (2018). *Semi-structured interviews*. KnowHow. https://know.fife.scot/__data/assets/pdf_file/0028/177607/KnowHow-Semistructured-interviews.pdf

Bargen, C., Edwards, A., Hartman, M., Haslett, J., & Lyons, A. (2018). *Serving crime victims through restorative justice: A resource guide for leaders and practitioners*. Alberta Restorative Justice Association.

Benjet, C., et al. (2016). The epidemiology of traumatic event exposure worldwide: Results from the World Mental Health Survey Consortium. *Psychological Medicine*, 46(2), 327–343. https://doi.org/10.1017/S0033291715001981

Block, P. (2008). *Community: Restoring the possible*. Berrett-Koehler.

Chapman, T., Nascimento, T., & Tata, C. (2022). *Restorative justice training needs analysis for Scotland: Report to the Scottish Government*. University of Strathclyde.

Charuvastra, A., & Cloitre, M. (2008). Social bonds and posttraumatic stress disorder. *Annual Review of Psychology*, 59, 301–328. https://doi.org/10.1146/annurev.psych.58.110405.085650

Clear, T. (2007). The impacts of incarceration on public safety. *Social Research: An International Quarterly*, 74, 613–630. https://doi.org/10.1353/sor.2007.0070

Council of Europe. (2018). *Recommendation CM/Rec(2018)8 of the Committee of Ministers to member States concerning restorative justice in criminal matters*. https://search.coe.int/cm?i=09000016808e35f3

Crisis and Trauma Resource Institute (CTRI). (2019). *Trauma-informed care: Building a culture of strength*. CTRI.

Crisis Prevention Institute (CPI). (2017). *Trauma-informed care for health care professionals: Resources guide*. https://institute.crisisprevention.com/Refresh-Trauma-Informed-Care-For-Health-Care.html

De Jonckheere, M., & Vaughn, L. M. (2019). Semistructured interviewing in primary care research: A balance of relationship and rigour. *Family Medicine and Community Health*, 7(2), Article e000057. https://doi.org/10.1136/fmch-2018-000057

European Forum for Restorative Justice (EFRJ). (2021). *Manual on restorative justice values and standards for practice*. www.euforumrj.org/sites/default/files/2021-11/EFRJ_Manual_on_Restorative_Justice_Values_and_Standards_for_Practice.pdf

Feasy, S., & Williams, P. (2009). *An evaluation of the Sycamore Tree Programme: Based on an analysis of Crime Pics II Data*. Sheffield Hallam University.

Gilligan, J. (2003). Shame, guilt, and violence. *Social Research*, 70(4), 1149–1180.

Harris, R. D., & Fallot, M. (2001). *Using trauma theory to design service systems*. Jossey-Bass/Wiley.

Herman, J. L. (1997). *Trauma and recovery: The aftermath of violence, from domestic abuse to political terror*. Basic Books.

Institut Français pour la Justice Restaurative (IFJR). (2021). *Enquête nationale sur la justice restaurative 2020*. IFJR.

Institute on Trauma and Trauma-Informed Care (ITTIC). (2021). *Trauma-informed organizational change manual*. Buffalo Center for Social Research.

Johansen, V. A., Milde, A. M., Miodini Nilsen, R., Breivik, K., Øystein Nordanger, D., Morten Stormark, K., & Weisæth, L. (2022). The relationship between perceived social support and PTSD symptoms after exposure to physical assault: An 8 years longitudinal study. *Journal of Interpersonal Violence*, 37(9–10), 7679–7706. https://doi.org/10.1177/0886260520970314

Keenan, M. (2014). *Sexual trauma and abuse: Restorative and transformative possibilities?*University College Dublin.

Keenan, M. (2018). Training for restorative justice work in cases of sexual violence. *International Journal of Restorative Justice*, 1(2), 291–302.

Kim, J., Merrill, C., & Suharan, D. (2018, September 6). *Building a trauma-informed research practice*. Ad Hoc. https://adhoc.team/2022/09/06/building-trauma-informed-research-practice

Klinic Community Health Centre. (2013). *Trauma-informed: The trauma toolkit* (2nd ed.). Health Canada.

Lanni, A. (2021). Taking restorative justice seriously. *Buffalo Law Review*, 69(3), 635–681. https://digitalcommons.law.buffalo.edu/buffalolawreview/vol69/iss3/2

Liebling, A., & Maruna, S. (Eds.). (2005). *The effects of imprisonment* (1st ed.). Willan. https://doi.org/10.4324/9781843926030

New World Encyclopedia. (n.d.). *Dialogue*. www.newworldencyclopedia.org/entry/Dialogue

NHS Education for Scotland. (2022). *Trauma – national trauma training programme*. www.nes.scot.nhs.uk/our-work/trauma-national-trauma-transformation-programme

NHS Education for Scotland and Scottish Government. (2019). *The Scottish Psychological Trauma Training Plan*. https://transformingpsychologicaltrauma.scot/media/5lvh0lsu/trauma-training-plan-final.pdf

Online Etymology Dictionary. (2023). *Restoration*. www.etymonline.com/word/restoration

Romney, P. (n.d.). *The art of dialogue*. Animating Democracy. https://animatingdemocracy.org/sites/default/files/documents/reading_room/art_of_dialogue.pdf

Substance Abuse and Mental Health Services Administration (SAMHSA). (2014). *SAMHSA's concept of trauma and guidance for a trauma-informed approach*. HHS publication no. (SMA) 14-4884. SAMHSA.

Scottish Government. (2021). *Trauma-informed practice toolkit*. www.gov.scot/publications/trauma-informed-practice-toolkit-scotland

United Nations Office on Drugs and Crime (UNODC). (2020). *Handbook on restorative justice programmes* (2nd ed.). www.unodc.org/documents/justice-and-prison-reform/20-01146_Handbook_on_Restorative_Justice_Programmes.pdf

Wilson, J. (2005). Victim-centered restorative justice: An essential distinction. *Crime Victims Report*, 9(4). https://justalternatives.org/VCRJ.pdf

Wilson, J. M., Fauci, J. E., & Goodman, L. A. (2015). Bringing trauma-informed practice to domestic violence programs: A qualitative analysis of current approaches. *American Journal of Orthopsychiatry*, 85(6), 586–599. http://dx.doi.org/10.1037/ort0000098

Zhang, Y., & Wildemuth, B. M. (2005). Qualitative analysis of content. *Human Brain Mapping*, 30(7), 2197–2206.

2 Situating restorative dialogues in context

Introduction

At a time when traditional justice systems often fail to address the emotional and social impact of crime, leaving both victims and offenders with unresolved pain, restorative dialogues offer a promising alternative. These dialogues provide a safe environment in which victims and offenders can openly discuss the harm and its consequences. By facilitating deep and meaningful exchanges, restorative dialogues go beyond legal boundaries to address the broader impact of crime and promote mutual understanding.

As restorative dialogues are not as well known as other restorative justice processes, this chapter aims to introduce them and explain their unique features and contributions to the field of restorative justice. It begins by examining the different aspects of restorative dialogues, including their different forms and how they are used in other European settings. This overview highlights the different practices and adaptations used to address various forms of harm. The chapter then discusses the necessity and value of restorative dialogues, focusing on small group settings and storytelling, which will be explored in more detail later. It also provides theoretical underpinnings, emphasising the role of restorative dialogues in trauma recovery and desistance. The chapter concludes with a brief summary of the main findings.

Contextualising restorative dialogues

The implementation of restorative justice varies considerably from country to country. Some approaches focus primarily on interactions between the victim and the offender, while others use community-based models. Community-based processes often include methods such as circle processes, family group conferences (FGC) or restorative conferences, although variations of these methods are common. These approaches typically involve not only the victim and offender but also family members, supporters or other community members, and professionals with specialist roles.[1]

Within community-based approaches, restorative dialogues play an important role. These dialogues involve group discussions between victims and offenders

DOI: 10.4324/9781003271611-2

who have experienced or perpetrated similar crimes, and promote an exchange of perspectives. A notable example of this approach is the Sycamore Tree Project, developed in 1996 by Dan Van Ness and a multinational team from Prison Fellowship International. According to Prison Fellowship International's info letter from January 2024, the Sycamore Tree Project is actively implemented in 37 countries worldwide. This underscores the global recognition of the importance and potential impact of such dialogue programmes.

Although dialogue groups between unrelated victims and offenders have not been as widely used as restorative justice processes involving directly related victims and offenders, it is an approach that has been growing and attracting increasing interest in recent years. In Europe, various forms of such dialogue groups can be found in several countries, including the UK, Belgium, France, Italy, Germany, Spain, Switzerland and the Czech Republic. This reflects a growing recognition of the value that these programmes bring to the wider range of restorative justice processes. As the field continues to develop, the interaction of directly related and unrelated victims and offenders in dialogue settings is expected to make a significant contribution to the ongoing development of restorative justice processes, as such dialogues broaden access to restorative justice for victims and offenders.

Given the limited literature on group processes involving unrelated victims and offenders, this book focuses exclusively on these types of restorative processes. Restorative dialogues provide a well-structured but adaptable framework that encourages open discussion and promotes shared understanding among those involved. Trained facilitators who create a safe and respectful environment for all participants lead these group processes. As described in more detail later in this book, the process begins with careful preparation in which facilitators meet with victims and offenders separately to understand their perspectives and set expectations. During subsequent group meetings, participants share their experiences and feelings and have the opportunity to ask each other questions. The sharing of personal narratives often begins with victims describing the impact of the crime on their lives. Offenders then have the opportunity to ask questions, offer support, but also to share their stories and acknowledge the harm they have caused. In turn, victims can ask questions and make comments. This exchange is crucial in humanising both parties and fostering understanding and empathy. The dynamic of these dialogues is one of equal participation, where every voice is heard and validated. Through this process, participants explore together how crime affects victims, offenders and their communities, and discuss ways to address the harm caused and experienced. The aim is to provide a safe space to share their stories, find closure, experience a sense of community and support each other in their respective journeys of recovery and transformation.

The methodology of restorative dialogues is not intended to compete with other restorative processes, but to provide an alternative in cases where a restorative process between the direct victim and offender is not possible or advisable. The main aim of its implementation is to ensure that victims and offenders have the opportunity to participate in a restorative process if they so wish.

Given the diversity of approaches to restorative dialogues across different programmes and countries, the following section aims to provide an overview of some programmes currently existing in Europe.

How different forms of restorative dialogues are implemented in Europe

As explained in Chapter 1, the term 'restorative dialogues', as used by the Swiss RJ Forum in Switzerland, refers to group discussions between victims and offenders of mostly serious crimes who are not linked by the same crime. However, care is taken to ensure that the crimes suffered by the victims and those committed by the offenders are as similar as possible to facilitate mutual understanding. Although such dialogues take place in many countries, the term used to describe them varies.[2] In France, for example, the expression 'rencontres condamnés – victimes' (meetings between convicts and victims) is used, while in other countries terms such as 'surrogate victim–offender community dialogue' or specific programme names, such as 'Sycamore Tree Project®', are used.[3] The core principle remains the same: groups of unrelated victims and offenders come together to engage in a dialogue to discuss their crime-related experiences and collectively address the impact of the crime on their lives and their loved ones. This joint dialogue lies at the heart of such restorative processes.

Implementation may vary depending on the country and the implementing organisation. The following overview of examples of restorative dialogue programmes implemented in several European countries is based on interviews with facilitators directly involved in these initiatives. While these examples provide some insight into the different approaches and methodologies used in different contexts, it is important to recognise that these programmes represent a subset of the broader landscape of restorative dialogues not only in Europe but worldwide, as such dialogues are implemented internationally. Other programmes and variations exist, tailored to the specific needs and circumstances of their respective communities. Nevertheless, the first-hand perspectives shared by these facilitators offer valuable insights into the design and implementation of restorative dialogue programmes in their respective countries.

Examples of restorative dialogue programmes in Germany, Belgium and France

In Germany, Belgium and France, restorative dialogue programmes share a number of similarities in their structure and aims, but there are also clear differences in their implementation and emphasis. All programmes aim to promote healing and understanding between victims and offenders through facilitated sessions that focus on personal storytelling, emotional exploration and mutual reflection. The discussion begins with an exploration of the overarching mechanisms and dynamics common to these programmes, before highlighting their unique characteristics.

All three countries favour a structured but flexible approach, emphasising the importance of preparation and establishing trust. They involve several sessions in which victims and offenders share their experiences, discuss the impact of the crimes and work towards understanding each other's perspectives and emotional healing. Facilitators play a crucial role in creating a safe and supportive environment, ensuring that the sessions are productive and respectful.

In each programme, the initial sessions are dedicated to introductions and relationship building, paving the way for deeper engagement in subsequent sessions. Storytelling is a central component, allowing participants to express their experiences and feelings, followed by group discussion and reflection. Programmes typically culminate in a celebratory session that recognises participants' journeys and achievements, fostering a sense of closure and reinforcing community support.

In Germany, the restorative dialogue programme is structured into six two-hour sessions. The first session focuses on building rapport and trust between the four to five victims, four to five offenders and two facilitators. Subsequent sessions focus on the impact of the crimes on participants' lives, exploring emotions, repercussions and personal experiences. From the second session onwards, victims and offenders alternate in telling their stories, followed by open discussion and reflection. The final session is a celebratory gathering where participants reflect on their journey and invite guests to celebrate their achievements.

A notable feature of the German programme is its integration into a wider range of services. One of the services offered is the victim support offices, where victims have access to free counselling. This also serves as extended preparation for those interested in restorative dialogues. Offenders are required to complete a 12-session victim empathy training and undergo individual interviews before participating in the dialogues, thus ensuring thorough preparation and commitment.

The Belgian programme consists of five three-hour sessions and involves two to three victims, two to three offenders, two community representatives, two support persons from the victim or offender's circle (e.g. mother, partner, child, etc.) and two facilitators. The community representatives play a unique role in listening, representing the community and supporting the participants in their individual recovery process. The programme is guided by a manual developed in collaboration with various professional services, but remains flexible to adapt to the needs of the participants.

The first session focuses on introductions and relationship building, followed by storytelling in the second session. Subsequent sessions cover topics tailored to the group's interests and needs, such as emotions, responsibility, boundaries and recovery. The programme concludes with a celebratory session, and participants have the opportunity to meet again approximately one year later to discuss the impact of the programme and address any outstanding issues.

In France, the restorative dialogue programme consists of five three-hour sessions, similar to the Belgian model. Before the programme starts, victims and offenders meet separately to get to know their peers and the setting. The sessions are facilitated by two professionals and accompanied by two community members. Unlike the other programmes, the facilitators in the French model take a minimal intervention approach during the sessions, focusing more on the preparation phase to build trust and rapport.

Storytelling starts from the first session and the agenda is set by the participants themselves, allowing for a more organic and participant-driven discussion. There is no pre-determined list of topics. The agenda for the discussions is set by the participants themselves, so the programme does not have a handbook of pre-determined topics or activities. Instead, the group collectively decides on the topics for discussion. The programme concludes with a debriefing session six to eight weeks later, which allows participants to reflect on their experiences and assess the impact of the dialogue process on their lives. In Belgium, the debriefing session is an individual session.

While the restorative dialogue programmes in Germany, Belgium and France share the core principles of preparation, storytelling and facilitated discussions, they differ in structure, duration and the specific roles of facilitators and community representatives. Germany's programme includes extensive preparation work for offenders; Belgium involves community representatives in the process and limits storytelling to one or two sessions. France, while also involving community representatives, adopts a minimalist approach to facilitator intervention during sessions, allowing participants to guide the topics of discussion. These variations reflect how diverse restorative dialogues can be. Variations can be even greater when specific forms of harm are addressed, as illustrated by the following, specialised programmes.

Specialised programmes

The Belgian programme and the international initiative described below seek to address the specific needs of victims, offenders and the community in the aftermath of political violence. Once more, it becomes evident that such initiatives can differ considerably. The first programme described is called 'Retissons du lien' and is implemented in Belgium. The 'Encounter of Encounters', presented subsequently, is a multicultural cross-border initiative, which may take a slightly different form in each participating country. To provide further insight into the two specific initiatives, which differ from other approaches to restorative dialogues, facilitators from both programmes as well as a participant of the 'Encounter of Encounters' were willing to share some of their reflections and experiences.

'Retissons du lien'

The Belgian programme 'Retissons du lien' (Re-establishing ties) focuses specifically on the individual and collective recovery in the aftermath of terrorism. It takes a broader approach that goes beyond victims and offenders to include affected relatives and citizens. This programme, accompanied by two facilitators, differs in its philosophy in that the facilitators see themselves not only as professionals but also as fellow citizens deeply affected by societal events.

Their role goes beyond facilitation; they actively participate in the group as affected members of the community while at the same time fostering a safe environment where participants can freely express their feelings and engage in calm, respectful discussions.

The programme consists of five sessions of three hours each, followed after six weeks by what is known as a 'legacy review session'. The first session is dedicated to building trust and creating a safe space, laying the foundation for deeper discussion in subsequent sessions. The topics for discussion are identified collectively and reflect the interests and concerns of the group. Participants have the opportunity to take the time they need to share their stories without interruption, and the other participants are invited to respond to their stories in a respectful way. During the first session, participants also articulate their hopes, fears and expectations, which are revisited during the closing session to honour the shared journey. Importantly, the legacy review session is co-constructed with the group during the fifth meeting, allowing participants to co-create the format and purpose of the session together. This collaborative approach extends to decisions about sharing their experiences with the wider community, if all participants agree. The aim is to have a wider impact within the community, emphasising collective empowerment and healing.

To gain a broader understanding of this programme and its focus on the aftermath of acts of terrorism, two of its facilitators, Salomé Van Billoen and Roland Prévot, were willing to share some of their reflections and experiences.

Box 2.1 Reflections from two facilitators

These restorative justice dialogues, like a pluralistic narrative voiced by those affected, offer clues to better understand how to heal and how to reflect on the fragile foundations of individual and collective recovery in the aftermath of terrorism.

As facilitators, we ask ourselves, together with the participants, what has happened to us and what this violence says about our society. Together we recognise ourselves in our individual stories and gain a clearer view of the landscape of suffering and the complexity of the needs involved. In the process of meeting each other, we come to realise how the diversity of participants' stories – and especially the ways in which they are articulated – nourish the path to justice, individual and societal healing, and contribute to the field of collective memory.

Creating these spaces for plural expression places a responsibility on us: to facilitate an environment of respect and trust that is essential for these narratives to emerge; to move beyond binary and categorical thinking that limits both thought and practice; and to dare to take paths that allow us to embrace complexity and work together to co-construct a renewed common humanity.

In a sense, we are privileged witnesses to the inner transformations triggered by the sharing of stories. We see people expressing themselves, understanding and talking about what has suddenly entered their lives. We see them connect and regain a sense of agency. At the same time, almost imperceptibly, we see the same people moving forward together in the process of reparation, empowerment, restoration and healing – not denying, of course, the obstacles and doubts along the way.

How precious it is to see each person reclaim their place in the collective narrative and in the eyes of others. It is a challenge to work through the echoes of suffering, guilt, shame, stigma, sadness, fear and feelings of responsibility and powerlessness. Yet, in daring to embark on this ambitious journey, a glimmer of life and hope emerges, born of a heightened collective consciousness, a healing word and a transformative process.

Restorative justice is perhaps everything that society, including the legal system, does not naturally encourage. However, to experience it is to encounter moments of such profound humanity that their importance can no longer be denied – an importance that should now be seen as a demand.

Mobilising the resources and intelligence of human communities is perhaps one of the greatest strengths of the 'Retissons du lien' collective, which constantly offers different forms of exchange and encounter, where different forms of expression can be used, all embodying a diversity of narratives that respect people, their integrity and the different dimensions of their identity. It is a choice for society, for each individual, for the community, for tomorrow.[4]

The reflections highlight that one aspect which significantly distinguishes this programme from other forms of restorative dialogues is the involvement of the facilitators themselves. They do not take on the role of 'outsiders' but participate fully in the conversations. This aspect is also reflected in the 'Encounter of Encounters'.

Cross-border initiative: the 'Encounter of Encounters'

Launched in 2019, the 'Encounter of Encounters' is a unique international initiative that promotes dialogue between people affected by terrorism, political violence, violent extremism and armed conflict. Named after its purpose, the 'Encounter of Encounters' brings together regional and national groups that have participated in restorative encounters following such events to share their experiences.[5] Roberto Moreno, one of the facilitators of the group in the Basque Country, explains the initiative as follows.

Box 2.2 Insights from a facilitator

Participants meet face to face on an annual basis, recognising the need for an ongoing exchange of stories and experiences as the pain experienced by victims continues. It helps them to share their stories in a variety of contexts different from their own. The presence of community members is crucial to this, as the attentive listening of the international community acts as a healing force in the aftermath of extreme violence. A notable consequence observed is the mirroring effect across contexts. Participants gain insight into other approaches to accountability that are often not available within their own national frameworks. Seeing their experiences reflected in those of others helps victims to heal and fosters a sense of solidarity and understanding.

To accommodate the large groups, which often exceed 50 participants, innovative tools such as the 'spiral model' have been developed, as the use of traditional circles would be too difficult with such a large group. In this model, directly affected victims and offenders sit in the centre, while community members sit in the outer circles. This structure prioritises space for those directly affected while still including community members.

The meetings, which last between two and four days, allow for deep sharing over an extended period of time. However, for this to happen, it is first necessary to build trust to create the safe space required for the vulnerable nature of the discussions. The first day is dedicated to creating confidential spaces that also help to integrate the new groups that arrive each year. Art is used as a valuable communication tool, bridging linguistic and cultural barriers that can make verbal communication difficult.

Participants emphasise the importance of informal interactions after they have had a chance to share their deepest pain. Moments such as sharing a meal can help to break down preconceived roles of victim or offender, as everyone has a plurality of roles. Victims often no longer see themselves as victims but as survivors. So even such convivial moments are times of deep learning and sharing.

The programme remains open to new groups with similar experiences across Europe and focuses on creating safe, confidential spaces for deep sharing and listening. Participants acknowledge the transformative nature of the encounters, seeing them as crucial to supporting reintegration into the community and fostering a culture of peacebuilding over polarisation. In addition, the programme places a strong emphasis on engaging the younger generation, with the aim of raising awareness of past violence and preventing future occurrences through dialogue and understanding.

A distinctive feature of these restorative meetings is the group of young people, consisting of victims, offenders and community members representing new generations, who meet monthly online, accompanied by a facilitator. Some of these participants have publicly shared their personal experiences in larger settings with youth and university audiences, with the aim of sharing their narratives and restorative processes with the new generations as a contribution to peace. This initiative seeks to ensure the right to non-repetition of violence in post-terrorism contexts.

One of these younger members was willing to share her testimony openly to provide insight into the initiative from the viewpoint of a participant.

Box 2.3 Arianna's testimony: The impact of 'Encounter of Encounters'

As the daughter of two alleged Italian right-wing terrorists, I grew up with the prejudices of my parents' past. Although my parents had nothing to do with the Bologna massacre,[6] they served 20 years in prison and 10 years on probation for their crimes. Despite the stigma and social ostracism, my family provided a foundation of love and resilience.

At the age of 16, my life took a decisive turn when I joined the 'Encounter of Encounters' initiative. Accompanied by my mother and other influential people, I travelled to Israel and Palestine to meet with the Parents' Circle.[7] This is an organisation that promotes dialogue and reparation and is also a member of the 'Encounter of Encounters'. The experience was transformative, providing me with a community that shared my commitment to restorative justice.

The 'Encounter of Encounters' allowed me to share my story in a supportive environment where my experiences were actively listened to and respected. This participation reinforced my belief in the therapeutic value of restorative practices, where victims and offenders can share their experiences, build a collective memory and reintegrate into their communities. Through the 'Encounter of Encounters', I found a space to heal, contribute and advocate for a broader collective project of reparation, transforming my personal pain into a powerful force for community restoration and justice.

The Swiss programme

In contrast to the aforementioned specialised programmes, our programme in Switzerland is comparable to the previous programmes described. The programme consists of eight two-hour sessions. Each group comprises approximately three victims and three to four offenders, accompanied by four facilitators. While a manual outlines a possible programme structure, it is used flexibly to meet the individual needs and interests of the group. Individual preparation sessions for all participants and group preparation for offenders precede the first meeting between victims and offenders. The first three sessions are dedicated to co-creating a safe environment and fostering trusting relationships, laying the groundwork for the sharing of personal stories and experiences.

Subsequent sessions focus primarily on participants' narratives, allowing time for reactions, questions and discussions about the impact of the crime on all involved. The facilitators contribute actively during these first sessions, similar to the approach of 'Retissons du lien'. However, from the fourth session onwards, the focus of the programme shifts entirely to the participating victims and offenders, with the facilitators taking on a supportive role in maintaining the safe space and offering support as needed. The programme culminates in a celebration session, often attended by two to four people from prison management or social services, to recognise the collective progress made by the group. It is possible to hold a debriefing session several weeks or months later if desired, but this is a decision made by the participants based on their needs.

This brief presentation of restorative dialogue programmes shows that there exists a wide variety of approaches. To fully appreciate the value of restorative dialogues, however, it is essential to address a fundamental question: why are these programmes necessary? Exploring the reasons for the need for restorative dialogues will clarify their importance and help to understand their role in the broader context of restorative justice.

Why are restorative dialogues needed?

There are several reasons why restorative dialogues between unrelated victims and offenders are necessary, such as:

1 Widening access to restorative justice
2 Generating a pluralistic narrative about experiences of harm and suffering
3 Providing a safe and healing space in a group environment to facilitate sharing

1. Widening access to restorative justice

Restorative dialogues serve as an important means of widening access to restorative justice, particularly in cases where a dialogue between the direct victim and offender is not possible. Such circumstances may arise due to a number of factors, including the unknown identity of the victim or offender, particularly in cases involving unidentified offenders, or the reluctance of one of the parties to engage in the process. These barriers may make traditional restorative justice processes infeasible, given the voluntary nature of participation required. For both victims and offenders, it may be difficult to accept that in their case, it is not possible to have a restorative process with the other party as they may have many questions or things they would like to say but are unable to do so. When such an exchange is not possible, it can be more challenging to come to terms with the past.[8]

There are also cases where a direct process may not be in the best interests of either the victim or the offender. This could be due to the offender's lack of insight into the harm caused or severe psychopathology that prevents him or her from showing respect and empathy towards the victim, thereby risking re-traumatisation. There may also be legal restrictions in place, which prohibit direct contact. Several victims and offenders participated in the Swiss programme who were willing but unable to speak directly to the other party. This can be challenging and even painful for both parties. Victims often feel re-victimised, and offenders can suffer under the burden of not being able to explain why they did what they did or to apologise.

Victims may also prefer not to engage in direct dialogue with their offender, but still wish to communicate with others. This sentiment was expressed by several victims during the interviews. One reason for this preference is fear, while another is the perception that such dialogue may not be beneficial for them. The challenge is particularly pronounced when the crime has occurred within the family. In these cases, victims may be afraid of encountering resistance or of causing negative consequences for the family dynamic. Also, when the offender is part of the victim's intimate circle, there is often a reluctance to confront him or her for fear of repercussions from other family members or friends. In addition, some cited the group setting as providing a sense of security that they felt would be lacking in an individual process. As they had never participated in a direct victim–offender dialogue, this feeling was not based on experience, but rather on the fears based on preconceptions.

Finally, there are people on both sides who prefer to participate in a group process first and then decide whether they are ready for a direct encounter. Such a process can therefore also serve as a first preparatory step for a future direct process. This is an option offered by several of the programmes interviewed for this book, including our programme in Switzerland.

The aim to broaden the range and access to restorative justice services, even in cases where a face-to-face meeting is not possible or advisable, is in line with the Council of Europe's recommendation. The recommendation states that restorative justice should be a universally available service that includes a variety of methods that can be flexibly adapted to the needs of those involved.[9] The implementation of restorative justice should therefore include both direct and indirect methods to offer a wide range of options to all those affected by crime. As Umbreit and Armour (2011) explain,[10] the methodology of restorative dialogues:

> can be a partial response to the large volume of crime victims whose offenders are never caught. Such victims are equally in need of gaining a greater understanding of why people commit such crimes and letting others in the community know about the impact of these crimes on their lives.

They emphasise that such dialogues have been shown to be beneficial to all participants at low cost.

2. *Generating a pluralistic narrative about experiences of harm and suffering*

As Van Billoen and Prévot mentioned in their reflections, restorative dialogues are also needed to generate a pluralistic narrative of experiences of harm and suffering. Without this, victims and offenders can remain stuck in their singular, often polarised views of the crime and its impact. The objective of developing a pluralistic narrative is firmly rooted in the tenets of social constructionism, which emphasises the collaborative nature of learning. This theory posits that our understanding of reality is constructed through social interactions and shared meanings.[11] In restorative dialogues, victims and offenders share their experiences, feelings and perspectives, creating a shared understanding of the impact of crime. This process allows participants to challenge their pre-existing ideas and assumptions about harm and justice, leading to a more nuanced and holistic understanding of each other.

Language plays a crucial role in this interaction, as it is not just a means of expression but also a tool through which reality is constructed. As both sides share their stories, they collectively build a narrative that reflects the complexity of their experiences. This shared narrative, constructed through dialogue, promotes mutual understanding and learning.[12] Victims gain insight into the factors that contributed to the offender's behaviour, while offenders understand the profound impact of their actions on victims. The knowledge and understanding co-created through their interactions and exchanges can help both victims and offenders to work through their experiences constructively and find ways to move forward.

3. Providing a safe and healing space in a group environment to facilitate sharing

Another important reason that emerged from the interviews with victims was that restorative dialogues provide a safe community where they feel heard and supported by others. Being part of a group or community can provide a sense of belonging and support for both victims and offenders, promoting healing and empowerment through shared experiences and a deeper understanding of each other's perspectives. As one interviewee expressed, the opportunity to engage in restorative dialogues provided a safe space where her voice was not only welcomed but also accepted without rejection or judgement. This is an experience she has not had in her own community. Validation is crucial for participants who have felt isolated in their trauma.[13] As several of the interviewees said, it reassured them that their experiences were not abnormal, which meant that they themselves were 'normal'. This realisation provides a feeling of relief.

Similarly, the group setting provides a healing space for offenders. Many offenders have also experienced trauma,[14] and lack a sense of community and belonging, particularly during their time in prison. Their testimonies reveal they have rarely encountered such a supportive community, even on the outside, and so time spent in the group is a valuable and healing experience for them on their way to rehabilitation.

For anyone who has experienced trauma, whether victim or offender, restorative dialogues provide a platform to share their stories. The group setting can give them a sense of solidarity, collective strength and hope for a better future. For many of them it may have been difficult to share personal experiences within their own community because they may have felt fearful or ashamed to do so. It can therefore be easier to open up in this 'established' community where other group members have had similar experiences. One interviewee who had suffered deeply from shame said:

> The group is divine. Because … some people cannot express themselves on their own. They are afraid. But, in a group, when everyone else is sharing something, something bad … I don't know how to put it, but then you want to join in and talk about it.

This kind of dialogue and shared support can therefore allow participants to find comfort in knowing that they are not alone in their suffering and their journey to recovery.[15] This was a significant factor for Matt, who had experienced a profound sense of isolation due to his suffering.

Case study 2.1: A victim's perspective

Matt's daughter Laura was killed on a trip abroad. The family were told that she was in the wrong place at the wrong time and that the killing was not personal. However, such reassurances were of little comfort to the grieving family. The weight of not being able to say goodbye weighed heavily on them. For both her parents and Laura's siblings, the unexpected and painful loss had a profoundly traumatic impact on their daily lives. Desperate for closure, Matt felt the need to confront the offenders and contacted the criminal justice professionals handling his daughter's case. Unfortunately, his attempts were met with a vehement refusal of access to the offenders. This left Matt feeling re-victimised by the system, which aggravated his post-traumatic symptoms.

Many years later, Matt learned of an opportunity to engage in restorative dialogues with other victims and offenders who had suffered or caused similar losses. Despite the anticipated pain of telling his story, he felt the need to share his suffering with others who could empathise. This need was reinforced by his community's waning interest in the tragedy. They felt that Matt should be 'over it' by now and did not want to hear about the murder or even Laura. This left Matt feeling isolated in his grief. He also had questions he wanted to ask people who had taken someone else's life; he wanted to understand how someone could come to the point of killing another human being.

Participating in the dialogues was not easy for him, but he felt accepted, part of a community that understood, recognised and validated his pain. This experience allowed him to grieve, and the community grieved with him, over the loss of his beloved daughter. What helped him most was the presence of the offenders. Through his sharing, he saw how his story affected them and witnessed them begin to understand the enormous impact a murder has on a family and their community. In the end, it was the honest and sensitive dialogue with the offenders that brought him the most healing. While a direct restorative process was not viable for Matt, he was grateful to have had the opportunity to participate in a process with unrelated offenders.

However, it is not only the victims who need a safe and healing space to share their stories, their suffering, their journey. Many of the offenders are in need of healing too and only find out, once they are allowed to share in such a supportive community, how their own trauma and offending behaviour are connected. This was John's story.

Case study 2.2: An offender's perspective

John's life was marked by a history of violence and loss. Orphaned at a young age, he had a violent upbringing, bouncing from foster home to foster home, where he was physically and emotionally abused. He ran away from these homes several times and lived on the streets where the violence continued. As an adult, the scars of his past manifested themselves in a violent incident in which he inflicted serious, permanent injuries on another man. The gravity of his actions began to weigh heavily on him while he was in solitary confinement in his prison cell. As he began to grasp the enormity of the consequences, he felt devastated. He longed for a way to help his victim. However, the authorities prohibited any direct communication, fearing further harm to the injured man. Therefore, John decided to join a restorative dialogue group.

As John told his story, his emotions overwhelmed him, and the pain of his past showed itself in violent trembling and unceasing tears. As he recounted the traumas of his childhood, he realised that the rage burning within him had led him to commit a terrible crime that mirrored the abuse he had suffered as a child. This realisation was a heavy burden to bear, but it was a crucial revelation for John to understand how his victimisation had affected his actions.

Through the restorative dialogue process, John began to recognise the importance of confronting his past and working through his own victimisation and anger. He understood that addressing these deep-rooted issues was essential to reduce the burning anger within him and thereby reduce the risk of repeating similar acts of violence. It was crucial for John to feel that the group neither justified nor minimised the harm he had caused. Instead, they treated him as a human being, offering support while holding him accountable for his actions. This approach allowed him to reflect on his life choices and begin the process of self-analysis.

These case studies demonstrate the necessity of restorative dialogues to address some critical needs of victims and offenders in the aftermath of crime. A commonality between victims and offenders is the need for a supportive community that is willing to listen to their narratives. Therefore, it can be argued that the experience of community is a significant value of restorative dialogues.

The value of restorative dialogues to participants: the importance of a community for recovery

The distinctive feature of restorative dialogues is that they provide individuals with an opportunity to engage in a safe and protected group setting. According to the unanimous responses of the research participants, this feature seems to be particularly important for victims. This may be because recovering from trauma requires safe and trusting relationships with others.[16]

Humans are fundamentally social creatures. Safe and nurturing relationships with others are crucial for personal development and psychological well-being.[17] However, trauma, particularly trauma inflicted by others, as in the case of criminal acts, challenges fundamental human relationships. It shatters an individual's sense of safety in the world and their basic sense of trust, making it difficult to experience safe and meaningful relationships. This can ultimately lead to social withdrawal. Disempowerment and disconnection from others are therefore key experiences for trauma survivors, leaving them with a sense of isolation and abandonment and even causing them to lose their sense of self.[18] The damage is particularly severe when the traumatic event was caused within close relationships, as this is experienced as a betrayal and breach of trust.[19] Victims may feel abandoned by other relatives, who sometimes withdraw from them or do not allow them to talk about what has happened and do not want to hear about their suffering. Such negative social reactions increase feelings of isolation and loss of trust.[20]

Just as trauma does not occur in isolation, neither does recovery from trauma. Recovery can only take place in the context of relationships and is therefore highly dependent on the ability to reconnect with others. Capacities such as "trust, autonomy, initiative, competence, identity and intimacy … [which] are originally formed in relationships with other people" need to be rebuilt in such relationships after trauma.[21]

The damage to relational life is not a secondary effect, but has a direct impact on both the psychological structure of the individual and his or her attachment to the community. While supportive relationships can mitigate the effects of trauma and promote healing, negative reactions can increase the damage and exacerbate traumatic symptoms.[22] Regrettably, this is a challenge that some victims face, particularly in cases of abuse, where instead of empathy and support they face denial, minimisation or even blame.[23]

Because of the relational damage caused by trauma, the responses of an individual's community of care, including family, friends, significant others, those with shared experience or even professionals, are crucial. Their reactions have the power to influence the ultimate outcome of the trauma, as safe and caring relationships not only support recovery but also serve as a protective factor against the development of post-traumatic symptoms.[24] Such relationships are an important resource in fostering resilience, as Diane Fosha notes: The "roots of resilience... are to be found in the sense of being understood by and existing in the mind and heart of a loving, attuned and self-possessed other".[25] As a result, individuals struggling with trauma need the support of others to navigate their experiences and mitigate its impact on their lives. By creating spaces where victims with similar experiences can confide in each other and form meaningful relationships, they may become better prepared to reconnect with society. Patton and Goodwin emphasise that these relationships are essential for trauma survivors to feel supported and understood, facilitating their journey toward healing.[26]

Given the challenges some victims face in receiving adequate support and understanding from their communities, restorative dialogues can offer comfort and empowerment in a safe group setting where experiences can be shared without fear of judgement or dismissal. The collective understanding and empathy fostered in these settings provides a stark contrast to the isolation and invalidation experienced elsewhere. As Van der Kolk notes, "our capacity to destroy each other is matched by our capacity to heal each other".[27] This insight underlines the transformative potential of restorative dialogues, where both victims and offenders who have suffered traumatic experiences can find healing and connection through engaging in dialogue with others who understand and empathise with what they have been through. Nevertheless, for this to occur, it is vital to pay close attention to the dynamics required, namely those of the small group.

The dynamics of the small group

Understanding the dynamics of restorative dialogues requires acknowledging the pivotal role of the small group setting in fostering healing and connection. When implementing the first restorative dialogues in Chile, I encountered Peter Block's book *Community: The Structure of Belonging* (2008),[28] which significantly shaped my perspective on community dynamics. Block's exploration of the 'power of the small group' prompted me to contemplate why such dialogues are most effective in small group settings. His definition of community as the 'experience of belonging' and the antithesis of belonging as 'feeling isolated' deeply resonates with participants in the context of restorative dialogues. Participants, whether victims or offenders, often grapple with feelings of isolation following criminal incidents. Victims, particularly those who have endured traumatic experiences, may feel disconnected from their communities and struggle with the reactions of those around them. Similarly, offenders, especially those who are incarcerated, often experience profound isolation from the outside world, intensifying their sense of disconnection. Therefore, the fundamental need for belonging and connection serves as a primary motivator for participants to engage in these discussion groups.

Block posits that 'ownership' is intrinsic to belonging, defining it as one's role as a creator and co-owner of the community. This concept resonates deeply in restorative dialogues, as observed in various European programmes mentioned earlier. The objective is to empower participants to shape their interactions, address needs and promote empowerment – a core value of restorative approaches. While it requires courage to trust in the process and relinquish control, allowing participants to identify and resolve issues independently is crucial. This approach helps them to regain agency lost through traumatic experiences or incarceration.[29]

The significance of keeping the groups small is a question often raised. According to Block, small groups of three to 12 people foster intimacy, ensuring that each voice is heard and each person's uniqueness is valued, thus promoting a sense of belonging.[30] It is not surprising, then, that all the programmes presented emphasise small groups – a sentiment echoed by interviewed participants. For instance, a victim noted the stark difference between attending a larger group versus a smaller group in a restorative dialogues programme, feeling safer and easier to open up in the latter setting. Therefore, small groups provide an intimate and supportive environment where survivors can share their experiences authentically, fostering trust and solidarity among participants. Additionally, the smaller group size allows for more meaningful interactions, individual support and a deeper focus on each participant's needs.[31]

As a result, the intimate group setting embodies care – care for others, and the community's well-being. Block emphasises that care and accountability are intertwined and essential for creating a healthy community. He believes that when people care for each other, they become accountable to each other. This is a crucial aspect in the context of restorative dialogues, as victims often seek accountability from offenders, expressing a desire for them to acknowledge their actions. Even those interviewees whose cases had gone through a legal process felt that the level of accountability from their offenders fell short of their expectations.

According to Block, this lack of accountability is not surprising because the retributive system does not provide for accountability. True accountability arises out of concern for others, leading individuals to recognise their role in creating or perpetuating harmful conditions and fostering a sense of responsibility.[32] It is this form of accountability that victims often seek when they participate in restorative dialogues. The relationships and sense of belonging fostered in these groups enable participating offenders to develop a deeper understanding of the harm caused and foster a genuine desire to make amends voluntarily.

Focusing on people's strengths rather than their deficits is fundamental to building community, as highlighted by Block. This approach contrasts with many professional medical and therapeutic services, which tend to label individuals according to their weaknesses.[33] Victims and offenders alike frequently experience this labelling as pressure, judgement and blame. However, within restorative dialogue groups, these labels gradually dissolve, and participants begin to perceive these spaces as environments of giving and receiving. Cozolino (2006) suggests that this exchange of care, as seen in Japanese thought, is closely linked to mental well-being.[34] In my experience, restorative dialogues offer participants liberating opportunities to shed limiting labels and interact authentically as human beings, supporting one another.

Furthermore, Block emphasises the importance of conversations in fostering a sense of community, suggesting that community essentially revolves around dialogue. This notion holds particular significance in the context of restorative dialogues, where deep, vulnerable and honest conversations are vital. Block argues that all transformation stems from linguistic shifts, identifying the small group setting as the locus of transformation. As relationships deepen within these groups, conversations gradually shift from focusing on fears and retribution to embracing possibilities, generosity and restoration. Moments of shared laughter and conviviality within these groups also play a crucial role in promoting healing and strengthening the sense of belonging. Block's definition of restoration as healing our woundedness and incivility resonates deeply, linking restoration to connectivity[35] – an essential aspect of recovery for trauma survivors.[36]

Thus, the small group dynamic inherent in restorative dialogues addresses core needs of both victims and offenders: the need for safe and supportive relationships, validation of experiences, and a community that fosters healing and growth. By offering a space for dialogue that transcends preconceived labels, restorative dialogues empower individuals to recognise their strengths and resources, facilitating both individual and collective transformation. Because the small group and the role of the community in recovery is so central to restorative dialogues, it was also a topic of discussion during the expert interviews.

Experts' reflections on the small group setting

The interviewed experts agreed that the group setting offers participants a unique sense of community that may be difficult to find elsewhere. As one of the experts expressed:

> I think that talking in a group is very important for processing, no matter which side is involved. I think it is important for both sides to put their own story, their own experience into words, to talk about it – and to be able to talk about it in such a setting, in such a group. I think that helps with the processing and also with the reflection … I think that everybody who takes part gets a lot out of it … in the chance that something can still be healed in them. So, I believe that it can support the healing process. I think it is really important that people feel supported and protected.

This dynamic not only fosters individual recovery but also promotes collective transformation, underscoring the profound impact of community in the restorative process. At the heart of this process lies storytelling. Through the supportive interactions, victims and offenders alike are able to share their stories, which allows them to gain insight and find mutual support. The importance of this process is further explored in the next section.

The role of storytelling in the recovery of trauma and desistance from crime

Storytelling plays a central role in the process of recovery from trauma. Traumatic events profoundly affect individuals, disrupting their life narrative, sense of oneself, understanding of the world and perception of life's meaning. This disruption can lead to a 'crisis of meaning' where individuals struggle to make sense of the chaos.[37] Typically, the brain organises and recalls life events chronologically, allowing individuals to contextualise their experiences within familiar thought patterns.[38] However, when confronted with trauma, the brain's cognitive processes are disrupted, inhibiting rational thinking and processing – processes that would be essential for making sense of lived experiences. During traumatic events, while sensory input is vividly recorded, the brain's rational centres remain inactive, overwhelmed by the intensity of the experience. Consequently, traumatic memories often remain fragmented, characterised by their intensity and difficulty of verbal expression, making it even more challenging for individuals to make sense of their experiences.[39]

These memories, coupled with intense emotions, vivid images and physical symptoms, perpetuate a sense of ongoing trauma.[40] Victims often feel that the traumatic event is never-ending, due to the absence of chronological order. Thus, it is unsurprising that several interviewees found it difficult to put their experiences into words. One respondent mentioned the difficulty of verbalising his experience even decades later, with attempts to do so triggering somatic symptoms such as intense pain. Despite these challenges, storytelling is a powerful tool for individuals to confront and integrate their traumatic experiences into a coherent narrative.[41]

By sharing their stories in a safe and validating environment, trauma survivors can begin the process of reconstructing their identities and finding meaning in their experiences. Though painful, this narrative reconstruction facilitates emotional distancing from the trauma and empowers individuals by giving them control over their experiences. In addition, storytelling can alleviate post-traumatic symptoms by helping individuals recognise that the event is in the past and no longer a threat.[42]

This resonates with interviewees' experiences, who felt that the process of storytelling has brought them additional healing and closure. For many, it has been a challenging yet necessary process. One participant likened the experience to a metamorphosis from a caterpillar to a butterfly, arduous but ultimately liberating, releasing her from her inner prison and restoring her ability to embrace life anew. Despite the difficulty of articulating complex emotions and experiences, engaging in storytelling can empower victims.[43]

In addition, some individuals experience a transformation as they share their stories, moving from seeing themselves as *victims* to recognising their resilience and strength as *survivors*. This shift in perspective fosters resilience,[44] and it supports others in their journey of recovery, exemplifying post-traumatic growth.

Given that a substantial number of offenders have themselves experienced trauma,[45] the process of storytelling can have a significant impact on their lives. Therefore, it is of utmost importance that facilitators of restorative dialogues actively encourage offenders to engage in the sharing of both the harm they have caused and also of their personal lives and the traumas they have endured.

In sum, storytelling serves as a powerful tool for integrating traumatic experiences into one's life narrative. By reconstructing a chronological order, trauma survivors can regain agency over their experiences. Through storytelling, individuals can also reconnect with others, overcoming isolation and building supportive relationships, which are crucial aspects of the healing journey. In addition, storytelling can reduce stress symptoms, negative thinking, and promote resilience.[46]

Furthermore, storytelling represents an invaluable tool for offenders on their journey towards desistance.[47] Sharing their narratives can help them to:

1. understand the meaning behind their past actions and the motivations that led to offending behaviour;
2. gain insight into the impact of their actions by hearing the stories of victims affected by their crimes or similar crimes;
3. develop a sense of ownership and responsibility for their past actions and be accountable for their wrongdoings;
4. create a new 'redemptive personal narrative' by shedding stigmas and labels associated with their criminal behaviour and committing to new values that support a crime-free life. This process also enables them to regain agency over their lives, giving them a sense of control over their choices and actions.[48]

Consequently, storytelling can not only support survivors in their journey of recovery but also offenders in the process of desistance.

Conclusion

This chapter has introduced various forms of restorative dialogues practised across Europe, emphasising their importance and adaptability. These dialogues are crucial for extending restorative justice to cases where direct interaction between victims and offenders is not feasible. A significant feature of these dialogues is the group dynamic, which participants highly value. For victims of crime, who frequently experience trauma and isolation, and for incarcerated individuals, the sense of belonging and support from a group can be profoundly healing and facilitate societal reintegration.

For victims, validation and non-judgemental listening offered within the group are particularly important. Feeling believed and understood in a safe, intimate space promotes healing and transformation. Similarly, for offenders, these groups provide a platform for reflection and accountability in a community setting. The small group environment is key to creating this sense of belonging and safety, providing the intimate space necessary for vulnerable sharing and transformation. In these groups, victims and offenders courageously share their stories, exchange perspectives and develop a deeper understanding of harm and justice. It is a space where they co-create knowledge and understanding and grow in empathy for each other.

In examining the need for restorative dialogues, this chapter has also identified several needs experienced by both victims and offenders. The next chapter will explore these needs in more detail and discuss how restorative dialogues can effectively address them.

Notes

1 For more on processes, see UNODC (2020).
2 O'Mahony and Doak (2017); UNODC (2020).
3 Crocker (2015); Umbreit and Armour (2011); UNODC (2020).
4 Translated from French to English by the author.
5 For more on the Encounter of Encounters, see EFRJ. (n.d.).
6 On 2 August 1980, a powerful bomb exploded in Bologna's railway station, killing at least 75 people and injuring over 200 others.
7 The Parents Circle – Families Forum (PCFF) is a joint Israeli–Palestinian organisation of over 700 bereaved families who have lost an immediate family member to the ongoing conflict. It was founded in 1985.
8 Van Ness and Strong (2015); Zehr (1990).
9 Council of Europe (2018).
10 Umbreit and Armour (2011), p. 83.
11 Burr (2015).
12 Burr (2015).
13 Bolivar (2010); Herman (1997).
14 See, for example: Levenson et al. (2021).
15 See also Blanch et al. (2012).
16 Herman (1997); Van der Kolk (2014).
17 Greenfield and Marks (2010); Herman (1997); Van der Kolk (2014).
18 Bolivar (2012); Herman (1997).
19 Herman (1997); Van der Kolk (2014).
20 Bolivar (2012).
21 Herman (1997), p. 133.
22 Herman (1997).
23 Bolivar (2012); Todahl et al. (2017).
24 Bolivar (2012); Calhoun and Tedeschi (2006); Herman (1997).
25 Cited in Van der Kolk (2014), p. 125.
26 Patton and Goodwin (2008).
27 Van der Kolk (2014), p. 44.
28 Block (2008).
29 Block (2008).
30 Block (2008).
31 Block (2008).

32 Block (2008).
33 Block (2008).
34 Cozolino (2006).
35 Block (2008).
36 Herman (1997); Van der Kolk (2014).
37 Janoff-Bulman (2010); Manda (2019).
38 Van der Merwe and Gobodo-Madikizela (2008); Wigren (1994).
39 Van der Kolk and Van der Hart (1995); Manda (2019).
40 Van der Kolk (2014); Van der Merwe and Gobodo-Madikizela (2008).
41 Van der Kolk and Van der Hart (1995).
42 Betancourt (2010); Herman (1997); Manda (2017); Van der Kolk (1996); Van der Kolk (2014); Van der Merwe and Gobodo-Madikizela (2008).
43 Meichenbaum (2006).
44 Tedeschi (2020); Tedeschi and Moore (2016).
45 See, for example: Brown et al. (2021); Kerig et al. (2016).
46 Calhoun and Tedeschi (2006); Meichenbaum (2006).
47 Maruna (2001, 2016).
48 Marsh (2011); Maruna (2001); Stone (2016); Vaughan (2012).

References

Betancourt, I. (2010). *Even silence has an end: My six years of captivity in the Colombian jungle*. Penguin Press.

Blanch, A., Filson, B., & Penney, D. (2012). *Engaging women in trauma-informed peer support: A guidebook*. NCTIC.

Block, P. (2008). *Community: Restoring the possible*. Berrett-Koehler.

Bolivar, D. (2010). Conceptualising victims' 'restoration' in restorative justice. *International Review of Victimology*, 17, 237–265. https://doi.org/10.1177/026975801001700301

Bolivar, D. (2012). Community of care from a victim-perspective: A qualitative study. *Contemporary Justice Review*, 15(1), 17–37. https://doi.org/10.1080/10282580.2011.589671

Brown, S. L., Wanamaker, K. A., Greiner, L., Scott, T., & Skilling, T. A. (2021). Complex trauma and criminogenic needs in a youth justice sample: A gender-informed latent profile analysis. *Criminal Justice and Behavior*, 48(2), 175–194. https://doi.org/10.1177/0093854820964513

Burr, V. (2015). *Social constructionism* (3rd ed.). Routledge.

Calhoun, L. G., & Tedeschi, R. G. (Eds.). (2006). *Handbook of posttraumatic growth: Research & practice*. Lawrence Erlbaum Associates.

Council of Europe. (2018). *Recommendation CM/Rec(2018)8 of the Committee of Ministers to member States concerning restorative justice in criminal matters*. https://search.coe.int/cm?i=09000016808e35f3

Cozolino, L. (2006). *The neuroscience of human relationships: Attachment and the developing social brain*. W.W Norton & Company.

Crocker, D. (2015). Implementing and evaluating restorative justice projects in prison. *Criminal Justice Policy Review*, 26(1), 45–64. https://doi.org/10.1177/0887403413508287

European Forum for Restorative Justice (EFRJ). (n.d.). *The encounter of the encounters: Restorative dialogues with witnesses of political violence and violent extremism*. www.euforumrj.org/en/encounter-encounters

Greenfield, E. A., & Marks, N. F. (2010). Sense of community as a protective factor against long-term psychological effects of childhood violence. *The Social Service Review*, 84(1), 129–147. https://doi.org/10.1086/652786

Herman, J. L. (1997). *Trauma and recovery: The aftermath of violence, from domestic abuse to political terror*. Basic Books.

Janoff-Bulman, R. (2010). *Shattered assumptions*. Simon & Schuster.

Kerig, P. K., Chaplo, S. D., Bennett, D. C., & Modrowski, C. A. (2016). "Harm as harm": Gang membership, perpetration trauma, and posttraumatic stress symptoms among youth in the juvenile justice system. *Criminal Justice and Behavior*, 43(5), 635–652. https://doi.org/10.1177/0093854815607307

Levenson, J. S., Prescott, D. S., & Willis, G. M. (2021). Trauma-informed treatment practices in criminal justice settings. In E. L. Jeglic & C. Calkins (Eds.), *Handbook of issues in criminal justice reform in the United States* (pp. 483–502). Springer International Publishing. https://doi.org/10.1007/978-3-030-77565-0_24

Manda, C. B. (2017). Healing and reconciliation as a pastoral ministry in post-conflict South African Christian Communities. *Verbum et Ecclesia*, 38(1), a1562. https://doi.org/10.4102/ve.v38i1.1562

Manda, C. B. (2019). *Re-authoring life narratives after trauma: A holistic narrative model of care*. AOSIS.

Marsh, B. (2011). Narrating desistance: Identity change and the 12-step script. *Irish Probation Journal*, 8, 49–68.

Maruna, S. (2001). *Making good: How ex-convicts reform and rebuild their lives*. American Psychological Association.

Maruna, S. (2016). Desistance and restorative justice: It's now or never. *Restorative Justice: An International Journal*, 4(3), 289–301. http://dx.doi.org/10.1080/20504721.2016.1243853

Meichenbaum, D. (2006). Resilience and posttraumatic growth: A constructive narrative perspective. In L. G. Calhoun & R. G. Tedeschi (Eds.), *Handbook of posttraumatic growth: Research & practice* (pp. 355–367). Lawrence Erlbaum Associates Publishers.

O'Mahony, D., & Doak, J. (2017). *Reimagining restorative justice: Agency and accountability in the criminal process*. Bloomsbury.

Patton, M., & Goodwin, R. (2008). *Survivors helping survivors: A study of the benefits, risks, & challenges of peer-support with survivors of sexual violence in the province of Ontario*. https://wayback.archive-it.org/16312/20211208220147/https://www.attorneygeneral.jus.gov.on.ca/inquiries/cornwall/en/report/research_papers/Party_RP/3_Peer-Support-Guide_en.pdf

Stone, R. (2016). Desistance and identity repair: Redemption narratives as resistance to stigma. *British Journal of Criminology*, 56, 956–975. https://doi.org/10.1093/bjc/azv081

Tedeschi, R. G. (2020). Growth after trauma. *Harvard Business Review*. https://hbr.org/2020/07/growth-after-trauma

Tedeschi, R. G., & Moore, B. A. (2016). *The posttraumatic growth workbook: Coming through trauma wiser, stronger, and more resilient*. New Harbinger Publications.

Todahl, J., Olson, D., & Walters, E. (2017). Survivor insight: A study of family, friend, and community response to interpersonal violence. *Journal of Aggression, Maltreatment & Trauma*, 26(4), 391–410. https://doi.org/10.1080/10926771.2017.1278732

Umbreit, M. S., & Armour, M. (2011). Restorative justice and dialogue: Impact, opportunities, and challenges in the global community. *Washington University Journal of Law & Policy*, 36(1), 65–89. http://digitalcommons.law.wustl.edu/wujlp/vol36/iss1/5

United Nations Office on Drugs and Crime (UNODC). (2020). *Handbook on restorative justice programmes* (2nd ed.). www.unodc.org/documents/justice-and-prison-reform/20-01146_Handbook_on_Restorative_Justice_Programmes.pdf

Van der Kolk, B. (1996). Trauma and memory. In B. Van der Kolk, A. C. McFarlane, & L. Weisaeth (Eds.), *Traumatic stress* (pp. 279–302). Guilford Press.

Van der Kolk, B. (2014). *The body keeps the score: Mind, brain and body in the transformation of trauma.* Penguin Books.

Van der Kolk, B., & Van der Hart, O. (1995). The intrusive past: The flexibility of memory and the engraving of trauma. In C. Caruth (Ed.), *Trauma: Explorations in memory* (pp. 158–182). John Hopkins University Press.

Van der Merwe, C., & Gobodo-Madikizela, P. (2008). *Narrating our healing: Perspectives on working through trauma.* Cambridge Scholars Publishing.

Van Ness, D., & Strong, K. (2015). *Restoring justice: An introduction to restorative justice* (5th ed). Anderson Publishing, Ltd.

Vaughan, B. (2012). Subjectivity, narration and desistance. In M. Mohammed (Ed.), *Sortir de la délinquance: Théories, enquêtes, perspectives internationales* (pp. 89–111). La Decouverte.

Wigren, J. (1994). Narrative completion in the treatment of trauma. *Psychotherapy*, 31(3), 415–423. https://doi.org/10.1037/0033-3204.31.3.415

Zehr, H. (1990). *Changing lenses.* Herald Press.

3 Exploring restorative dialogues through the voices of lived experiences

Introduction

The true impact of restorative dialogues is not in its theory but in the lived experience of its participants. This chapter delves into the personal journeys of victims, offenders and facilitators who have engaged in restorative dialogues, revealing their underlying motivations and the perceived benefits that drive their involvement.

While the previous chapter laid the groundwork by exploring the principles and dynamics of restorative dialogues, this chapter turns to the lived experiences of participants. For many victims, the decision to participate stems from a deep sense of unmet or inadequately addressed needs within their communities. Offenders, too, are often motivated by personal needs and a desire to make amends.

Drawing on qualitative interviews with victims and facilitators, as well as insights from anonymous participant evaluations conducted after each Swiss programme, this chapter offers a comprehensive exploration of the impact of restorative dialogues. It also includes comments from offenders shared during final meetings, providing a rounded understanding of the process.

The chapter begins by examining the needs and motivations of victims, followed by an analysis of the benefits they perceived from their participation. The focus then shifts to the needs and motivations of offenders, before considering the challenges that both groups may face, with particular emphasis on the role of shame. Insights from the facilitators are added, culminating in a conclusion that summarises key findings and reflections.

Exploring victims' needs and their community's response to their needs

In the aftermath of crime, victims experience a myriad of needs essential for their recovery and overall well-being. Among these needs, establishing trusting relationships emerges as paramount, providing victims with a safe space to open up and be vulnerable. This profound desire for companionship and emotional support from their community of care is often the first and most pressing need. As one interviewee aptly put it: "I think I just wanted someone to be there. That was the biggest thing". Victims seek reassurance that they are not

DOI: 10.4324/9781003271611-3

alone, that their voices are heard and understood with compassion by their community. The need to be taken seriously was repeated throughout the interviews: "[I needed] understanding and, above all ... that they took me seriously and supported me".

Unfortunately, this essential need often remains unmet, leaving victims feeling isolated, misunderstood and abandoned. Where the need for trusting and supportive relationships is unfulfilled, it significantly affects another prominent need – the need to share their story. Whether this need arises immediately or subsequently, the need to express oneself, seek understanding and derive meaning through storytelling is common among victims. Yet, not all victims receive the empathy they long for: "You tell your story, you'd like to be understood, you'd like to have compassion and then you often encounter... incomprehension". Faced with such reactions, victims may be discouraged from fully disclosing their experiences for fear of judgement or disbelief, as articulated by one participant: "... people just looked at me like I'm crazy, so I ... just decided to share a little bit of information and, um ... not the whole story".

In instances where the crime occurred within the family, victims also have a need to communicate with their family members to understand how much they knew about the incident at the time, as well as their reactions, or lack thereof. This could involve directly confronting the offender or engaging with other family members who may have been aware of the situation but chose not to intervene. Yet, as reported by interviewees, this need is often met with resistance. Several victims described how their families withdrew from them, even though the crime was not the victim's fault. They wanted nothing to do with them, did not want to talk about what had happened or even decided to never speak to the victim again. As one victim expressed: "I felt all alone ... abandoned, actually. I felt like everyone had abandoned me because they didn't take me very seriously". Not surprisingly, several participants expressed that the reactions of their support networks hindered rather than supported their recovery and exacerbated their trauma. Some expressed that the reactions they were faced with were almost as traumatic as the crime itself.

Some participants were even blamed for their traumatic experiences, which exacerbated their suffering. A typical reflection on this experience was:

> You've suffered the act and then ... afterwards it's the blame that's hard to swallow because you didn't do anything in particular to make it happen. And then there's a feeling of guilt because you say, I could have done that, I should have done this, I should have done that. And then often ... they say "Yeah, but still, you could have done this, and so on" so, once again, we feel guilty. By ... people who weren't there at all, who've never experienced it and that was the difficulty at the time, at least for me. ... I actually lost people in these relationships because they didn't ... support me ... they got over it, and then they said well, we won't talk about it anymore, it's not worth it.

In other cases, the sheer scale of the stories was overwhelming for others to comprehend, which in turn compounded the pain for the victims. This was particularly distressing for one interviewee who felt that her community viewed her as vulnerable and fragile because of the severity of her experiences, rather than recognising her resilience. She vividly described feeling constantly burdened with the need to prove her ability to function despite her trauma, rather than being recognised as a resilient survivor deserving of support. As a result, although many felt the urge to share their experiences, they refrained from doing so because of these negative reactions. As one victim put it: "If you have to defend the fact that this has happened ... [then] I'm not really tempted to talk about it with a lot of people". Repeatedly hearing dismissive statements such as "Oh, if it's true [what happened to you], then it's really hard to live [with it]" not only caused pain, but also conveyed a lack of belief from friends, further discouraging victims from discussing their trauma. As one respondent poignantly put it, "No one understood what was happening to me inside". As a result, several interviewees felt that their trauma had been trivialised and that their experiences were insignificant, leading many victims to keep their trauma to themselves.

These adverse reactions were not limited to personal relationships but extended to interactions with professionals involved in their post-crime care. One interviewee poignantly recalled feeling re-traumatised by police interactions: "It was when the police came that I really had the feeling that I was reliving what had happened a second time". From the beginning, the police indicated that they would not be able to assist the victim significantly, and that it was unlikely that those responsible would be identified. For the victim, to hear this just after the crime was a significant source of distress. Another victim said she felt completely unacknowledged as someone who had experienced trauma: "In my case it was the police too, they didn't even say hello. I said hello but they didn't speak to me. It was as if I was nobody". Some struggled to find the psychological help they needed, and even where they did, some victims felt that the psychologists they spoke to were overwhelmed with their story and lacked the skills to effectively manage the emotional consequences arising from the incident. For others, they felt their cases were not handled professionally because the psychologist appeared to be more interested in the details of the incident rather than addressing their emotional needs. One victim from a highly publicised case lamented the media's lack of emotional intelligence in telling her story and she emphasised the need for more sensitive media portrayals.

As a result, interviewees often expressed frustration with the sporadic and inadequate positive responses from their community, including professionals. They deeply yearned for support and believed that their community could have significantly contributed to their recovery, yet such assistance was largely absent. This absence of support posed challenges for interviewees in coping with and healing from their experiences, compelling them to seek alternative sources for both support and answers to their questions. Many interviewees expressed a desire to directly confront their offender and seek answers to their questions. However, with the exception of one case, this was not possible due to the offender's unwillingness, safety concerns or the inability to identify the offender.

Ultimately, the responses of the interviewees demonstrate the crucial role of supportive relationships for individuals affected by trauma. Research indicates that survivors of trauma require compassionate listening, acknowledgement of the impact of the traumatic event and effective support. They seek interactions that are free of judgement, blame, coercion or labelling. Furthermore, survivors value having a support network that includes professionals and organisations that are well informed about trauma and able to provide appropriate support. While discussing trauma can be challenging, survivors value the opportunity to share their experiences and insights into coping and healing in a safe and supportive environment.[1] This is one of the reasons why they may wish to participate in restorative dialogues.

Why do victims want to participate in restorative dialogues?

Crime victims struggle with a wide range of needs, emotions and questions following the harm suffered. At the heart of their struggle is a deep need to make sense of their experience and to understand why it happened to them. As expressed in the interviews, the decision to engage in restorative dialogues with offenders often stems from this need to understand the motivations and rationales underlying the perpetration of harm. As one interviewee expressed, "I wanted to hear why offenders do what they do". Similarly, another participant expressed a desire for the opportunity to ask questions and gain insights to aid their recovery. When victims are left with unanswered questions, it becomes difficult for them to find closure and move on from the incident as they may feel trapped in their experiences and fears.[2]

Beyond the search for answers lies a much deeper longing for authentic engagement and dialogue. For victims who have not been in contact with the person who offended against them, meeting others who have committed similar crimes can help to humanise the person who hurt them. One interviewee stated, "I wanted to have a discussion with the offenders; to talk to someone who has caused harm. I wanted to look them in the eye". This underlines the importance of direct interaction. Some victims construct an image of their offender as a monstrous figure, unable to comprehend how any human could commit such grievous acts. These perceptions only heighten the fear experienced by victims. Meeting other offenders face to face can help victims to recognise their shared humanity, alleviating their fear and aiding healing and closure.

This was reflected in the victim interviews: "My hope was to heal more. I thought that by understanding them better, I might be able to heal some more". By sharing their stories and experiences with offenders, victims hope to find a sense of closure and empowerment. "I had the conviction that it could be helpful for me to share with others", said another interviewee, "to share my story, my experiences, my pain".

There is also a need to share their own story, as many victims have not had the opportunity to share their full story with their community of care for fear of their reactions or overwhelming them. Some tried to share but found their community unresponsive or unwilling to listen. One interviewee said that her "goal was to talk and see that it is okay to talk about it". Another shared that she had "never talked about it with others but had the need to talk". In addition, victims often seek the opportunity to confront offenders with the consequences of their actions: "I felt the need to show the offenders the damage they were causing to the victim and the family". Another added: "I wanted to see their reactions when I shared my story". There can also be a need to address the offender's side: "I needed to not only work on myself but also deal with the other side and deal with my feelings towards them".

For other victims, the motivation to participate in restorative dialogues stemmed from the inability to engage in a direct restorative justice process with their own offender, or from feeling disillusioned with, and unsupported by, the criminal justice system. One interviewee explained: "I decided to participate because the criminal justice system had not been helpful and restorative for me". The reasons why victims want to participate thus reflect a multi-layered quest for connection, understanding, support and validation. They are motivated by a deep desire for genuine dialogue, which is often lacking in their personal communities, and an urgent need to confront and understand the circumstances of their victimisation. This was also Michael's case.

Case study 3.1: Michael's questions

Michael's house was broken into during the night while the family were asleep. He was the first to get up in the morning and discover the havoc the burglars had left behind. The entire family was in shock and fear. Michael later said that it was not so much the shock of what had happened, but what might have happened if someone had woken up to find the burglars. It seemed that they had been frightened off and left. Michael was afraid that they might have got into their rooms and hurt them.

Another big fear was that they might come back another night, knowing what was in the house and not having taken everything. This fear followed him every step of the way. His wife did not even want to live in the house anymore and went to stay with other family members. Eventually, they decided to sell the house and move elsewhere, no longer feeling safe in the house that had been in their family for decades.

However, even with the move, the questions remained. Why me? Why did they choose our house? Had they been watching us? Would they come back to the new house? Michael could no longer live with these questions. He desperately wanted to talk to the burglars and get answers to his questions, but they had not been identified and arrested. Nevertheless, the questions were making it difficult for Michael to get on with his life. Therefore, he decided to take part in restorative dialogues, hoping to get some answers from others who had committed similar crimes. After his participation he said: "I wanted to participate because I had the big question of 'why'. How does someone become a criminal? Why did they choose me? It helped me to see that I had a person in front of me, with his fears, his anxieties, his qualities, his faults, just like me, and above all with his hopes".

Michael's experience illustrates how restorative dialogues can address some of the questions and emotional needs of victims. The opportunity to work through personal fears and insecurities in a safe group environment is one of the potential benefits of such processes, yet there are more, as the following section will reveal.

Perceived benefits for victims in participating in restorative dialogues

Participating in restorative dialogues can be a transformative experience for victims of crime, providing a unique space where individuals can openly express their experiences, share their pain and find solace in connecting with others. A fundamental need that is satisfied through this process is the need to be heard and to have their experiences and suffering acknowledged. Yet, this is just one of many benefits they perceive.

1. *Enriched understanding through different perspectives*

Interviewees confirmed that exposure to different perspectives played an important role in their participation. They experienced how these shared narratives enriched their understanding of the complexity of their experiences. Victims expressed that the presence of offenders was as important as that of other victims. One participant reflected: "I quickly became convinced that sharing between victims and offenders could really help both sides".

2. *Empowerment and reconnection through dialogue in a group setting*

Many interviewees emphasised the importance of the dialogue taking place within a group, particularly in a small group setting. This setting helped them to reconnect with others and break down barriers of fear. For instance, one respondent recounted how her experience of crime and the subsequent reactions of her community had eroded her trust in others. However, participating in the group setting helped her to overcome this fear and allowed her to reconnect with others and share openly. Moreover, the group setting proved particularly beneficial for victims who felt isolated within their communities. It provided a space not only for sharing but also for listening, observing and receiving feedback. This exchange within the group offered valuable insights into different viewpoints, allowing participants to learn from each other's stories and experiences.

3. *Validation through shared experiences*

Meeting fellow victims and hearing their stories served as a source of comfort and validation for the interviewees, normalising their own experiences and traumatic reactions. Knowing that they were not alone and that others shared similar experiences had a healing impact on many participants. As one victim said:

> I've never come out of a session the same way I went in. And, I say to myself, well, I'm not alone in the world. So, for me it's actually a positive thing … for me it's almost like therapy … it was reassuring to hear the stories of other victims because you can tell yourself that you're not alone.

4. *Impact of engaging with offenders*

For some participants, the presence of offenders was equally as important as, if not more than, the presence of victims. Engaging with offenders gave victims the opportunity to listen to their stories, to understand their perspectives and emotions, and to see them take responsibility for their crimes. Many victims found it significant to witness the impact of their stories on offenders, particularly when discussing how the consequences often extended to their family members, leading to a profound change in their understanding of the consequences of their actions. Victims reported witnessing a notable transformation in the offenders' outlook as they engaged in deep introspection and reflection on their actions and the harm they had caused. One victim expressed certainty that offenders would be unable to forget the stories shared by victims, while another believed that sharing these stories could have a preventative effect and encourage dialogue rather than violence. Consequently, several victims claimed that these dialogues made a real difference, transforming their negative experiences into a catalyst for positive change such as reducing the likelihood of further crimes being committed by those offenders.

5. *Recognising shared humanity and moving beyond labels*

Moreover, interacting with offenders enabled victims to move beyond the label of 'offender' and recognise their shared humanity. When victims discovered that they had much in common with offenders, especially shared experiences of victimisation, it helped to alleviate their anger and support their recovery. During the meetings, offenders often shared they had been victims themselves and felt similar emotions. This realisation fostered a sense of shared humanity and bridged the gap that had previously existed.

Removing the 'offender' label was not the only important aspect; removing the 'victim' label was equally significant. One interviewee finally felt valued as a human being rather than a fragile, vulnerable victim whom others outside the group were reluctant to engage with openly. She emphasised her need for open, honest and sometimes confrontational conversations – conversations that were always respectful in the group setting. Even when difficult, she valued hearing the unvarnished truth over delicate treatment. The group environment provided a safe space for these discussions, and she appreciated the opportunity to engage with others in this way. For her, real growth and understanding occurred during these challenging moments.

6. *Support of community members*

In some programmes, unrelated community members joined victims and offenders as supportive participants. One interviewee emphasised the importance of their presence, seeing it as a vital and comforting element. The involvement of community members filled a gap he keenly felt throughout his recovery process. Their willingness to volunteer their time without expecting anything in return deeply touched him and contributed to a sense of resolution and healing. He saw their involvement as a positive step towards healing, allowing his wounds to begin to mend.

7. *The healing power of storytelling*

A central aspect of restorative dialogues is the act of storytelling, serving as a tool for victims to share their experiences, pain and memories. Storytelling fulfils the need to be heard, one of the most important benefits of restorative dialogues, according to victims. For many, the need to tell their story and have it acknowledged is paramount. There is a sense of validation and understanding in receiving responses such as "We have received your story; we have heard you". In addition, seeing the empathy and understanding in the eyes of offenders, sometimes shimmering with tears as they begin to grasp the impact of the crime on victims and their families, further validates victims' experiences. "You could feel the empathy ... they were also affected when they heard what had happened to me". The validation and recognition received during these dialogues contributes to a sense of empowerment and facilitates victims' recovery.

8. *Transformative potential and contribution to positive change*

Verbalising their pain and witnessing its impact on the offenders, as well as the impact of their stories on them, was particularly powerful for victims and was perceived as a healing experience. Feeling genuine empathy and emotional resonance from offenders validated their experiences and provided a sense of closure. The act of being listened to and validated by offenders was deeply moving, as expressed by one victim who found unexpected comfort in a prisoner's sincere response to her distress. Another interviewee described how, throughout the process, she felt her pain begin to diminish. She recognised that it was possible to heal further and that through the process of sharing she felt that some more healing had already taken place in her life. It was a privilege for her to share in this group and to witness the reactions of the offenders:

> I didn't expect them to believe in me, to believe in my cause. But it is healing for me – [providing] remembrance and healing and closure. A little bit of the wound that was open is closed. It doesn't hurt as much when I talk about it ... That they understood what I was saying, that gave me security and closure, such an inner closure that I could say it's going to be okay now. Now I can talk about it – I wouldn't have been able to before.

9. *Contributing to prevention*

Some interviewees also highlighted the transformative potential of sharing negative experiences for what they considered 'constructive purposes'. Through storytelling, victims not only find validation and closure, but also the sense that they can contribute to a wider dialogue about violence and its impact on individuals and communities. One victim reflected on how his negative and very painful story could help offenders understand the consequences of their actions, leading to a constructive dialogue and mutual growth. It can be encouraging for victims to observe how their painful experiences can sensitise offenders to the impact of their crimes and foster an understanding of the far-reaching consequences. As one interviewee put it, this realisation can give victims a sense of empowerment, enabling them to see their suffering as a catalyst for positive change, in the hope that it will help prevent future crimes.

Summary

Victims of crime perceive several benefits from participating in restorative dialogues. The opportunity to share their stories in a safe and supportive environment satisfies their need to be heard and validated, fostering a sense of empowerment and promoting healing and recovery. Storytelling thus plays a crucial role. Furthermore, witnessing the offenders' empathy and understanding as they listen to the victims' experiences provides further validation and closure. Victims also appreciate the transformative potential of sharing their negative experiences in the hope of sensitising offenders and preventing further crime. Finally, participating in restorative dialogues helps victims come out of the isolation they may be feeling and reconnect with others, learning to trust others again and forming safe and supportive relationships.

Having gained insight into the needs and perceptions of victims, it is important to consider the same aspects from the offenders' perspectives.

Exploring offenders' needs

Like victims, offenders may feel a need to reconnect and come to terms with the offence and its consequences. During the considerable time they often spend alone in the cell, some may begin to reflect on their actions. This reflection may lead to an awareness of the potential harm their actions may have caused to their victims. This growing awareness can cause distress and trigger a need to work through what has happened with the victim. Some offenders feel the need to take responsibility, express remorse and explore ways to mitigate the harm they have caused. Unfortunately, it is not always possible to engage in such a process directly with those they have harmed.

As part of the process of coming to terms with the past, we often hear offenders in interviews express a desire to understand. It is not uncommon for them to grapple with deep questions about 'why'. They may ask themselves how they came to offend in the first place, or how they could have reacted in such a way as to cause so much harm and pain to another person. While they seek to understand the reasons for their actions, there is often a need to comprehend what the offending has caused in their victims. In interviews, offenders often state that they need contact with victims to gain a true understanding. They hope that this will help them to recognise and accept the consequences of their actions and thus reduce the likelihood of reoffending.

Like victims, offenders may long for closure. There may be a desire to apologise and seek forgiveness, although they are often aware that they never 'deserve' it and should not demand it. There is also often a need to be able to explain to victims how the offence happened and why.

While it is important for offenders to understand the consequences of their actions, they also need help in dealing constructively with their feelings of guilt. Taking responsibility for one's actions towards victims can be an important step in this direction and is a serious concern for some. However, where this is not possible, it may be beneficial for offenders to express at least symbolic remorse to victims of similar offences.

The isolation and separation from loved ones that results from imprisonment, as well as the tendency to be labelled as an 'offender' by society, often makes it difficult to satisfy basic needs such as relationships and belonging. As with victims, there is also a deep sense of loneliness and isolation and a need for community – the need to feel part of a community, to belong and to be seen not just as an 'offender' but as a human being. This need extends to the sharing of experiences.

An often overlooked need is the ability to deal with personal trauma. As will be discussed in the next chapter, studies show that a significant proportion of serious offenders have themselves been victims of serious crime, often in childhood or adolescence. Unresolved trauma is a significant risk factor for violent offending against self and others.[3] It is therefore important to be able to deal with one's own past and any trauma to reduce recidivism.

The primary needs of offenders can be broadly categorised into two main areas: firstly, an understanding of their own actions and the reasons behind them; and secondly, an understanding of the impact of their actions on victims. In addition, offenders also have a need for connection and belonging, as well as the opportunity to share their experiences and emotions, including their own pain. This can be seen as a way of coming to terms with the past and finding ways to address the harm caused and experienced, as well as to act and react differently in the future.

Why do offenders want to participate in restorative dialogues?

When interviewing offenders interested in participating in restorative dialogues at the Swiss RJ Forum, we always ask them about their motivations for taking part in these dialogues. Most often, their motivation is connected to the need to hear victims' stories first hand to understand the impact of their crimes on the lives of others. As stated above, many offenders find it difficult to grasp the full extent of the consequences of their actions without direct contact with their victims or victims of similar crimes. In cases where victims were not physically harmed, offenders often admit that they did not consider the harm they may have caused. It is only with time spent reflecting in their prison cells that they begin to consider the impact of their actions on the lives of their victims. For those who have caused physical harm, this awareness may come sooner and manifest as remorse or even nightmares. However, they claim that without talking to their victims, or victims of similar crimes, they cannot fully grasp the impact of their actions.

Motivations for participating in restorative dialogues vary. Some offenders want to understand the consequences of their crimes in the hope that this awareness will deter future reoffending. There are cases where offenders acknowledge that without understanding the victims' perspective and suffering, their risk of reoffending remains high. This acknowledgement is particularly notable in cases of armed robbery and burglary, where offenders may rationalise their actions by claiming that they did not intend to harm the victims. Despite the seemingly detached reasoning, I have observed that such recognition serves as a central motivator for participation in the programme. After listening to the victims' stories, offenders typically show visible shock as they acknowledge the serious consequences of their actions, not only for the victims but also their loved ones.

Others express a desire to support victims of similar crimes by being available to answer their questions, listen to their stories, and show respect and empathy, believing this could help victims in their recovery process. Several participants reflected that this programme was the most difficult thing they had ever done. One person said: "Hearing the victims' stories, seeing their faces, their pain; it was like a slap in the face". Many offenders never imagine the impact their crimes could have on victims and their community. These conversations allow them to understand the far-reaching effects of crime on individuals and their loved ones, and encourage them to reflect critically on their actions. In some cases, offenders feel the need to rationalise their actions in order to live with themselves. Many struggle with sleepless nights after hearing the victims' stories. And yet, they do not feel judged or condemned by the group; instead, they sense that the participants are there to support each other, to walk a path of recovery together – painful though it may be, it is also healing for both sides.

Therefore, the primary motivations for offender participation in restorative dialogues typically include a need for understanding, a desire to support unrelated victims of crime, and an opportunity for personal growth aimed at preventing future recidivism. In some instances, offenders also use the group process to prepare for possible direct victim–offender dialogues with their own victims in the future. Anthony's case provides a vivid illustration of the motivations that offenders may display.

Case study 3.2: Anthony's eye-opening moment

Anthony came to Switzerland as a child refugee. He found it difficult to integrate. He says he fell in with the wrong crowd at an early age and was soon moving in criminal circles. As a young adult, he began committing armed robberies and for a long time he remained unidentified. One day, when he was walking home, he suddenly saw a person pointing a revolver at him. He says he saw his life flash before his eyes and thought it was over. Even more so when he recognised that he was surrounded by a group of people. Only after a while did he realise that the person in front of him was trying to tell him something, but that he could not hear because he had air pods in his ears. He slowly took them out and heard the person shouting: "Police, surrender". The relief he felt was enormous because he was convinced that the Swiss police would not shoot him.

Sitting in his solitary cell, he suddenly understood that his victims must have felt the same way when he committed armed robberies. He had never thought about it before. He believed that everyone at the location of the robbery understood that the robbers were only interested in stealing money from the bank, not in harming the people inside. As the robberies were brief, he was also confident that there would be no adverse consequences for those involved. Now, however, he was overcome with doubt and wondered if he had caused harm to others. If the victims experienced the same fear and uncertainty as he did when he was apprehended by the police, how much more terrifying must it have been for them to be confronted by robbers. The victims could not be sure of the robbers' intentions and certainly feared for their personal safety. These doubts led him to participate in restorative dialogues. He recognised that he needed to hear directly from the victims of armed robbery what the experience was like for them and how it affected their lives. After attending the dialogues, he said it was brutal to hear their testimonies and comprehend the incredible damage he had done, not only to the victims but also to their families. He admitted: "In those moments I never thought of you, only of myself. But I will not be able to do that in the future because I will always be thinking of you. I have no words to express how touched and grateful I am that you were willing to come and talk to me – to us – when you had suffered so much. I have learned so much from you".

Anthony's case illustrates the profound effect that exposure to victims' stories can have on offenders. Through this process, offenders are often confronted with the real consequences of their actions, fostering a deeper understanding and empathy for those they have harmed. This ability to learn from victims and their experiences is one of the key benefits that offenders perceive in restorative dialogues, and it is a theme that will be explored further in the following section.

Perceived benefits for offenders in participating in restorative dialogues

Participation in restorative dialogues offers offenders a unique opportunity for personal reflection and growth. These dialogues create a space where offenders can directly confront the impact of their actions, gain insight into the experiences of victims, and receive support from a community setting. This section explores the range of benefits reported by offenders, highlighting how these dialogues promote empathy, accountability and the development of key skills, ultimately contributing to rehabilitation efforts.

1. Community and support

One of the most important benefits cited by offenders participating in restorative dialogues is the opportunity to experience a sense of community. In prison, where isolation is prevalent, being part of a group that treats them as human beings and not just as offenders resonates deeply. Many express that the dialogue group becomes like a supportive family where they feel safe to open up about their lives, crimes and personal traumas. This environment of trust and openness fosters hope and motivation for personal change.

2. Insight into the victim's experience

Participation in restorative dialogues exposes offenders to first-hand accounts of victims' experiences. Confronted with the tangible effects of their actions, offenders gain insight into the emotional and psychological scars caused by their crimes. This experience often triggers empathy, leading to personal reflection, remorse and a genuine desire to make amends and prevent future harm.

3. The healing power of storytelling

Participation in restorative dialogues allows offenders to share their personal stories in a supportive environment. Many offenders find it both challenging and cathartic to articulate their stories, often for the first time. This process not only helps them come to terms with their own traumatic experiences, but also begins a process of healing. The compassionate listening and support of the dialogue group provides validation and encouragement, enabling offenders to process their feelings and experiences. By acknowledging their past and sharing it with others, offenders can experience a sense of relief and empowerment, which can contribute positively to their rehabilitation.

4. *Encouraging self-reflection and understanding of personal triggers*

Sharing their own narratives also helps them to explore the underlying motivations for their offending in a supportive, non-judgemental environment. By exploring their stories and receiving feedback from others in the group, offenders gain valuable insights into their behaviour, including identifying personal triggers and understanding the root causes of their actions. This process of self-reflection is crucial for taking critical steps towards desistance and personal growth, as it enables offenders to confront their past and make informed decisions about their future.

5. *Acceptance and restoration of self-esteem*

Another important benefit is the acceptance and support that offenders receive from the group. This acceptance helps to rebuild their self-esteem and challenges the stigma and isolation they often face in prison. Feeling valued and respected in the community encourages offenders to take responsibility for their actions and commit to positive change.

6. *Accountability and responsibility*

The process of sharing and listening in restorative dialogues can instil a sense of accountability and responsibility in offenders. A clear comprehension of the tangible consequences of their actions, not only on victims but also on their own families and communities, can result in a strong motivation to desist from crime, as they become more aware of the broader implications of their actions.

7. *Communication and emotional regulation skills*

Finally, restorative dialogues can assist offenders in developing better communication and emotional regulation skills. By participating in structured discussions and listening empathetically to others, offenders learn to express their emotions constructively and understand the perspectives of others. These skills are essential for personal development and successful reintegration into society.

Summary

In summary, restorative dialogues provide offenders with an opportunity to experience community, gain insight into the impact of their crimes, reflect on their own lives and receive support from others. Collectively, these elements facilitate personal growth, empathy and a motivation to change, which in turn can potentially contribute to the rehabilitation of the individual and a reduction in recidivism.

However, engaging in restorative dialogue can also present challenges that need to be taken seriously, despite the benefits perceived by participants.

Challenges experienced by participants in restorative dialogues

In my research, I sought to explore not only the benefits but also the perceived challenges faced by participants in restorative dialogues. While interviewees consistently stated they had not experienced any disadvantages from the process itself, they did highlight some challenges they faced during their journey that need to be considered when implementing restorative dialogues.

1. Intensity and length of sessions

Participants, particularly victims, find the emotional intensity challenging and demanding. Although restorative dialogue programmes typically last 15–16 hours, many feel that this is not enough time. They need time to adjust to the group dynamics and topics, and often feel that discussions with other participants could last much longer. They acknowledge the finite nature of the programme, but stress the importance of careful planning to avoid feeling rushed. They stress the need for sufficient time between meetings to reflect on and digest the discussions. While some prefer weekly meetings, others favour longer intervals. One option might be to include a break somewhere in the programme, so that at least once there is a break of more than a week.

Likewise, offenders frequently express a similar sentiment regarding the programme's intensity, with many initially feeling that eight meetings is a considerable number. However, they soon come to realise the swiftness with which time passes during the course of the programme, and often express at the conclusion that they would have liked the opportunity to continue, as they perceive there is still much to be discussed and that being in a community is of significant value for them. Consequently, the conclusion of the programme can be a challenging experience for participants.

2. Timing and readiness

Given the emotional intensity of the journey, interviewees stressed the importance of carefully assessing whether a victim is ready for such a programme. While they unanimously believe that these dialogues are beneficial and healing for victims, they stressed the importance of timing. Soon after the crime may be too soon, as victims often need time to process the experience with the help of their community or professionals. Victims should therefore enter the programme when they feel ready and well prepared. Adequate assessment and preparation must ensure that they have a detailed understanding of what to expect throughout the programme.

3. *Participation with offenders before sentencing*

Some victims noted that they had participated in restorative dialogues with offenders who had not yet been sentenced. This was a significant challenge as there was a concern that offenders might exploit the programme to secure a lighter sentence. One victim said he would not have participated in the process if he had known that an offender would take part before sentencing. "My feeling was, I'm getting abused again! Because my fear is okay, you are going to use those days in front of the judge ... and I don't want to participate in that process." Others, while less concerned about this aspect, observed that offenders awaiting sentencing were less forthcoming with their own stories and therefore more reluctant to respond to victims' questions. There was a consensus among victims that if pre-sentence offenders were to take part, this should be communicated to victims prior to the start of the programme so that they could either accept or refuse their or the offender's participation in the group.

For those who participate in the programme prior to sentencing, the process can also be challenging. They fear that what they say in the groups will be used against them in court. Consequently, many of them are reluctant to engage in the programme or share their stories. This can result in a lack of openness, which presents challenges for the victims.

4. *The need for openness*

A lack of openness among offenders in general is a major challenge for victims, not only when participating with offenders who are still awaiting their trial. Victims rely on offenders to be open and honest about their lives, actions and motivations, and to take responsibility for these. When this transparency is lacking, it hinders genuine dialogue, which can be emotionally distressing for victims. It is therefore also imperative that offenders are adequately prepared, understand the expectations and commit to open communication.

5. *Transparency in participant information*

Interviewees highlighted the challenges they faced when they did not have prior information about the offenders involved. Although they did not need personal details such as names, it would be helpful to know the types of crimes participating offenders had committed. Without this information, victims may be reluctant to raise certain issues or ask specific questions for fear of upsetting offenders. As a result, this hesitation can hinder the victims' ability to participate freely in discussions. In addition, prior knowledge helps victims to prepare internally. It can be unsettling to walk into a room with no prior information and suddenly find yourself sitting next to someone who has committed a serious crime such as murder. Knowing the offender's background in advance allows victims to prepare mentally for such encounters, making it easier to face the situation.

Similarly, offenders also require information regarding the types of offences that will be represented within the group. This helps them to prepare emotionally for the encounter. Furthermore, they require to be informed if there is no victim who has experienced the same type of crime they have committed, as this may cause them to become dissatisfied with the programme. This is easily perceived by the group, which could have negative consequences for the group dynamics.

6. *Matching offender and victim experiences*

Understanding the range of crimes represented in the group is equally important for victims, especially if there is no offender present who has committed the same type of crime that they experienced. While some victims are open to dialogue with offenders of crimes that differ from their own, others have a specific need to talk to someone who has committed a similar crime. Therefore, providing this information in advance allows victims to determine whether the group is appropriate for their needs. This consideration also applies to offenders, who may find it challenging if they want to talk to a victim of a particular type of crime but find no one available. This mismatch can lead to frustration and potentially affect their attitude towards the group and their own participation. Therefore, transparent communication about the types of crime represented in the group is essential for both victims and offenders to have a positive experience.

7. *Managing breaks and informal interactions*

The inclusion of breaks during sessions to allow opportunity for informal sharing and interaction was perceived as beneficial by participants. However, in groups dealing with politically motivated crimes, facilitators need to be particularly attentive during breaks. They need to keep an open ear during ongoing discussions and monitor interactions closely. One victim reported feeling re-traumatised during a break when a participating community member, who had not experienced victimisation, failed to grasp the profound and devastating impact of such crimes on victims' families. This person minimised the impact during the conversation, causing significant hurt to the victim. For this reason, it is vital that the group establishes a set of agreed-upon ground values, which also apply to the breaks. However, it is crucial that the facilitators remain alert during the breaks to prevent such occurrences and to maintain a supportive environment for all participants.

8. *Managing storytelling*

The topic that received the most attention during the interviews was storytelling. While it was recognised as the most beneficial aspect for both victims and offenders, it was also recognised as the most challenging. Participants agreed that listening to each other's stories, while emotionally draining, is essential to understanding and making sense of one's own experience. Offenders' stories can be just as difficult to absorb as victims' stories, as they often recount their own experiences of victimisation, typically experienced during childhood or adolescence. Immersing oneself in the painful stories shared by participants can feel like riding an emotional rollercoaster.

It is therefore imperative that participants feel they are adequately supported during this phase. For example, for victims, it may be important to debrief outside the group sessions. Facilitators thus need to establish prior to the start of the programme whether victims have ongoing support from a therapist throughout the programme. If not, they should ensure that victims are aware of the facilitators' availability for discussion between sessions. If facilitators notice that a participant, whether victim or offender, appears to be deeply affected, it is important to proactively approach them to make sure they are okay and get the support they need. Some interviewees suggested that optional online meetings between sessions could be beneficial, particularly when stories are difficult to digest. In the case of offenders, it is of the utmost importance to ensure that they have access to support in prison should they require it following the storytelling sessions. In the absence of such support, it is the responsibility of the facilitators to discuss, prior to the commencement of the programme, the means by which offenders can reach them to obtain support between meetings. This is of significant importance also for the safety of the programme, as listening to the victims' stories and sharing one's own traumatic story can be profoundly distressing.

As participants can easily feel overwhelmed if too many stories are shared at once, they also suggested that the stories should be spread out over several sessions, with time for a break between each story to digest it and prepare for the next one. Sharing stories simultaneously carries the risk that participants will not listen fully, which can feel disrespectful to other group members. They know from their own experience how important it is to genuinely hear and acknowledge stories – to truly 'receive' them – and to treat them with the respect they deserve, which means being fully present.

Participants emphasised that listening to each other's stories was also a moment to be there for each other, to support each other, even to hold each other. Thus, despite the challenge of storytelling, it remains the most important element of the dialogues. Some interviewees said that it is important to have the courage not to close one's eyes to reality, to acknowledge that crimes happen every day and that it is no use denying this fact and not wanting to face reality. At the same time, it is important that offenders are well prepared to tell their story in a way that does not cause further harm to the victims. Therefore, facilitators need to spend enough time with them to discuss this aspect of the programme and prepare them to share their stories respectfully, taking into account the victims' emotions and personal experiences.

9. Addressing shame and providing emotional support

Finally, it is important to consider how challenging it may be for participants to share their own experiences, especially if it is the first time they are opening up and fully disclosing their story. Shame is an emotion that many people struggle with deeply, making it very difficult to speak out and be honest with themselves and others. Participants, therefore, need support throughout this process, and it can be very helpful if the issue of shame is addressed before the storytelling phase begins. It is also crucial for participants to receive reassurance that what they have shared will be received with an open mind and that they will not be rejected, as this may be a fear they have. One victim said that after sharing her narrative, she panicked thinking about how her community had reacted to her story. She was afraid that she would get the same reaction from this group: "I had this whole panic that everyone is going to think I'm crazy and that no one will ever want to talk to me again and that they want me out of this group". She thought it would be better if she never went back to the group. However, talking it through with the facilitator helped her to see that it was okay and that she could openly share her experience and fear with the group at the next meeting. She did this, and it was very helpful to receive this affirmation from the group, that they did not judge her, and that she was still accepted. Therefore, shame is an issue that needs to be considered for all participants, and facilitators need to know how to deal with it.

Why victims may experience shame after traumatic events

Understanding why victims struggle with shame can be challenging for those who have not experienced similar situations first hand. However, shame is a common experience for many individuals who have experienced trauma and is included as a possible symptom in the DSM-V criteria for trauma and stress-related disorders. Traumatic events such as sexual violence, multiple traumatic events or intimate partner violence with emotional abuse are known to trigger feelings of shame.[4] These experiences can lead to feelings of powerlessness and shame, which may exacerbate post-traumatic stress symptoms. Addressing shame, particularly in the context of trauma treatment, has been shown to reduce symptoms and promote recovery.[5] Therefore, it is important to consider shame when working with victims, as it can lead to negative coping behaviours.[6]

This was confirmed by interviewees who said that they either did not talk about their traumatic experiences or did not seek help because they felt ashamed. Several also described how they suffered from the shame inflicted on them by their relatives, which they found extremely painful and, in some cases, more distressing than the traumatic event itself. Some explained they had been accused by their relatives of not reacting appropriately or even of being responsible for the crime. One interviewee reported that his children were ashamed of him because of the traumatic symptoms he displayed after the crime. This was one of the most distressing and shameful experiences for him.

A review of the research literature enabled Dolezal and Gibson to identify several factors that may contribute to the experience of post-traumatic shame:[7]

- The traumatic event itself can directly trigger feelings of shame, which may subsequently lead to the individual internalising blame and holding themselves responsible for what happened.

- Ongoing reflection on one's behaviour and reactions during the traumatic event can serve to reinforce these feelings. This is further compounded by the perception of being damaged, defiled and unlovable, particularly in the context of complex traumatic experiences in childhood.
- Survivors may also perceive that they have failed to uphold personal ideals and standards, which can contribute to feelings of shame. Furthermore, the symptoms, coping strategies and identity labels associated with the trauma can also increase feelings of shame.
- The taboo surrounding the trauma and the associated shame can reinforce these feelings, which are further exacerbated by social stigmas associated with the type of trauma experienced and fear of judgement from others. Even in a therapeutic setting, shame can potentially interfere with the ability to discuss the event and its impact.

According to Scheff,[8] shame is the 'master emotion' that is often hidden due to the social stigma and taboo surrounding it. As such a powerful, negative and self-conscious emotion, it can prevent people from seeking help. In contrast to guilt, where individuals feel that their actions or behaviour were wrong ('I *did* a terrible thing'), people who feel shame judge themselves as inherently bad ('I *am* a terrible person'). This self-judgement fosters a fear of negative judgement from others and promotes a negative self-image. As a result, individuals may invest considerable effort in concealing their true selves for fear of being seen as flawed or immoral.[9] Shame is thus a complex emotion that includes a range of negative self-perceptions such as embarrassment, guilt, humiliation and shyness. These feelings may arise from the person's fear that their social connections with others are in jeopardy.[10] Shame has a profound impact on a person's sense of self-worth, reinforcing negative beliefs about themselves and creating barriers between them and others, potentially leading to isolation and hindering recovery from trauma.[11]

Recognising chronic shame can be challenging, even for the person experiencing it, as it is often hidden behind other emotions and maladaptive behaviours. Chronic shame involves a persistent sense of anticipated shame or fear of experiencing shame, leading to compensatory behaviours aimed at avoiding, masking or coping with its distressing effects and the pain it can cause. These coping mechanisms (i.e. isolation, disengagement, withdrawal, hiding, suppressing or limiting one's emotions) can damage interpersonal relationships and make it difficult to ask for help.[12] Given the central role of relationships in trauma recovery, it is easy to see how shame can be a significant barrier to recovery.

Shame is also closely linked to anger,[13] sometimes leading to self-harm or violence against oneself or others.[14] This relationship sheds light on why people who have experienced harm, such as abuse, may exhibit aggressive behaviour, as their anger often results from the shame they have endured. Furthermore, shame can have a significant impact on both mental and physical health, contributing to conditions such as low self-esteem, depression, anxiety and eating disorders.[15] It can also manifest in physical ailments,[16] and fuel behaviours such as perfectionism, people-pleasing tendencies, addictions, self-harm and compulsive behaviours, perpetuating a harmful cycle.[17] Shame is thus a possible consequence of trauma that needs to be carefully considered when working with people who have experienced traumatic events. How to do this will be explored in Chapter 5.

While this text discusses shame from the perspective of victims and the reasons why they may experience shame, it is important to remember that a significant proportion of offenders have also experienced trauma. As a result, they can be equally affected by shame, as they themselves may have been victims in the past. As mentioned in the previous paragraph, shame can also trigger anger and violence, which then can lead to causing harm to others.[18] Consequently, shame represents a risk factor for offending behaviour, as will be discussed in Chapter 4. For this reason, it is necessary to adopt a shame-sensitive approach with both victims and offenders in restorative dialogues. What this entails will be discussed in Chapter 5.

Facilitators' thoughts on addressing feelings of shame and self-blame

During the interviews, facilitators also emphasised the crucial role of restorative dialogues in providing a safe space for participants to confront feelings of shame and self-blame. One facilitator highlighted the profound impact of shame on victims, which often leads them to withhold their experiences for fear of being judged. However, in the protected environment of group dialogues, victims find comfort in opening up about their shame, as they start to trust others and gain a sense of solidarity and reassurance. This trust enables participants to realise that they are not alone in their struggles, which can help them to gradually reduce their feelings of shame and regain their agency. A facilitator emphasised the importance of guiding victims to recognise "I am the victim and it's not my fault that this happened to me". This acknowledgement can empower them and challenge their self-blame.

In her experience, victims often internalise feelings of blame and powerlessness, which can hinder their recovery. Their community's response can either exacerbate or alleviate these feelings, depending on the presence of supportive individuals. As a result, victims seek understanding and support from those who offer non-judgemental acceptance, even if they are not part of their immediate social circle. Many victims express a desire to connect with others who understand their experiences and find solace in participating in restorative dialogues where they can engage with other victims and share their feelings with offenders.

The exchange with the offender's perspective is critical and can help to overcome feelings of shame and place the blame where it belongs – on the person who has harmed them. This interaction fosters mutual understanding and empathy that contributes to the recovery process of both victims and offenders. The facilitator thus highlighted the reciprocal nature of restorative dialogues, where participants not only receive support but also give support to others, creating a sense of solidarity and empowerment.

Facilitators' views on the role and benefits of restorative dialogues

While this chapter has outlined what victims and offenders perceive to be the benefits of participating in restorative dialogues, it is now time to look at what facilitators have to say on the subject.

The facilitators echoed victims' views that these dialogues can foster a sense of belonging, rebuild trust and enable individuals to move on from their traumatic experiences. They are often impressed by the connections that form within these groups. One facilitator said: "There is really this expression of the importance of being able to recreate a form of community – where we feel safe, where we are able to move forward because we are recognised and we recognise each other in our story, in our respective stories".

Furthermore, facilitators agreed that these dialogues provide a platform for individuals to share their stories in a supportive environment:

> They all say how good it makes them feel to be able to hear each other's stories, how much it soothes them, and how it enables them to get out of their own narrow and restrictive vision, which is also confining. So something is clearly opening up again.

This sharing transcends the typical victim–offender dynamic and creates a connection that resonates on both sides, meaning that both victims and offenders feel understood and validated not only by their peers but also by the other group. Interestingly, it is in this exchange between the two groups that participants often find help where they least expect it. As they listen to each other and share their stories, they often uncover insights and perspectives that might otherwise elude them in more conventional therapeutic settings. Restorative dialogues thus create a space that "acknowledges their capacity to act … and to act together" because as participants experience a sense of belonging in this community, it also helps them "to rebuild security and regain the ability to act".

Restorative dialogues also benefit offenders by providing a space for reflection, empathy and acceptance within this community created by the group. They often approach these dialogues with questions such as:

> If I go there, what will they think of me and will they even talk to me? They will hate me … and then to experience that someone is accepted and that there is a community and yes, people who listen with appreciation, I think that is also very good for the offenders.

The conversations also challenge offenders' preconceptions and encourage them to rethink their actions: "Hearing what other offenders think about the offence … encourages them to reconsider their own actions". Importantly, however, the depth of reflection would not happen if they were simply sitting with a professional or in a peer group. According to one of the facilitators, there is something unique and powerful about

> the mix of offenders and victims that is very helpful and that I ... hadn't really thought about before or couldn't imagine what would happen and that it would actually ... It's more than just a support group afterwards. We have had peer support groups for a long time, but this mix brings about unexpected and profound changes [in perspectives]. It wasn't until I attended a session that I really realised the transformative potential of this interaction.

The facilitators therefore believe that restorative dialogues provide invaluable support and promote significant personal development for both victims and offenders.

Conclusion

According to the experiences shared by victims and offenders, and the findings of the facilitators, restorative dialogues provide a safe and supportive environment where participants can openly share their stories, experiences and emotions. This co-created space fosters a sense of belonging that participants may not have found, or may have lost, in their own communities. While opening up can be challenging, the presence of peers with similar experiences facilitates this process, allowing for deeper connections and mutual understanding.

Storytelling is proving to be a powerful and effective tool for both victims and offenders in their journey of recovery and desistance, helping to rebuild trust and empathy. However, the experience of shame can be a significant barrier to vulnerability and connection, highlighting the need for careful management of these dialogues. In addition, the profound impact of crime on personal relationships and the often lack of supportive confidants highlights the importance of restorative spaces in providing crucial support and understanding.

Despite the potential challenges, the benefits of restorative dialogues are evident. The experiences shared in this chapter illustrate the profound impact these dialogues can have on all participants. To overcome these challenges and maximise the effectiveness of restorative dialogues, it is essential that they are carefully prepared and led by trained facilitators, as will be discussed in subsequent chapters.

The following chapter presents some initial lessons from my own experience in developing and implementing restorative dialogues. These reflections will include suggestions and considerations for improving future practice to ensure that these dialogues continue to serve as a vital tool for all participants.

Notes

1 Todahl et al. (2017).
2 Van Ness and Strong (2015); Zehr (1990).
3 See, for example: Brown et al. (2021); Kerig et al. (2016).

4 Dolezal and Gibson (2022); Saraiya and Lopez-Castro (2016).
5 Saraiya and Lopez-Castro (2016); Taylor (2015).
6 Klinic Community Health Centre (2013).
7 Dolezal and Gibson (2022).
8 Scheff (2003).
9 Dolezal and Gibson (2022); Saraiya and Lopez-Castro (2016).
10 Scheff (2003).
11 Dolezal and Gibson (2022); Saraiya and Lopez-Castro (2016).
12 Bradshaw (2005); Dolezal and Gibson (2022); Taylor (2015).
13 Scheff (2003).
14 Nathanson (1992).
15 American Psychological Association (2018).
16 Thoresen et al. (2018).
17 Cuncic (2023).
18 Gilligan (2003); Nathanson (1992).

References

American Psychological Association. (2018). Shame. In *APA dictionary of psychology*. https://dictionary.apa.org/shame

Bradshaw, J. (2005). *Healing the shame that binds you*. Health Communications.

Brown, S. L., Wanamaker, K. A., Greiner, L., Scott, T., & Skilling, T. A. (2021). Complex trauma and criminogenic needs in a youth justice sample: A gender-informed latent profile analysis. *Criminal Justice and Behavior*, 48(2), 175–194. https://doi.org/10.1177/0093854820964513

Cuncic, A. (2023). *The psychology of shame*. Verywell Mind. www.verywellmind.com/what-is-shame-5115076

Dolezal, L., & Gibson, M. (2022). Beyond a trauma-informed approach and towards shame-sensitive practice. *Humanities and Social Sciences Communications*, 9(214), 1–9. https://doi.org/10.1057/s41599-022-01227-z

Gilligan, J. (2003). Shame, guilt and violence. *Social Research*, 70(4), 1149–1180.

Kerig, P. K., Chaplo, S. D., Bennett, D. C., & Modrowski, C. A. (2016). "Harm as harm": Gang membership, perpetration trauma, and posttraumatic stress symptoms among youth in the juvenile justice system. *Criminal Justice and Behavior*, 43(5), 635–652. https://doi.org/10.1177/0093854815607307

Klinic Community Health Centre. (2013). *Trauma-informed: The trauma toolkit* (2nd ed.). www.ctctbay.org/application/files/3615/4160/0382/The_Trauma-Informed_Toolkit_Second_Edition.pdf

Nathanson, D. (1992). *Shame and pride: Affect, sex, and the birth of the self*. Norton.

Saraiya, T., & Lopez-Castro, T. (2016). Ashamed and afraid: A scoping review of the role of shame in post-traumatic stress disorder (PTSD). *Journal of Clinical Medicine*, 5(11), 94–115. https://doi.org/10.3390/jcm5110094

Scheff, T. J. (2003). Shame in self and society. *Symbolic Interaction*, 26(2), 239–262.

Taylor, T. F. (2015). The influence of shame on posttrauma disorders: Have we failed to see the obvious? *European Journal of Psychotraumatology*, 6(1). http://dx.doi.org/10.3402/ejpt.v6.28847

Thoresen, S., Flood Aakvaag, H., Frugård Strøm, I., Wentzel-Larsen, T., & Skogbrott Birkeland, M. (2018). Loneliness as a mediator of the relationship between shame and health problems in young people exposed to childhood violence. *Social Science & Medicine*, 211, 183–189. https://doi.org/10.1016/j.socscimed.2018.06.002

Todahl, J., Olson, D., & Walters, E. (2017). Survivor insight: A study of family, friend, and community response to interpersonal violence. *Journal of Aggression, Maltreatment & Trauma*, 26(4), 391–410. https://doi.org/10.1080/10926771.2017.1278732

Van Ness, D., & Strong, K. (2015). *Restoring justice: An introduction to restorative justice* (5th ed). Anderson Publishing.

Zehr, H. (1990). *Changing lenses*. Herald Press.

4 Implementing restorative dialogues

Reflections from Switzerland

Introduction

My venture into restorative dialogues and the field of restorative justice began in 2012 during my work as a volunteer in Chilean prisons. My responsibilities included teaching courses on conflict resolution and the prevention of sexual and domestic violence, among other topics. One day, my supervisor handed me the manual for the original Sycamore Tree Project®, developed by Prison Fellowship in 1996, and expressed the need to implement this programme. Given the proximity of the initiative to my area of work in conflict resolution and crime prevention, he felt it would be most appropriate for me to oversee the initiative.

With no background in restorative justice, I was faced with the daunting task of implementing the Sycamore Tree Project®. As expected, there was a steep learning curve ahead, marked by significant milestones and turning points. Even now, after more than a decade, this journey remains an ongoing process of continuous reflection and adaptation. In the following pages, I would like to highlight the key lessons learned during this dynamic process and explore their implications for the current implementation of restorative dialogues in Swiss prisons.

In this chapter, I will first discuss the need to collaborate with prison staff to ensure the effective delivery of the programme. The next section will emphasise the importance of individual preparation for participants. I will then explain the changes made to the methodology and how an understanding of the prevalence of trauma in both victims and offenders has further influenced these changes. This discussion will naturally lead into the final section, which addresses the need for specialised training, including comprehensive trauma education.

The very first steps and lessons

The Sycamore Tree Project® was presented to me as just 'another programme' to be implemented. However, when I realised that it was a programme that facilitated encounters between victims and offenders, it became clear that it was unlike anything I had done before. As a former crime victim myself, my interactions with prisoners convicted of serious crimes had already provided opportunities for profound conversations that shaped my own healing process. I was

DOI: 10.4324/9781003271611-4

intrigued by the idea of bringing victims and offenders together, though I remained concerned about the potential distress experienced by victims entering prisons for the first time and meeting unfamiliar inmates. This concern was reinforced by my years of work outside prisons with victims of sexual and domestic violence.

Lacking a background in restorative justice, I struggled with the challenge of delivering the programme without causing unintended harm to the participants. To fill this gap, I enrolled in a one-year certificate programme in restorative justice at Simon Fraser University in Canada. Simultaneously, I initiated a pilot programme outside the prison walls to familiarise myself with restorative justice. By avoiding the added stress of entering the prison environment, my aim was to minimise the risk of inadvertent re-traumatisation of victims. The first group consisted of criminal justice professionals who had been victims of crime, were familiar with the system and experienced in working with offenders. This small-scale trial aimed to understand how the programme worked and to identify considerations for future implementation.

Despite diligently following the manual and engaging in deep discussions, the early efforts felt more like 'doing a programme' than fostering real dialogue. The programme was designed to include many topics for discussion, but the time allotted did not give participants enough opportunity to engage in free dialogue or to honour their personal stories in a respectful way by allowing sufficient time for them to do so. This lack of time meant that we had to share their stories in smaller groups rather than with the whole group. As a result, although we followed the prescribed programme, I felt that the group needed more time to enter into a genuine dialogue – a dialogue that facilitates a deep and meaningful understanding of oneself and of the other participants, ultimately fostering mutual respect and understanding. Soon after this pilot, I found myself preparing for the first implementation of the programme in a high-security prison. To address my ongoing concerns about the potential for re-traumatisation, I continued to recruit prison professionals who had been victims of crime.

As I immersed myself in my studies at Simon Fraser University, I began to reflect deeply on the nature and goals of restorative justice. My initial perception was that at the heart of this philosophy was an open and honest dialogue that focused on the stories and experiences of participants, rather than simply following a programme. This insight marked the beginning of a profound journey of self-reflection that has evolved over more than a decade. In 2013, it led me to evaluate not only my first implementation of the Sycamore Tree Project® in prison as part of my coursework but also subsequent implementations in Chile and Switzerland. From these initial reflections and subsequent implementations, key lessons emerged to inform future practice:

1 It became clear that it is essential to collaborate closely with prison staff, ensuring they are well informed about restorative justice and the programme, and actively involved in the preparations preceding each programme's implementation.

2 Individual preparation of participants also emerged as a critical factor.
3 Another key aspect was the methodology used during the meetings. I recognised that for restorative dialogues to be effective, it was not enough to simply follow a manual; it was important to cultivate genuine dialogue among participants and to empower them to shape the process according to their needs.
4 With each programme, I also became increasingly aware of the prevalence of trauma among the participants, extending beyond the victims to include the offenders. This led to the understanding that a trauma-informed approach with all participants was essential. Consequently, this highlighted the need for facilitators to receive specialised training to deal with the complexities inherent in restorative dialogues.

The following section discusses each of these lessons in more detail.

1. The need to collaborate with prison staff

When I implemented the first programme in Chile, I underestimated the importance of gaining the support of prison staff. I quickly learned that their involvement was crucial, as prison staff are the initial point of contact for victims entering prison and can significantly influence prisoners' willingness to participate. Their attitude towards restorative justice can both help and hinder access to the programme. In many cases, prison staff may lack familiarity with restorative justice principles, leading to misconceptions about its effectiveness. This knowledge gap can hinder the integration of restorative dialogues, resulting in resistance from staff and potential discouragement of prisoner involvement. It may also lead to undignified treatment of victims entering the prison. Effective collaboration with prison governors and staff is therefore essential for the successful implementation of restorative dialogues in prisons.

When I relocated to Switzerland, I began cultivating relationships with prison governors and staff based on my previous experience of successfully implementing restorative justice initiatives.

A key lesson learned was the importance of providing staff with comprehensive information about restorative justice and the programme itself, along with sensitisation to the needs of victims. Challenges arose in ensuring the physical and psychological safety of victims during security procedures, transiting through the prison and for the duration of their stay at group meetings. These initial challenges highlighted the necessity of careful consideration and collaboration in navigating implementation complexities with prison staff. To ensure effective implementation and staff support, it is crucial that those directly involved are educated about restorative justice principles, programme specifics and given the opportunity to ask the programme facilitators questions. Clear communication about what the programme entails, what it offers to both victims and offenders, and how its implementation can affect the day-to-day dynamics of prison life are essential for staff to understand the nuances of the programme, anticipate potential challenges and adapt conventional prison measures where needed. This ensures prison staff feel more involved and that they have a role to play in the success of the programme. In my experience, the prisons where this happens are also the ones where victims feel most welcome and safe.

Staff should also be knowledgeable about the specific needs of victims and how to address them within the prison setting. Understanding the impact of trauma on victims is essential for staff to respond empathetically and to create a safe environment. Failure to recognise trauma-related responses may lead to misunderstandings and hinder victim participation in restorative processes. In maintaining security measures or other procedures, staff must prioritise the welfare of victims. Sensitive procedures, such as body checks, require careful handling to minimise discomfort and preserve dignity. Restorative justice facilitators need to explain these processes in detail to victims so that they can prepare accordingly and, wherever possible, non-contact alternatives should be explored to alleviate anxiety and promote participation. If physical contact is necessary, the presence of both male and female staff is recommended.

Overall, staff awareness and support are crucial for the success of restorative justice initiatives in prisons. In my experience, in prisons where staff lack information about restorative justice and the specific programme, there can be a noticeable decrease in prisoner interest sometimes. At times, their involvement is even ridiculed by staff. By fostering understanding and collaboration, correctional facilities can create an environment where victims feel safe and respected, ultimately enhancing the effectiveness of restorative dialogues.

However, I realised that it is not only the preparation of the prison staff that is important but also the individual preparation of the participants.

2. Individual preparation of participants

I learned this lesson the hard way while implementing the first prison programme in Chile. At that time, I had not individually prepared the participants but grouped them together. This was mainly due to the fact that there was no mention of individual preparation in the manual I was given. Consequently, I missed the chance to connect with each participant, assess their motivations for taking part and understand insights into the level of harm caused, particularly in the case of prisoners.

During the storytelling phase, a situation escalated when a prisoner, convicted of a double murder, declared he was the true victim because he acted in self-defence. His narrative lacked insight into the harm he had caused, triggering disbelief and anger from the victims. This experience taught me the importance of individually preparing participants before the start of the programme. Additionally, we now prepare offenders in groups to address key issues and detect any underlying tensions before involving victims thorough a three-stage preparation process:

1 They attend an information session on restorative dialogues, where they are given detailed insight into the programme and have the opportunity to ask questions.
2 They take part in individual interviews in which they express their motivations for taking part and briefly tell their story.
3 Facilitators assess whether the individual accepts responsibility for his or her actions, with a particular focus on identifying signs of deflection, minimisation or denial, which could potentially cause further harm to victims if conveyed during the group setting.

The aim of these discussions is to support offenders in preparing to share their stories responsibly and sensitively with victims, minimising the risk of re-traumatisation. The aim is not only to recount the details of their crimes but also to provide insight into their lives, upbringing and the factors that contributed to their criminal behaviour. This multifaceted exchange can help victims understand the root causes of criminal behaviour and may provide answers to their questions. It can also provide offenders with personal insights into potential triggers for offending behaviour, helping them to identify areas where they need further support to desist from future offending.

Victims also have individual preparatory sessions with one or two facilitators to establish rapport, to identify needs and additional support they may need outside of the restorative dialogue process, and to ensure their expectations align with programme objectives. In my experience, the way victims tell their stories provides facilitators with valuable information about their psychological well-being and readiness for the programme. A crucial lesson for me came from working with a new restorative justice facilitator who assumed a victim did not feel comfortable telling me her story in person and suggested that she provide it in writing. I was uncomfortable with this, but I did not want to contradict my colleague in front of the victim.

The written statement gave me detailed insight into what had happened, but not into her emotional state and her recovery. During the subsequent group meetings, she was overwhelmed when participants asked her questions, and she became very upset. It became evident that she was not ready and that she needed more time and support before she could meaningfully engage with the process. Since then, we insist that victims tell us in person what they want to share during the programme so that we can gauge their readiness and provide the necessary support before the group sessions. By prioritising individual preparation and fostering open dialogue, we strive to create a safe and supportive environment for all participants in our programme. Recognising that reciprocal dialogue is key within this safe environment, I realised that changes were needed to encourage genuine exchange between participants.

3. Changes to the methodology used

When I first began implementing restorative dialogues in Chile, my practice was guided by a manual. However, I quickly realised that genuine dialogue between participants does not emerge through a pre-determined schedule but through deep conversations between victims and offenders, which aid their process of recovery. Participants need space to share their stories, their pain, to work through the consequences they have suffered or caused, along with confronting each other with their questions, emotions and experiences. Recognising this, I centred the process around the participants, understanding it as a flexible journey tailored to each group's unique needs and responsive to those involved.

Before engaging in this challenging work, participants need time to build relationships, trust and a safe environment. Without these foundations, participants may feel vulnerable or reluctant to engage authentically, hindering the effectiveness of the dialogue. This insight led to adjustments in the methodology, aiming to make the programme flexible while ensuring participants' ownership of the process. One significant change I made was introducing circle processes at the beginning and at the end of sessions. Circle processes are structured dialogues guided by a 'talking piece', encouraging equal participation and deep listening, creating a respectful environment for profound and sometimes difficult exchanges. At the beginning of the session, we start with questions that are related to the theme of the meeting but are also designed to foster deeper connections between participants. These questions can be childhood memories or light-hearted anecdotes. Not every question needs to be serious to serve the purpose of community building and deep listening. By giving everyone the opportunity to share without interruption, circle processes promote equality and respect, encouraging even reluctant participants to contribute. This approach fosters empathy and understanding, building trust and rapport within the group.[1]

The introduction of circle processes proved transformative, particularly in the initial sessions of each group. Witnessing the respectful and caring dynamic between participants, a journalist attending one of our meetings was deeply moved by how the participants responded to each other with care and compassion when this type of interaction is missing in so many communities and even families outside the prison walls. Instead of just attending this one meeting, she asked if she could join the group for subsequent meetings – which she did. She subsequently joined the programme as a facilitator, underscoring the profound impact of these processes. Since implementing circle processes, participants have also consistently commended their positive impact, noting their role in fostering safety, trust and attentive listening.

Another change to the process that moved away from the manual involved creating more space for storytelling, recognising the importance of authentic exchange between participants. Although these changes required removing some programme content, participants appreciated the increased focus on spontaneous conversations and storytelling at the heart of restorative dialogues. With the groundwork laid by circle processes, participants become used to deep listening without interruption and storytelling begins in session four of the programme. This kind of attentive listening is deeply comforting and healing for participants as they feel truly understood and accepted. This was also Lucy's experience.

Case study 4.1: Lucy's questions

Lucy's life was shattered when a family member committed murder within their own family. As soon as the justice system permitted, she bravely confronted the offender. She wanted answers to her questions, but she also needed to express her feelings and make him understand the enormous impact his crime had on the family. Despite this challenging, direct confrontation, Lucy also decided to take part in a restorative dialogue. The close relationship with the offender made it difficult to get certain answers, so she sought further understanding through the group process. She hoped to gain insight into the motivations behind such heinous acts and believed that sharing her story with others who had experienced similar tragedies could offer her support. While unable to fully disclose her story within her community, the environment of restorative dialogues provided a sanctuary for her to share her unvarnished truth.

Yet, Lucy's search for understanding went beyond storytelling. Recognising the power of entering into a two-way dialogue, she took the opportunity not only to share her story but also to ask the participating offenders questions. In this exchange, she discovered an unexpected source of insight – the questions the offenders asked *her*. Through these questions, Lucy was confronted with memories she had long suppressed, and felt that it was time to face them. Though a painful process, it ultimately brought great relief and marked a significant step forward in her journey to recovery.

4. The prevalence of trauma and its connection to offending behaviour

The more stories I listened to, I discovered that the line between victims and offenders was often blurred. Many of the offenders in our dialogues had themselves suffered serious harm, often during their formative years. It dawned on me that they were grappling with their own traumas, and storytelling served a dual purpose for them. It not only helped them make sense of their own painful experiences; it also shed light on the journey that led them to offend. As facilitators, we increasingly acknowledged the pervasive impact of trauma on both victims and offenders, intricately shaping their lives and relationships. Victims, in addition to bearing the trauma of the crime they had experienced, often carried the weight of past burdens, with the crime serving as a visible manifestation of deeper suffering or a tipping point for their resilience.

This realisation led me to delve deeper into the study of trauma, revealing its staggering prevalence within society. Research indicates that 70% of the world's population will experience at least one traumatic event in their lifetime, with 30.5% experiencing multiple traumas.[2] While 'only' a fraction (4–5%) develop PTSD, the enduring ramifications of trauma reshape lives and can even alter brain functions.[3] In the implementation of restorative dialogues, we found it imperative to address two facets of trauma:

1. Trauma inflicted by others, especially through violent acts, is most likely to have profound and lasting effects.[4] Given most victims participating in restorative dialogues will have experienced this type of victimisation, sensitivity to this reality is paramount to prevent further harm or re-traumatisation.
2. A considerable proportion of offenders in prison have themselves experienced significant trauma, particularly during childhood and adolescence.[5] Studies reveal a higher prevalence of PTSD among inmates compared to the general population,[6] underscoring the vulnerability of this population. Sensitivity to their traumatic experiences is therefore just as important as it is for victims.

Research has also revealed a link between trauma and offending behaviour,[7] and between PTSD and an increased likelihood of reoffending.[8] Certain types of traumas (e.g. childhood experiences of complex trauma and betrayal, poly-victimisation, adolescent maltreatment and racism) undermine a child's sense of safety and are known risk factors for the development of antisocial or offending behaviour.[9] Consequently, individuals who engage in offending behaviour may have grown up without a sense of safety and protection, exposed instead to continual threat and danger. This experience can impair the functioning of the prefrontal cortex, which affects an individual's control over behaviour, impulses, emotions, thought processes and interpersonal relationships.[10] This difficulty in effectively regulating actions and emotions increases vulnerability to offending behaviour, mental health conditions, substance abuse and efforts to find belonging outside the home.[11]

Reflecting on the stories I have heard over the years, my personal experience aligns with these research findings. A significant proportion of the offenders I have worked with have grown up in families marked by abuse and violence and a lack of safety, and this shaped their understanding of relationships. Often, violence perpetrated by parents or carers led them to internalise the notion that such behaviour was a manifestation of love and the acceptable norm in relationships. Consequently, they mirrored these patterns in their interactions, fostering resentment and a resolve to wield power and violence to protect themselves from further harm. This cyclic pattern perpetuates a spiral of violence.[12]

In light of these complexities, it is crucial to approach restorative dialogues in a trauma-informed way with all participants. Dividing them into groups of victims and offenders oversimplifies their experiences, which are often shaped by trauma. Embracing a holistic perspective can foster healing and potentially mitigate violence and recidivism.[13] This insight underscores the need for an approach that recognises each individual as a complex being shaped by their life experiences, including trauma, so that individuals like Manuel can be supported in their recovery process alongside their desistance journey.

Case study 4.2: Manuel's triggers

Growing up in a war-torn country, Manuel experienced several armed conflicts during his early childhood and teenage years. He lived in constant fear, witnessing the deaths of school friends during breaks while playing on the school football pitch. Manuel and his friends were repeatedly ambushed by the occupying forces on their way to and from school. Over the years, he lost several close family members, including his father, and he, his mother and his siblings were seriously injured on several occasions. After their home was occupied by enemy forces, the family sought refuge in another country.

Manuel was 15 when they arrived in their host country. Despite being severely traumatised, the family received no support to deal with their traumatic experiences. Manuel's brain and body remained attuned to the constant threat, and his nights were plagued by nightmares in which he relived the horrors. As an adult, Manuel explained that he lacked the cognitive capacity to learn a new language or concentrate at school because of his trauma. However, these signs were not recognised, and he was expected to learn the language and attend regular classes appropriate for his age.

The challenges for Manuel went beyond the classroom. At his new school, there were many children from the country that had occupied his own. Every time he saw one of these children, his anger would flare up, resulting in violent outbursts. He was soon labelled a 'problem youth' and expelled from school. Without a proper education, he ended up on the streets, where he continued to start fights whenever he encountered someone from the 'enemy side'. He was arrested for the first time as a minor, and from then on, he was in and out of prison. No one ever asked or understood why he was triggered every time he met someone from the other side. No connection was made between his traumatic experiences and his angry outbursts.

During his participation in restorative dialogues, Manuel was finally able to share his experiences openly and he recognised the connection to his offending behaviour. It was the first time he had shared his experiences with others openly and although it was a painful process, it was also liberating. This process helped Manuel to understand his triggers and where they came from. He hoped that this insight would help him to react differently in the future and stay out of prison.

This case highlights the urgent need for a trauma-informed approach not only within the criminal justice system but also across public services. Failure to understand the profound impact of trauma can perpetuate victimisation and cause further harm. Integrating trauma awareness into public services is essential to ensure that survivors like Manuel receive the support they need early on, potentially preventing future imprisonment. By adopting a trauma-informed approach, it is possible to better address the underlying issues that contribute to offending behaviour and support individuals on their journey towards healing and reintegration. Thus, over time, I concluded that we needed to be much better prepared to respond to trauma and start working in a trauma-informed way with all participants. Restorative justice practitioners need to understand trauma and its effects so that they do not inadvertently cause more harm, but rather learn how to support participants in their journey of recovery and be able to create a safe process for everyone. For this, however, specific training is required.

The need for specific training

As mentioned earlier, my journey with implementing restorative dialogues was akin to being thrown in at the deep end. Reflecting on this experience, I remember feeling unprepared when I took on the role of facilitator. While my background in working with victims and offenders, coupled with my experience in mediation, provided a foundation, I soon discovered that navigating restorative dialogues required a more specialised skill set. Although I was enrolled in SFU's certificate in restorative justice during the initial implementation phase, my primary learning occurred through hands-on experience. Looking back, I am grateful that no significant mistakes occurred that could have harmed the participants. Nevertheless, this highlighted the critical need for comprehensive facilitator training.

Facilitators require not only deep knowledge to ensure the safety and effectiveness of restorative dialogues but also personal qualities conducive to building trust and comfort among participants. Their role is essential as they guide the participants through complex emotions, power dynamics and diverse perspectives, creating a space where all participants feel safe, valued and supported. Thus, the impact of facilitators goes beyond mere skill; their personal qualities profoundly influence the tone and outcome of the dialogue.

Despite the rapid growth of restorative justice, international standards for facilitator training are lacking, leading to variations even within countries, and raising concerns about accreditation or certification. This lack of standards is particularly concerning for services dealing with individuals who have had complex life experiences,[14] and questions are raised about the extent to which restorative justice facilitators are sufficiently prepared to provide the safe and competent support required, particularly for victims.[15] This scepticism is justified given that the quality of the restorative process is largely dependent on the quality and skills of the facilitator.[16] Thus, questions remain about "who should facilitate dialogues or what qualifications are necessary".[17]

Since its inception, one of the primary goals of the Swiss RJ Forum has been to train facilitators in restorative justice philosophy and diverse implementation methods. Identifying the necessary components to adequately equip facilitators has proved challenging, but over time we have identified five key areas for effective facilitator training:

1 A deep understanding of the philosophy and values of restorative justice
2 Skills in facilitating restorative processes
3 Specific knowledge of different types of offending
4 Cultivating a humble and open mindset and attitude towards the work
5 Fomenting reflective practice
6 An understanding of trauma and trauma-informed practice

It might be easy to think that to facilitate restorative dialogues, facilitators only need a course in how to conduct these dialogues. However, my experience so far has shown that facilitators need to be competent in all of the above areas to facilitate restorative dialogues successfully. I outline the reasons for this position by discussing each element in turn.

1. *A deep understanding of the philosophy and values of restorative justice*

A comprehensive understanding of the philosophy and values of restorative justice is essential, as restorative dialogues operate within a broader spectrum of restorative justice practices. Facilitators must undergo training not only in the execution of restorative dialogues but also in the philosophy and theory of restorative justice, along with its various applications, to provide a holistic service to their clients. This understanding encompasses fundamental values and principles such as respect, voluntariness, confidentiality, inclusion, participation, restoration, honesty, trust, sharing and empathy.[18] Without a solid understanding of these core values and the underlying theory, facilitators risk deviating from the essence of restorative justice. Thus, facilitators need to reflect on their personal values, attitudes towards punishment and justice, and how these factors shape their approach to addressing harm and interacting with clients.

Proficiency in values and principles is essential for embodying and integrating them into daily practice. As emphasised during my studies at SFU, it is crucial to 'walk the talk', meaning that these values should be evident in our words, actions and attitudes. They serve as a compass guiding our practice and facilitating the creation of respectful and trusting relationships with clients, or, in the context of restorative dialogues, participants. Research by Pranis et al. (2003) highlights that while individuals may express values differently based on their cultural backgrounds, life experiences or religious beliefs, the underlying essence remains consistent: "the type of value is always the same: positive, constructive, healing values—values supportive of the best in ourselves and others".[19] Thus, values have the potential to unite people and foster a constructive and healing environment. The impact of grounding practice in core values is observable in the implementation of restorative dialogues. In the first session, participants identify the values they want the group to uphold, enabling everyone to feel safe, respected and authentic in their interactions. This exercise profoundly influences the dynamics of restorative dialogues, underscoring the imperative for facilitators to have this insight and engage in deep reflection to effectively lead these processes. Based on this foundation, the subsequent step is to develop facilitation skills.

2. Skills in facilitating restorative processes

Facilitation skills are paramount in training, providing facilitators with the necessary tools to guide restorative processes effectively, safely and with respect. While facilitators typically receive training in specific restorative justice methods, it is important to broaden this training to include various approaches. This broader skill set enables facilitators to respond comprehensively to the diverse needs and circumstances of all involved parties.

Consider a scenario where a participant initially engages in restorative dialogues but later expresses a desire for a direct process with their respective victim or offender. Continuity in facilitation is ideal in such cases, as it preserves the trust and rapport established between the facilitator and the participant. This underlines the importance of facilitators being skilled in a range of restorative approaches. Moreover, individuals approaching restorative justice services may be unsure about the best or most feasible approach for their situation. Facilitators need to have an understanding of the range of restorative interventions available, including victim–offender dialogue (victim–offender mediation), conferencing and circles. This knowledge enables facilitators to collaborate with clients in assessing which process best meets their needs, aspirations and safety concerns, enabling them to make informed choices.[20] However, in addition to knowledge of processes, specific knowledge of different types of crime is equally important.

3. Specific knowledge of different types of offending

It is generally accepted in the restorative justice field that it is not enough to master basic facilitation skills; facilitators also need to acquire specific knowledge and competencies relevant to the nature and seriousness of the crimes they are dealing with.[21] This includes understanding the dynamics of different types of crimes, the impact of specific crimes on victims and offenders, and the appropriate interventions and support services available to participants. Such expertise is important in restorative dialogues, where groups may delve into sensitive topics like sexual or domestic violence, as well as acts of terrorism. Ongoing training and support ensures facilitators to keep up to date with emerging issues, refine their skills and ensure they are effectively meeting the needs of participants in restorative processes. As such, consistent monitoring and supervision is vital to upholding high standards of practice.[22] However, there is another crucial aspect that is very personal – the facilitator's mindset and attitude

4. Cultivating a humble and open mindset and attitude towards the work

In addition to mastering practical skills, facilitators need strong relational skills, including the ability to build trust, create a safe environment, demonstrate empathy and compassion, and engage in active listening. These competencies require a high degree of self-awareness.[23] Facilitators not only need to understand the core values of restorative justice but also embody them in their interactions with participants. This involves treating others with respect, honouring their human dignity and consciously setting aside personal biases while maintaining a non-judgemental stance.[24] Equally important is demonstrating "unconditional positive regard", empathy and congruence, which fosters genuine presence.[25] Facilitators should encourage open dialogue and deep listening, allowing for moments of silence and uninterrupted storytelling, which are essential for participants to fully engage in the process.

A humble attitude is paramount in this context. Facilitators must refrain from assuming they know what victims or offenders need. Instead, they should empower participants to identify their own needs and goals, adapt the process accordingly and prioritise flexibility over rigid adherence to plans. Moreover, facilitators should acknowledge their own limitations and be willing to seek support when necessary, embracing a multidisciplinary approach to provide holistic care.[26] These personal qualities, combined with training, contribute to the facilitator's ability to create an environment conducive to healing and recovery. While some traits may be innate, training programmes can refine and nurture these qualities through reflective exercises, role-playing scenarios and mentoring opportunities. By integrating personal development with skills training, facilitators can effectively embody the values and principles of restorative justice in their practice. Another essential tool to support this is to engage in reflective practice.

5. Fomenting reflective practice

For us, as a new service, encouraging reflective practice was an essential part of our ongoing learning from the outset, but even over time, it has become clear how important it is to maintain this approach. As Bargen et al. (2018) highlight, "restorative justice is complex work, and even the most experienced practitioners have more to learn".[27] To deliver high-quality restorative justice services, it is necessary to engage in an ongoing process of "self-observation and self-evaluation" to understand our own actions and the responses they elicit in others. The purpose of reflective practice is therefore to continually observe and improve our practice.[28] Reflective practice requires a humble attitude, the kind of attitude described earlier. It can also be helpful to engage in the process with peers to support each other and learn together.

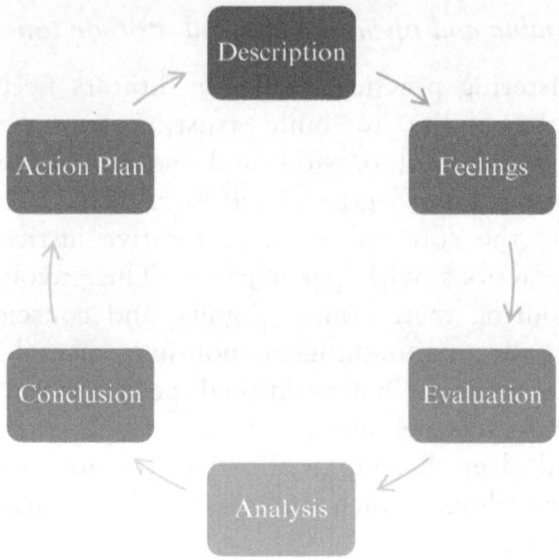

Figure 4.1 Gibbs' reflective cycle

There are many models that can be useful, one of which is 'Gibbs' reflective cycle' (1998), which can be used individually or as a group.[29]

The first three steps focus on what has happened and the next three steps focus on what can be improved. It is a circular, continuous process. The following questions are adapted from the University of Edinburgh's 'Reflection Toolkit':[30]

1 *Description*: The first stage consists of describing the situation and what happened in detail.

   - What has happened?
   - Who was involved and what was their role?
   - What was the context and background of the situation?
   - What did you do?
   - What did others do?
   - What did you want to happen?

2 *Feelings*: The next step is to explore the feelings and thoughts you had during the experience and reflect on how these might have affected the experience.

   - What were your feelings and thoughts during the experience?
   - How did you feel or think about the reactions of others?
   - Did your feelings change over time? If so, how?
   - How do you think the others feel or think about the situation now?
   - What do you think and feel about the situation now?

3 *Evaluation*: The aim is to evaluate what worked well and what did not. It is important to evaluate both the positive and negative aspects as objectively as possible.

- What do you think went well?
- What aspects did not go well?
- What did you or others contribute positively or negatively to the situation?

4 *Analysis*: This step is about making sense of what happened and drawing meaning from it. The aim is to analyse what went well or badly and to understand why it went that way.

- Why did things go well?
- Why did things not go well?
- Why do you think things turned out the way they did?
- What sense do you make of what happened?
- What were the key factors that influenced the outcome?
- What knowledge can help me understand the situation better?

5 *Conclusion*: The aim is to summarise what you have learned from the experience and identify changes you could make to improve future outcomes.

- What has this experience taught you about your practice?
- What could you have done differently to improve the outcome?
- What did you learn about the participants and their needs?
- What skills do you need to develop to be better prepared for similar situations in the future?

6 *Action plan*: The final step is to plan what you would do differently in similar situations in the future.

- If the same situation arose again, what would you do differently?
- How will you apply what you have learned to future meetings/programmes?
- What strategies will you use to deal with similar situations more effectively?
- Are there any general changes you plan to make in your approach to restorative justice practice?

This circular process can be used to reflect on personal practice as well as to evaluate and improve programmes. Since we started implementing restorative dialogues, we have been engaged in continuous reflection and adaptation of the programme. In addition to personal reflection, it is also important to involve participants in the process to draw on their lived experience. Engaging with participants' experiences often brings to light the significant role that trauma plays in their lives, underlining the need for facilitators to have a deep understanding of trauma and to work in a trauma-informed way, which is the final element of the training.

6. An understanding of trauma and trauma-informed practice

Given the prevalence of trauma, it is essential that restorative justice facilitators are knowledgeable about trauma and how to work in a trauma-informed way. Integrating trauma-informed practices into training programmes equips facilitators with the necessary skills to engage with participants in a supportive and understanding manner, thereby reducing the risk of causing further harm or re-traumatisation, and increasing the effectiveness and safety of services for all involved.[31]

In addition, self-care, awareness of mental health and well-being are essential components of restorative justice training. Constant exposure to traumatic stories, coupled with facilitators' own traumatic experiences, underlines the importance of self-care practices to protect themselves from burnout, emotional exhaustion and secondary traumatisation. Facilitators must, therefore, prioritise their own mental health so they can effectively support participants throughout the restorative justice process. However, as Chapter 7 will explore, the well-being of facilitators is ultimately not only their personal responsibility but also that of the organisation. Being trauma-informed involves caring for everyone involved in a restorative justice process, and this responsibility cannot be placed solely on the person affected.

Conclusion

This chapter has highlighted key steps and lessons learned both in my personal journey as a facilitator and in the development of our evolving restorative justice service. A fundamental lesson learned is the need for a collaborative approach when implementing restorative dialogues. This underlines the importance of effective communication and collaboration with other agencies involved, as working in isolation can hinder the success of the programme.

Other key lessons include the importance of individual preparation of participants and the flexibility to adapt the methodology to meet the diverse needs of participants. The prevalence of trauma and the need for specialised training emerged as other critical lessons. Restorative justice facilitators must be able to guide groups through emotionally charged processes while addressing their holistic needs. As such, comprehensive training that includes a mix of theoretical knowledge, practical skills, personal attributes and ongoing development is essential.[32] Effective training in restorative justice practice, therefore, involves a holistic approach that includes knowledge acquisition, practical application and adjustment of personal attitudes and mindsets.

Relying solely on theoretical instruction is inadequate and can hinder genuine engagement with participants, as Bussler (2004) notes. The aim is not to foster a sense of superiority among restorative justice facilitators,[33] but rather to equip them to empower participants and give them maximum autonomy and agency. Therefore, effective training should emphasise practical skills and the cultivation of a supportive and empowering facilitator mindset.

By integrating trauma-informed practices into training programmes, facilitators gain a deeper insight into the complex needs of participants and are better able to address them, thereby increasing the overall effectiveness of restorative justice processes and facilitating the well-being of the facilitators themselves. As the aspect of a trauma-informed approach is central to this book and crucial to the implementation of restorative dialogues, it is discussed in detail in the next chapter.

Notes

1 To learn more about Circle processes, see Pranis (2005).
2 Benjet et al. (2016).
3 Stark et al. (2015); University of Oxford (2015).
4 Benjet et al. (2016); Charuvastra & Cloitre (2008); Johansen et al. (2022).
5 Abram et al. (2004); Brown et al. (2021); Ford, Chapman, et al. (2012); Ford, Hartman, et al. (2008); Kerig et al. (2016); Levenson and Willis (2019).
6 Briere et al. (2016).
7 Godsoe (2022); Kerig et al. (2016); Maschi et al. (2015); Miller & Najavits (2012); Oudshoorn (2015); Vitopoulos et al. (2019).
8 Sadeh and McNiel (2015).
9 Ford, Chapman, et al. (2012); Willmot & Jones (2022).
10 Ford, Chapman, et al. (2012); Willmot & Jones (2022).
11 Ardino (2012); Ford, Hawke, and Chapman (2010); Honorato et al. (2016); Walsh (2007).
12 Willmot and Jones (2022).
13 MacNair (2015); Miller and Najavits (2012).
14 As highlighted in both editions of the *UNODC Handbook on Restorative Justice Programmes* 2006 and 2020.
15 Choi et al. (2012); Keenan (2018); Umbreit and Armour (2011).
16 Lanni (2021).
17 Umbreit and Armour (2011), p. 241.
18 EFRJ (2021); Pranis et al. (2003).
19 Pranis et al. (2003), p. 33.
20 Choi et al. (2012); Umbreit and Armour (2011); UNODC (2020).
21 Bolitho (2015); Council of Europe (2018); Keenan (2018); UNODC (2020); Umbreit and Armour (2011).
22 Choi et al. (2012); UNODC (2020).
23 Umbreit and Armour (2011); UNODC (2020).
24 Umbreit and Armour (2011); UNODC (2020).
25 Bolitho (2015), p. 273.
26 Bolitho (2015); Umbreit and Armour (2011); Umbreit et al. (2003); UNODC (2020).
27 Bargen et al. (2018), p. 85.
28 UCD Teaching and Learning/Resources (n.d.).
29 Gibbs (1998).
30 The questions are adapted from the University of Edinburgh (2020).
31 Bolitho (2015); Choi et al. (2012); UNODC (2020).
32 UNODC (2020).
33 Bussler (2004); Umbreit and Armour (2011); Zehr (2002).

References

Abram, K. M., Teplin, L. A., Charles, D. R., Longworth, S. L., McClelland, G. M., & Dulcan, M. K. (2004). Posttraumatic stress disorder and trauma in youth in juvenile detention. *Archives of General Psychiatry*, 61, 403–410.

Ardino, V. (2012). Offending behaviour: The role of trauma and PTSD. *European Journal of Psychotraumatology*, 3, 1–4. https://doi.org/10.3402/ejpt.v3i0.18968

Bargen, C., Edwards, A., Hartman, M., Haslett, J., & Lyons, A. (2018). *Serving crime victims through restorative justice: A resource guide for leaders and practitioners*. Alberta Restorative Justice Association.

Benjet, C., et al. (2016). The epidemiology of traumatic event exposure worldwide: Results from the World Mental Health Survey Consortium. *Psychological Medicine*, 46(2), 327–343. https://doi.org/10.1017/S0033291715001981

Bolitho, J. (2015). Putting justice needs first: A case study of best practice in restorative justice. *Restorative Justice*, 3(2), 256–281. https://doi.org/10.1080/20504721.2015.1069531

Briere, J., Agee, E., & Dietrich, A. (2016). Cumulative trauma and current posttraumatic stress disorder status in general population and inmate samples. *Psychological Trauma: Theory, Research, Practice and Policy*, 8(4), 439–446. https://doi.org/10.1037/tra0000107

Brown, S. L., Wanamaker, K. A., Greiner, L., Scott, T., & Skilling, T. A. (2021). Complex trauma and criminogenic needs in a youth justice sample: A gender-informed latent profile analysis. *Criminal Justice and Behavior*, 48(2), 175–194. https://doi.org/10.1177/0093854820964513

Bussler, D. (2004). Are 98.6 degrees enough? Reflections on restorative justice training and credentialing. *Hamline Journal of Public Law & Policy*, 25(2), 335–346.

Charuvastra, A., & Cloitre, M. (2008). Social bonds and posttraumatic stress disorder. *Annual Review of Psychology*, 59, 301–328. https://doi.org/10.1146/annurev.psych.58.110405.085650

Choi, J. J., Bazemore, G., & Gilbert, M. J. (2012). Review of research on victims' experiences in restorative justice: Implications for youth justice. *Children and Youth Services Review*, 34(1), 35–42.

Council of Europe. (2018). *Recommendation CM/Rec(2018)8 of the Committee of Ministers to member States concerning restorative justice in criminal matters.* https://search.coe.int/cm?i=09000016808e35f3

European Forum for Restorative Justice (EFRJ). (2021). *Manual on restorative justice values and standards for practice.* www.euforumrj.org/sites/default/files/2021-11/EFRJ_Manual_on_Restorative_Justice_Values_and_Standards_for_Practice.pdf

Ford, J. D., Chapman, J., Connor, D. F., & Cruise, K. R. (2012). Complex trauma and aggression in secure juvenile justice settings. *Criminal Justice and Behavior*, 39(6), 694–724. https://doi.org/10.1177/0093854812436957.

Ford, J. D., Hartman, J. K., Hawke, J., & Chapman, J. C. (2008). Traumatic victimization, posttraumatic stress disorder, suicidal ideation, and substance abuse risk among juvenile justice-involved youths. *Journal of Child and Adolescent Trauma*, 1, 75–92.

Ford, J. D., Hawke, J., & Chapman, J. C. (2010). *Complex psychological trauma among juvenile justice-involved youth*. University of Connecticut.

Gibbs, G. (1998). *Learning by doing: A guide to teaching and learning*. Further Educational Unit.

Godsoe, C. (2022). The victim/offender overlap and criminal system reform. *Brooklyn Law Review*, 87(4), 1319–1350.

Honorato, B., Caltabiano, N., & Clough, A.R. (2016). From trauma to incarceration: Exploring the trajectory in a qualitative study in male prison inmates from north Queensland, Australia. *Health and Justice*, 4(3), 1–10. https://doi.org/10.1186/s40352-016-0034-x

Johansen, V. A., Milde, A. M., Miodini Nilsen, R., Breivik, K., Øystein Nordanger, D., Morten Stormark, K., & Weisæth, L. (2022). The relationship between perceived social support and PTSD symptoms after exposure to physical assault: An 8 years longitudinal study. *Journal of Interpersonal Violence*, 37(9–10), 7679–7706. https://doi.org/10.1177/0886260520970314

Keenan, M. (2018). Training for restorative justice work in cases of sexual violence. *International Journal of Restorative Justice*, 1(2), 291–302.

Kerig, P. K., Chaplo, S. D., Bennett, D. C., & Modrowski, C. A. (2016). "Harm as harm": Gang membership, perpetration trauma, and posttraumatic stress symptoms among youth in the juvenile justice system. *Criminal Justice and Behavior*, 43(5), 635–652. https://doi.org/10.1177/0093854815607307

Lanni, A. (2021). Taking restorative justice seriously. *Buffalo Law Review*, 69(3), 635–681.

Levenson, J. S., & Willis, G. M. (2019). Implementing trauma-informed care in correctional treatment and supervision. *Journal of Aggression, Maltreatment & Trauma*, 28 (4), 481–501. https://doi.org/10.1080/10926771.2018.1531959

MacNair, R. (2015). Causing trauma as a form of trauma. *Peace and Conflict: Journal of Peace Psychology*, 21(3), 313–321.

Maschi, T. M., Viola, D., & Koskinen, L. (2015). Trauma, stress, and coping among older adults in prison: Towards a human rights and intergenerational family justice action agenda. *Traumatology*, 21(3), 188–200. https://doi.org/10.1037/trm0000021

Miller, N. A., & Najavits, L. M. (2012). Creating trauma-informed correctional care: A balance of goals and environment. *European Journal of Psychotraumatology*, 3, 1–8. https://doi.org/10.3402/ejpt.v3i0.17246

Oudshoorn, J. (2015). Trauma-informed rehabilitation and restorative justice. In T. Gavrielides (Ed.), *The psychology of restorative justice* (pp. 159–181). Ashgate.

Pranis, K. (2005). *The little book of circle processes: A new/old approach to peacemaking*. Good Books.

Pranis, K., Stewart, B., & Wedge, M. (2003). *Peacemaking circles: From conflict to community*. Living Justice Press.

Sadeh, N., & McNiel, D. E. (2015). Posttraumatic stress disorder increases risk of criminal recidivism among justice-involved persons with mental disorders. *Criminal Justice and Behavior*, 42(6), 573–586. https://doi.org/10.1177/0093854814556880

Stark, E. A., Parsons, C. E., Van Hartevelt, T. J., Charquero-Ballester, M., McManners, H., Ehlers, A., Stein, A., & Kringelbach, M. L. (2015). Post-traumatic stress influences the brain even in the absence of symptoms: A systematic, quantitative meta-analysis of neuroimaging studies. *Neuroscience and Biobehavioral Reviews*, 56, 207–221. https://doi.org/10.1016/j.neubiorev.2015.07.007

UCD Teaching and Learning/Resources. (n.d.). *Reflective practice models*. www.ucd.ie/teaching/t4media/reflective_practice_models.pdf

Umbreit, M. S., & Peterson Armour, M. (2011). Restorative justice and dialogue: Impact, opportunities, and challenges in the global community. *Washington University Journal of Law & Policy*, 36(1), 65–89. https://digitalcommons.law.wustl.edu/wujlp/vol36/iss1/5

United Nations Office on Drugs and Crime (UNODC). (2020). *Handbook on restorative justice programmes* (2nd ed.). www.unodc.org/documents/justice-and-prison-reform/20-01146_Handbook_on_Restorative_Justice_Programmes.pdf

University of Edinburgh. (2020). *Gibbs' reflective cycle*. www.ed.ac.uk/reflection/reflectors-toolkit/reflecting-on-experience/gibbs-reflective-cycle

University of Oxford. (2015). *Trauma experiences change the brain even in those without PTSD*. www.ox.ac.uk/news/2015-08-04-trauma-experiences-change-brain-even-those-without-ptsd

Vitopoulos, N. A., Peterson-Badali, M., Brown, S., & Skilling, T. A. (2019). The relationship between trauma, recidivism risk, and reoffending in male and female juvenile offenders. *Journal of Child and Adolescent Trauma*, 12, 351–364. https://doi.org/10.1007/s40653-018-0238-4

Walsh, F. (2007). Traumatic loss and major disasters: Strengthening family and community resilience. *Family Process*, 46(2), 207–227.

Willmot, P., & Jones, L. (2022). *Trauma-informed forensic practice*. Routledge.

Zehr, H. (2002). *The little book of restorative justice*. Good Books.

5 Being trauma-informed in restorative justice

Introduction

Trauma is a powerful force that shapes the lives and behaviours of survivors at all levels of society. Its pervasive nature means that trauma is not just an individual experience but also a social one, influencing how people interact within different systems, including restorative justice. For those working in the field of restorative justice, understanding the widespread impact of trauma is not only beneficial – it is essential. This is because people involved in restorative justice processes are more likely to have experienced significant trauma than the general population.

For victims, the trauma of crime often leaves deep scars, as trauma inflicted by others is often the type most likely to cause profound and lasting effects.[1] As discussed in the previous chapter, offenders also often carry the heavy burden of traumatic experiences, with the prevalence of trauma being significantly higher in prison populations.[2] As a result, many restorative justice facilitators work with clients who have been deeply affected by traumatic experiences. This underscores the importance of a trauma-informed approach, which enables facilitators to address the specific needs of trauma survivors and create a safe and empowering environment, even without specialised training in trauma therapy. Given its importance, this chapter is dedicated to outlining what a trauma-informed approach looks like in restorative justice practice.

The discussion begins by exploring the intersection of trauma-informed practice and restorative justice. It then outlines practical ways of incorporating trauma-informed principles into restorative justice practice, emphasising the importance of using trauma-sensitive language and adopting a shame-sensitive approach. The chapter concludes with a reflection on the need for these practices to promote more effective and safe restorative justice processes.

The relationship between trauma-informed practice and restorative justice practice

The difference between a trauma-informed approach and restorative justice practice is a recurrent question. While both approaches share some common principles, such as creating a safe space and promoting the empowerment of

DOI: 10.4324/9781003271611-5

individuals, their focuses and objectives differ significantly. Trauma-informed practice focuses on understanding the impact of trauma on individuals and communities, and it prioritises the creation of safe and supportive environments conducive to the healing and empowerment of trauma survivors. Key components include recognising the signs and symptoms of trauma, understanding the impact of trauma on behaviour and relationships, and responding in a way that prevents further harm or re-traumatisation.[3] Trauma-informed approaches are used in a variety of settings, including healthcare, social services, education and criminal justice.

In contrast, restorative justice focuses on bringing together those affected by harm to engage in a respectful dialogue aimed at addressing the consequences of the act. It emphasises dialogue, restoration, accountability, understanding and finding ways to address the harm caused.[4] While the primary aim is not necessarily to resolve trauma, restorative justice processes address harm, meet needs caused by the offence, and seek mutually acceptable and beneficial solutions.

Consequently, while trauma-informed practice focuses on understanding and addressing the effects of trauma, restorative justice focuses on addressing harm, promoting accountability, and building relationships through dialogue and engagement. Despite some potential similarities in principles and approaches, the different aims and focus set the two practices apart. Adopting a trauma-informed approach within restorative justice, therefore, requires a comprehensive understanding of trauma and its effects.

How to be trauma-informed in restorative justice

Integrating a trauma-informed approach into restorative justice requires several key elements:

1. Acquiring a deep understanding of trauma involves recognising the different reactions to trauma and behavioural manifestations. To achieve this level of competence, facilitators need specialised training to equip them with the necessary knowledge and skills to address trauma within restorative justice processes effectively.
2. Collaborative relationships between restorative justice facilitators and mental health professionals, along with other support services, are paramount. Such collaboration creates a holistic approach to addressing trauma, ensuring individuals receive comprehensive support beyond the confines of the restorative justice process. While this support may not be required in all cases, establishing and maintaining these collaborative networks is essential to ensure that it is readily available when needed.
3. A trauma-informed approach also involves ensuring the well-being of facilitators themselves. As previously discussed, the role of facilitating restorative justice processes can be emotionally demanding and challenging work, and thus, it is of the utmost importance that restorative justice services are trauma-informed with their facilitators. Without this level of psychological

support, facilitators are at risk of becoming emotionally exhausted, which could compromise their ability to provide safe and effective support to participants (this will be discussed in greater detail in Chapter 7).

4 As flexibility is a fundamental aspect of restorative justice practices, it is similarly vital in trauma-informed approaches. For individuals who have experienced trauma, this adaptability becomes even more crucial, as the distress associated with the restorative process can be intensified by the trauma. Flexibility may thus entail modifying the process, the pace, communication methods or the level of support provided, ensuring a more responsive and supportive environment for trauma survivors.

Laura's case demonstrates what trauma-informed flexibility might look like.

Case study 5.1: At Laura's pace

Laura, a woman in her forties, had experienced complex trauma during her childhood and adolescence, suffering multiple forms of abuse at the hands of caregivers and others close to her. Decades later, she felt compelled to confront one of her abusers, recognising that she could not move forward in her recovery journey without answers to certain questions. Engaging in a restorative justice process was daunting and anxiety provoking for Laura. She displayed a heightened sensitivity to the facilitators' reactions and shifts in mood, becoming distressed when triggered by her fears or reminders of her past traumas. The facilitators devoted considerable time to building a trusting relationship with her before preparing her for a possible encounter with her abuser. They also met with her therapist, in Laura's presence, to collaboratively discuss and determine the most effective way to support her during this challenging time. The aim was twofold: for the therapist to fully understand the planned restorative process to better support Laura, and for the facilitators to learn more about Laura's needs, how to support her and what triggers to look out for.

Given the enduring impact of Laura's traumatic experiences on her life, the trajectory of the restorative process was not as straightforward as in other cases. Confronted with life experiences that challenged her on a number of levels, Laura found it necessary to step back from the restorative process at times. The pace of preparation was therefore adapted to suit her needs. As her understanding of her traumatic experiences evolved with other life events, her perceptions of her past and the process changed along the way. The facilitators regularly reviewed her needs and expectations of the process, as well as the feasibility of addressing them through a restorative process. Preparation took about two years, and the interaction with the offender progressed gradually to help Laura overcome her fears. At first, communication occurred through verbal or written messages with the support of the facilitator. Then they moved to video messages, which allowed Laura to see the offender, whom she had not seen for many years. Finally, both parties were ready for a face-to-face meeting. This flexible and tailored approach enabled Laura to fully engage in the restorative process despite the enduring effects of her traumatic past.

Respecting the boundaries of individuals affected by trauma is vital when they engage with restorative processes. Trauma often results in a profound loss of trust, which can lead to anxiety in interpersonal relationships and an inability to open up and share freely or confront the other person. Honouring boundaries creates a sense of safety and trust in the facilitator, which is indispensable for meaningful participation in the restorative justice process. Facilitators need to recognise when participants require more space or time to process their emotions or to make decisions, and to empower them by giving them control over their involvement in the restorative justice process. By demonstrating sensitivity, facilitators can effectively manage these fluctuations and provide the necessary support without causing further distress.

This approach was crucial to Laura's journey. She felt heard, respected and involved in the process. The facilitators demonstrated trust in her choices and recognised her as the expert in her own life. As her case study illustrates, this approach can foster a sense of empowerment and agency, which is essential for survivors who may have felt disempowered by past experiences. Empowerment lies at the heart of successful restorative justice processes.

Incorporating trauma-informed principles into restorative justice

A practical and specific way to integrate a trauma-informed approach into restorative justice is to incorporate the six trauma-informed principles – safety, trust, choice, collaboration, empowerment and cultural humility. The following suggestions provide general ideas about how this can be done with the caveat that this is not a one-size-fits-all approach. Facilitators must adapt the approach to the specific context and needs of the individuals they are working with.

1. Safety

Creating a sense of safety is foundational to facilitating restorative justice processes, even more so for individuals affected by trauma. Traumatic experiences can profoundly disrupt an individual's feeling of safety, leading to feelings of fear, helplessness and powerlessness long after the event has occurred.[5] Such trauma often triggers dysregulation in the brain's stress response system, notably affecting the amygdala that processes emotions like fear and anxiety. This dysregulation can lead to a heightened state of arousal and hypervigilance, where even seemingly minor stimuli can trigger intense feelings of distress.[6] Consequently, individuals may struggle to fully engage in the restorative process, as their internal alarm system – the amygdala – is sensitive to any potential threats. To enhance feelings of safety, restorative justice facilitators may consider employing the following strategies.

- Co-create a safe space:
  - Involve individuals in identifying what they need to feel safe, recognising that each person may have unique triggers or safety requirements. Collaboratively establish a supportive environment that meets these needs.
- Ensure clear and transparent communication:
  - Maintain a calm demeanour and transparent communication style; be mindful of tone of voice and body language to convey a sense of reassurance. Avoid ambiguity and provide detailed explanations of the process to reduce anxiety and uncertainty, and clearly signpost other available services and support.
- Tailor the physical environment:
  - Allow survivors agency in selecting meeting venues where they feel comfortable, considering preferences such as outdoor settings or, in prisons, seating arrangements so they do not feel trapped. Strive to create a welcoming physical space with elements like comfortable furnishings and soothing aesthetics, prioritising privacy and comfort.
- Establish clear boundaries and guidelines:
  - Define acceptable behaviour and expectations for all participants to prevent further harm or re-traumatisation. Whenever possible, co-define these boundaries and guidelines *with* the participants. Clearly outline guidelines for respectful dialogue and confidentiality, ensuring participants understand privacy rights and professional conduct expectations.
- Provide resources:
  - Offer trauma survivors information on support services tailored to their needs, including counselling, support groups and crisis hotlines. Maintaining a directory of available resources promotes a sense of safety and well-being.
- Develop feedback mechanisms:
  - Establish channels for individuals to voice concerns and provide feedback on the process, prioritising their input and addressing any issues raised respectfully.

Box 5.1 Practice example

Susanna, a victim of an attempted homicide during an armed robbery, experienced heightened anxiety in enclosed spaces. To accommodate her need for safety, she chose her own store as the venue for preparatory meetings. For the encounter with the offender, she chose an open park setting where she felt less confined.

Luis, a survivor of long-term abuse, found it difficult to talk about distressing events indoors. Facilitators addressed this by explaining what the aim of the next meeting would be, allowing Luis to prepare. When anticipating distress, he preferred walking outdoors during preparatory meetings with the facilitators because nature had a calming effect on him.

2. *Trust*

Establishing trust is essential when working with trauma survivors, as it lays the foundation for meaningful relationships. However, due to past experiences of betrayal and broken trust, trauma survivors often grapple with trust issues and find it challenging to place trust in others, including themselves. This loss of self-esteem can profoundly affect their self-worth, leading to feelings of humiliation, guilt and helplessness.[7] Building trusting relationships therefore requires patience, empathy, understanding, unwavering effort and consistent interactions to demonstrate to trauma survivors that they "will not be abandoned again".[8] As demonstrated in the experiences of the interviewees in previous chapters, while supportive and compassionate responses can mitigate harm, negative responses can exacerbate it.[9] To foster trust in restorative justice interventions, facilitators should:

- Be there for trauma survivors, not only in a professional capacity but also as fellow human beings:
  - Engage with survivors on a personal level, investing time and effort to build relationships, demonstrating compassion, understanding and genuine care. Consistently fulfilling commitments and maintaining reliability can help survivors feel valued and supported.
- Provide focused, unhurried attention and active listening:
  - Allow survivors to express their experiences, concerns and emotions without judgement or interruption. Active listening involves giving survivors undivided attention, maintaining eye contact and conveying understanding through verbal and non-verbal cues.
- Allow survivors to communicate at their own pace:
  - Recognise that trauma survivors may require time and space to articulate their thoughts and feelings. Facilitators should exercise patience, refraining from pressuring survivors to share more than they are comfortable with and respecting their boundaries.
- Choose words carefully:
  - Language holds significant power, particularly for trauma survivors who may be sensitive to words and cues that suggest disbelief or

judgement (e.g. 'really?', 'I cannot believe this!', 'this is too horrible!', 'why did you react this way?'). Facilitators should use language that conveys belief, compassion and affirmation, ensuring that survivors feel heard and understood.

- Be reliable and transparent:
  - Trust is nurtured through consistent actions. Facilitators should uphold promises, agreements and deadlines made with survivors, remaining transparent about constraints and limitations to manage expectations effectively. Honesty and transparency regarding confidentiality and information sharing can further bolster survivors' sense of trust and security.
- Validate concerns and fears:
  - Acknowledge survivors' concerns and fears and collaborate with them to address and alleviate any issues. By validating their experiences, facilitators help survivors to feel heard and understood.
- Conduct regular check-ins:
  - Assess their level of trust and comfort with the restorative justice process and address any concerns or doubts they may have promptly.

Box 5.2 Practice example

Alice, having felt deeply re-victimised by her interactions with the criminal justice system, approached the restorative justice service with reluctance and uncertainty regarding the trustworthiness of the facilitators. Despite her desire for a restorative process, she feared a repeat of her previous negative experiences with criminal justice professionals, which made her interactions initially hostile. During the first meeting, she vented her anger at feeling hurt and dismissed. However, the facilitators patiently listened without interruption, allowing her to express herself freely. This attentive listening eased her distress, marking the first time she felt truly heard. In subsequent sessions, she gradually opened up, demonstrating willingness to fully engage with the process.

3. Choice

Traumatic experiences deprive individuals of their sense of autonomy, control and choice, leaving them feeling powerless and without agency. During traumatic events, their personal perspectives are disregarded, which increases their sense of helplessness. Therefore, the primary aim should be to restore the survivor's power and control.[10] It is important to consistently ask the person about their preferences and to give them "as much choice as is compatible with the preservation of safety".[11] In restorative justice, this can be done by empowering participants to co-construct the restorative process, keeping arrangements as flexible as possible to meet their needs. By offering choices, actively listening to their preferences, and acknowledging their wants and needs, facilitators can help survivors regain a sense of control and autonomy over their healing journey. To empower survivors, facilitators should:

- Offer choice and flexibility:
    - Allow survivors to make decisions whenever possible, such as choosing meeting locations, choosing attendees or determining their level of participation. Additionally, accommodate survivors' needs by offering virtual meetings, alternative communication methods or adjusting schedules to ensure accessibility. These options empower survivors and restore their sense of control over the process.
- Practice active listening:
    - Engage in active listening by asking targeted questions and genuinely considering survivors' responses. This information can guide decision-making and ensure that survivors' preferences are respected.
- Help survivors to identify priorities:
    - Assist survivors in identifying their priorities and needs after their experience, and discuss how these can be addressed in the restorative process. Facilitators can support individuals in expressing their desires, seeking recognition of harm, or communicating with the offender or their loved ones. Through open-ended questions, survivors can articulate their wishes and concerns, allowing facilitators to provide the support for them to feel safe and empowered.
- Provide information:
    - Offer clear and accessible information about available support services, therapeutic options and alternative pathways within the restorative justice process. Ensure that survivors understand their options and feel empowered to make informed choices.

Box 5.3 Practice example

The case of the sisters Lilia and Margot clearly illustrates the extent to which people's needs can differ. Both had experienced years of abuse from a relative during their childhood. Lilia's impression was that she did not want to confront the offender, as he would probably just deny or ridicule their suffering. It was important for her to confront other relatives with her questions, especially regarding the question of why no one protected the sisters. Margot, on the other hand, did not care whether and how the offender responded to her; she needed the confrontation with him and the opportunity to tell him to his face how much he had hurt her and shaped her life forever in a negative way. Even in the same case, needs can therefore vary greatly from person to person and this needs to be considered.

4. Collaboration

The principle of collaboration underscores the importance of survivors having a voice in their recovery process. It advocates the need to work *with*, rather than for, survivors, fostering a collaborative working relationship. Where such an approach is adopted, it shows the individual they are capable of acting on their own behalf and builds confidence. This counteracts the feeling of disempowerment created by trauma.[12] Facilitators can collaborate by doing the following.

- Co-design processes and services:
    - Collaborate with participants to tailor the restorative justice process to their individual needs, concerns and preferences. Involve them as equal partners in decision-making about the planning and design of the process, ensuring that their voices are heard and respected. Explore their desired outcomes for the restorative justice process and work together to integrate their requests, giving them a sense of control.
- Recognise survivors' unique insights into their own lives and experiences:
    - Respect their autonomy and choices by allowing them to make decisions about their involvement whenever possible, even if their decisions differ from the facilitators' initial suggestions. This collaborative approach ensures that survivors' perspectives are heard and valued throughout the process.
- Engage in regular case reviews:
    - Arrange reflective sessions with survivors to evaluate their experience in the restorative justice process and identify necessary adjustments.
- Establish peer support opportunities:
    - Facilitate peer support or mentoring programmes where survivors who have completed their restorative justice process can offer guidance and support to newcomers, especially in group processes such as restorative dialogues.

Box 5.4 Practice example

Roberto felt the need to confront the person who had caused him so much harm in his childhood. He expressed the need to see this person face to face to observe his reactions. Throughout the preparatory period, Roberto exhibited symptoms of the impact the trauma had on his life. His facilitators were concerned about how he would cope being in the same room as his abuser and the potential for it to overwhelm him. Nevertheless, Roberto insisted on facing his offender. After discussing various options, Roberto and his facilitators decided the restorative encounter would take place via video conferencing. This arrangement allowed Roberto to see his offender's face without being in the same room, thereby reducing his anxiety.

5. *Empowerment*

The principle of empowerment is closely intertwined with the principles of choice and collaboration. According to Herman (1997), the journey of recovering from trauma starts with empowerment since disempowerment lies at the core of trauma experiences, and so the individual should be the "author and arbiter of her own recovery".[13] Any intervention that diminishes the survivor's power is counter-productive, even if it may seem initially beneficial. Empowerment therefore involves restoring power to victims, reducing their sense of isolation and helplessness by increasing their range of choices in an environment that validates their experiences, and recognises and nurtures their strengths.[14] As highlighted in the UN Handbook (2020), restorative processes have been shown to be effective in empowering victims of serious crimes as they "may counter the humiliation, disempowerment, lack of information and loss of control that tends to result from mainstream criminal justice processes".[15] Many of the suggestions in the previous principles contribute to the empowerment of individuals in restorative justice processes. Additional strategies for promoting empowerment include the following.

- Trust and support the individual's capacities:
  - Recognise, affirm and nurture their inherent strengths, resilience and ability to actively engage in their own journey. By instilling confidence in their abilities and encouraging meaningful participation in the restorative justice process, facilitators empower survivors to regain a sense of self-efficacy, agency and control over their lives.
- Build resilience:
  - Trauma often erodes an individual's sense of resilience. Facilitators can provide information and resources to help survivors understand the impact of trauma and develop self-care strategies. Moreover, they can assist survivors in rebuilding and strengthening their resilience by

encouraging engagement in self-care practices and promoting self-compassion and self-acceptance. Survivors may struggle with judgement from others, self-blame and shame; therefore, fostering self-care and self-compassion is vital in helping them develop a positive and nurturing relationship with themselves.[16] Facilitators can help survivors in setting realistic and achievable goals for their recovery journey and celebrate their progress and successes, as they may struggle to recognise these themselves.

- Support survivors to find their voice:
  - Trauma can silence survivors and impede their ability to express their needs and advocate for themselves.[17] Facilitators can support survivors in finding and using their voice, actively listen to their perspectives and ensure that their views are respected. Additionally, some survivors may benefit from sharing their story with a wider audience or with other victims of crime.
- Strengthen social networks:
  - Social support is essential for recovery from trauma.[18] Facilitators can help survivors to identify and engage with supportive networks, including friends, family, support groups or community resources. They can also involve these individuals in the restorative process where feasible, or at least consider their involvement in the preparation or follow-up work offered by facilitators. Participation in restorative dialogues or other community approaches to restorative justice may also prove beneficial.

Box 5.5 Practice example

One of the most re-traumatising experiences for Alice during her journey through the criminal justice system was the way she was treated by the police as a rape victim. Rather than being recognised and supported, she felt violated again by the lengthy and harsh interrogation she endured. Recognising the gravity of this experience, the facilitators approached Alice and offered to help her share her experiences with the police, if she wished. Initially surprised, Alice agreed. Later, when she had the opportunity to express the shame, humiliation and anger she felt towards the police and explain how it had affected her life, she felt a profound sense of vindication. The police listened and validated her experience, allowing her to regain her voice and dignity.

6. *Cultural humility*

Cultural humility, often overlooked in discussions of trauma-informed practice, originates from the work of Melanie Tervalon and Jann Murray-García

(1998).[19] It underscores the significance of developing authentic connections across different cultural backgrounds, encompassing elements such as race, ethnicity, class, gender and sexual orientation. Professionals are encouraged to approach interactions with humility, curiosity and a genuine willingness to learn from others, thereby nurturing respect for the beliefs, practices and values that shape each person's worldview and lived experiences.[20]Wheeler (2018) outlines several key attributes of cultural humility, including openness, self-reflection/awareness, lifelong learning, institutional accountability, empathy, compassion, 'other-centredness', and acknowledgement and rectification of power imbalances.[21] In the context of restorative justice, cultural humility is essential for navigating the complex dynamics among participants of restorative processes who come from different cultural and social backgrounds.[22]

Integral to trauma-informed practice, cultural humility acknowledges the sway of cultural disparities on individuals' perceptions, interpretations and coping mechanisms concerning traumatic events. Sensitivity to these nuances is imperative, as overlooking or disregarding cultural contexts can inadvertently inflict additional harm through misunderstandings and misinterpretations.[23] For instance, in Switzerland where a substantial portion of the prison population comprises foreigners, addressing cultural disparities in interpretations of trauma is important. In one example, a victim who had lost his son to murder was approached by one of the participating prisoners during one of the restorative dialogue sessions. This prisoner tried to offer comfort based on his own cultural understanding of loss by saying that "God gives, and God takes away, and there's nothing we can do about it". Unfortunately, this statement was deeply hurtful to the victim and caused shock within our team. However, it was also a useful lesson in the importance of developing cultural sensitivity and awareness of divergent perceptions of trauma and its associated coping mechanisms when preparing victims and prisoners for restorative processes.

Cultural humility is challenging precisely because it is impossible to pre-emptively address all cultural differences. Yet, embracing humility entails acknowledging our limitations and maintaining an open attitude when we encounter difference. Several practices are relevant for restorative justice facilitators:

- Engage in continual self-reflection to identify personal biases and limitations:
    - Reflect regularly on your own beliefs, attitudes and assumptions about other cultures. Consider how your own cultural background and experiences may influence your interactions with, and perceptions of, others. Be open to exploring any biases or limitations you may have and actively work to challenge and overcome them. Self-reflection is an ongoing process that requires honesty, humility and a willingness to learn and grow.[24]

- Practise active listening and empathetic engagement:
    - Seek to understand different perspectives, feelings and needs, and respond with empathy and compassion. Such an open and non-judgemental approach can help to build trust and rapport between facilitators and clients.
- Be aware of power dynamics:
    - Recognise and address power imbalances that may exist in interactions and relationships, whether based on cultural, societal or historical factors. Strive to create an equitable environment where all individuals feel empowered to participate fully and have their voices heard. Be aware of your own privilege and use it responsibly to advocate for justice and equality.[25]
- Recognise individuals as experts in their own cultures:
    - Recognise and respect individuals as experts in their own cultures and lived experiences and encourage them to share their knowledge and insights with you.
    - Recognise the value of diverse perspectives and seek to learn from them as equals.

In sum, a trauma-informed approach to restorative justice accentuates the importance of fostering secure and empowering relationships, dovetailing with Herman's contention that recovery from trauma unfolds within relational contexts.[26] Such an approach assumes pivotal significance for all participants in restorative processes, especially given the high prevalence of trauma in society, notably among the prison population,[27] and its potential "to reduce crime and prevent future offending".[28]

Integrating trauma-sensitive language into restorative justice practice

An often overlooked yet important aspect of a trauma-informed approach lies in the sensitivity we employ in our language. Incorporating trauma-sensitive language into restorative justice practice plays an important role in creating a safe, respectful and non-judgemental environment. The use of trauma-sensitive language reflects professionals' awareness of the profound impact that words can have on people who have experienced trauma. The aim is to avoid blame, shame, stigmatisation or judgement, creating a space where individuals feel comfortable talking openly about their experiences, emotions and needs. Given each person is unique, it is important to explore with them which words may trigger stress, anxiety or pain and refrain from using them. Additionally, observing people during challenging conversations can offer valuable insights into words or expressions that may be difficult for them. Indicators such as cringing, withdrawal or changes in body language can signify such discomfort.[29] Some practical suggestions for integrating trauma-sensitive language into restorative practice are:

Be mindful in your use of words

Facilitators should carefully consider the impact of certain terms like 'victim', which can be unacceptable or distressing to some trauma survivors or victims of crime.[30] For instance, one interviewee said: "I'm allergic to this [word] because I don't want to be seen as just a victim". In her case, she associated the term with helplessness and vulnerability, contrary to how she wanted to be perceived. She wanted to be recognised and treated as a 'human being'. Alternative words like 'survivor' or 'person who has experienced trauma' recognise resilience without defining individuals solely based on their victimhood. However, it is best to ask the person how they would like to be addressed. Similarly, sensitivity is also important when referring to the person who has caused the harm. I once had a case where the victim only wanted facilitators to refer to the person who had harmed her as 'the offender', rather than use his name. As it was unacceptable for her to hear his name on our lips, we agreed to refer to him as 'her offender' when working with her, but explained that we would call him by his name when they met face to face. She understood our position and accepted it.

In some cases, such as when the offender is a family member, labels like 'offender' may evoke discomfort for the person harmed or affect the self-identity of the harmer and increase feelings of shame.[31] Moreover, the clear distinction between 'offender' and 'victim' may be blurred in some cases and some phrases may convey myths and stereotypes common in society, particularly in relation to intimate crime. Therefore, facilitators should ask individuals to choose words that feel acceptable to them and identify words they want to avoid.

Frame questions carefully

In trauma-sensitive communication, facilitators should ask open-ended questions that use neutral language and avoid making judgements or assumptions about the situation or the person's experience.[32] For example, rather than saying "That must have been terrible" or "How unbelievable" or "Why did you/didn't you?", it is more appropriate to ask questions like "Can you tell me how you felt at the time?" or "What was your experience like?" or "How did that affect you?".[33] Due to the fragmented nature of the memories of trauma survivors,[34] they may find it easier to describe their experiences in terms of sensory, emotional and physiological content.[35] These questions also invite people to share their feelings, experiences and perspectives in a non-threatening and validating manner. One interviewee shared that he was often confronted with phrases containing expressions of disbelief, which he experienced as hurtful, causing him to disengage.

Use positive, empowering language

Choosing positive and empowering language that highlights strengths and resilience is fundamental to a trauma-informed approach.[36] Acknowledging inner strength and resilience can be a powerful source of validation and support for trauma survivors, inspiring hope and optimism for the future. Phrases like "You have faced significant challenges, but your strength and resilience are evident by your presence here" honours the individual's journey, affirming their strengths and resilience.

Validate experiences

Traumatic experiences can foster feelings of isolation, making individuals believe that no one truly understands what they are going through. Therefore, it is vital to acknowledge and validate their experience,[37] without claiming to fully understand what the person has been through, as each experience is unique. Phrases like "I understand" or "I see" should be avoided, as they may diminish the individual's experience. Instead, phrases like "I can hear this has affected you deeply" or "I see how difficult this has been for you" may be helpful.

Respect boundaries

While inviting individuals to share their experiences is crucial, respecting their boundaries is equally important.[38] Individuals should have the autonomy to decide when and what to disclose. It is also important for facilitators to inform individuals about the confidentiality of their stories and any obligations to report certain details to relevant authorities or services. This is particularly important when working with offenders, as they may disclose information they have not previously shared with the authorities. I experienced this once when an offender in prison began to confess to a crime he had committed for which he had not been convicted. I stopped him to remind him of my obligation, but he said he was aware of it and knew he could be convicted again.

Allow for time

Recovery from trauma is a non-linear process that takes time. Rushing or pressuring survivors to share prematurely can exacerbate their distress. It is important to give survivors the time they need and encourage self-compassion and self-care throughout their process of recovery. In essence, trauma-sensitive language is about mindful communication, creating a safe and supportive environment that validates individual experiences and empowers them to make choices and take control of their recovery process. It is a testament to our respect, empathy and understanding, recognising the remarkable resilience and strength inherent in trauma survivors.

Complementing trauma-informed practice with a shame-sensitive approach

Chapter 3 drew attention to the common experience of shame among individuals who have suffered trauma, noting its significant role in post-traumatic stress. Similarly, in Chapter 4 shame was highlighted as a risk factor for offending behaviour. Therefore, it becomes imperative to address this emotion within a trauma-informed approach, given its profound impact and the detrimental effects on mental and physical health.

Identifying shame can be challenging because individuals may not immediately recognise it, and as restorative justice facilitators, it is easy to overlook it. Dolezal and Gibson (2022) explain how chronic shame often presents itself as shame anxiety, where individuals do not directly acknowledge feeling shame but instead engage in behaviours aimed at avoiding or concealing it. These behaviours include feelings of fear, anxiety, self-consciousness, stress, and a strong urge to withdraw or escape. People who struggle with chronic shame often go to great lengths to avoid situations or relationships that could potentially trigger shame. They may actively suppress feelings of shame and replace them with more manageable emotions or states, a phenomenon known as 'bypassed shame', effectively obscuring the experience of shame itself.[39]

The intensity of shame is often described as the 'fear of disconnection'. Individuals experiencing shame feel unworthy of love and belonging due to their past experiences or actions, threatening their relationships and undermining the basic human need for connection. Consequently, individuals may withdraw from others and hide their emotions and true selves, creating a sense of isolation.[40] Moreover, shame can act as a powerful trigger for anger, serving as a defence mechanism against vulnerability, allowing individuals to deflect or mask feelings of shame. Additionally, deep-seated beliefs of unworthiness may lead to powerlessness and humiliation, causing individuals to use anger to assert control and preserve self-esteem.[41] Renowned shame expert and researcher Brené Brown (2021) has identified common responses to shame:[42]

- Moving Away: Withdrawing, hiding, silencing ourselves, and keeping secrets.
- Moving Towards: Seeking to appease and please.
- Moving Against: Trying to gain power over others, being aggressive, and using shame to fight shame.

Rodrigo's narrative provides a compelling illustration of the adverse effects of unresolved shame, with potentially devastating consequences.

Case study 5.2: Rodrigo – masking shame with anger

Rodrigo faced significant challenges as a young boy when an infection deprived him of most of his sight. Initially cheerful, enjoying life in a quiet village surrounded by family and friends, he began to experience severe bullying due to his deteriorating vision. His peers could not understand his struggles – why he bumped into things, fell frequently and could not keep up, ride his bike or excel in school. Neither could the doctors understand his condition. Eventually, he had to leave his family and move to a residential school in the city. Shame became a constant companion, and he felt abandoned.

Two years later, a doctor finally diagnosed and treated his infection, restoring his sight and allowing him to return home. However, he still felt like an outsider and harboured deep-seated anger. Only as an adult did he begin to understand what had happened to him. He explained that during this time, he had decided that the shame he had suffered was unbearable, vowing that no one would ever bully or exercise power over him again. This determination led him down a destructive path, reacting aggressively whenever he felt shamed or disrespected. His behaviour escalated, resulting in several periods of imprisonment. When I met him, he was in prison for multiple murders. It was only when we addressed the issue of shame within the context of restorative dialogues that Rodrigo began to understand the profound impact of shame on his life.

Restorative justice facilitators hold a unique role because they can support people who are suffering from the impact of shame. Dolezal and Gibson (2022) propose three key principles for shame-sensitive practice:[43]

1. *Acknowledge shame*: Sensitivity to feelings of shame requires recognising its commonality, understanding its nature, mechanisms and the behaviours individuals employ to cope with it. It is essential not only to acknowledge others' experience of shame but also for facilitators to recognise their own shame and understand how it influences their thinking, actions, behaviour and attitudes.
2. *Avoid shaming*: Facilitators must be mindful of how easily shame can be triggered, especially when discussing traumatic experiences or harm inflicted on others. It is crucial to be aware of one's own reactions when people share their experiences and to consider language, question framing, reactions and emotional expressions to avoid exacerbating feelings of shame. When victims or offenders share their experiences with facilitators, they are vulnerable, which increases the risk of experiencing further shame. Thus, using trauma-sensitive language, as described previously, can be very useful. It is also essential to be mindful of "interpersonal dynamics based on gender, race, ethnicity, language-spoken, disability, age, and religious identification".[44] Facilitators should avoid stereotypes, labels and other stigmatising behaviours, remaining responsive to individuals' unique circumstances to create a safe, non-judgemental environment conducive to free and fearless sharing.
3. *Address shame*: To effectively address an individual's experience of shame, it is crucial to listen to their personal history and context to understand the root causes. Creating an emotionally safe environment where individuals feel comfortable discussing their experiences "without fear of judgement, criticism, or ridicule" is vital.[45] These experiences should be discussed in a non-judgemental, sensitive and empathetic manner. Careful selection of terminology is key, as even the word 'shame' can trigger more shame.

> Other, perhaps more suitable, terms such as 'feeling judged', 'feeling self-conscious' or 'embarrassment' may be used. Failure to acknowledge or discuss shame can reinforce harmful beliefs, while open acknowledgement presents an opportunity to reduce its impact on interactions. It is important to attend to a person's need for support and connection after sharing sensitive experiences or feelings of shame.[46]

To nurture shame resilience, it is vital that individuals can connect with others, receive and offer empathy, and talk about it with others – or "speak shame", as Brown (2006) calls it.[47] Therefore, it is important to provide individuals with the time and space to share at their own pace, to ask what they need to feel safe, understood and supported in sharing their story, and to listen carefully and empathetically.

Both self-compassion and empathy are considered important tools for coping with shame. Self-compassion means being kind to yourself and talking to yourself as you would to someone you care about. Embracing this approach can provide a constructive response to trauma and shame, potentially alleviating the intense stress responses, such as feeling constantly on edge or anxious. Self-compassion involves caring for oneself, validating one's suffering and setting boundaries.[48] As facilitators, it is possible to gently encourage individuals to practise self-compassion and explain how this can help them in managing shame. I have done this on several occasions, and although it is often a difficult exercise, people usually appreciate learning how this can support them in addressing the painful feeling of shame in their lives.

Empathy, another essential tool, involves connecting with others to understand their emotions. When individuals connect with others and empathetically listen to their story, it can reduce the sense of isolation in their struggles. Brown (2020) explains that empathy is a cure for shame because shame "cannot survive empathy".[49] Empathy is reciprocal; thus, receiving empathy from others for one's own experience of shame can increase, restore or even strengthen one's sense of connection and empowerment.[50] Restorative dialogues provide an excellent platform for this empathetic exchange. Interviewees have consistently highlighted how sharing their story with others and listening to them, giving and receiving empathy, has had a healing effect on their lives. The same is true for offenders, who often feel that it is one of the first times that others have listened to their (often shameful) stories, and that this has helped them to deal with their shame in a constructive way. It may not be easy to share these painful stories, but Brown (2019) notes that:

> Owning our story can be hard but not nearly as difficult as spending our lives running from it. Embracing our vulnerabilities is risky but not nearly as dangerous as giving up on love and belonging and joy – the experiences that make us the most vulnerable. Only when we are brave enough to explore the darkness will we discover the infinite power of our light.[51]

Another way to deal with the shame stemming from crime may be confronting the responsible individual through a restorative process. This can help to shift the shame and blame felt by the individual to the person who was responsible for the incident.

Conclusion

This chapter has outlined the relationship between trauma-informed practice and language and restorative justice practice, highlighting what is required to build shame resilience. The development of safe, respectful and trusting relationships has been at the heart of this chapter. As facilitators, it is vital to maintain ongoing relationships with clients to build meaningful connections based on familiarity, trust and empathy. Such relationships are fundamental not only to addressing the immediate impacts of trauma but also to fostering long-term recovery and resilience.

The quality of the relationship between facilitators and clients is key to both trauma-informed practice and shame resilience. By prioritising strong, empathetic connections, facilitators can create an environment where clients feel safe, understood and empowered. Continuity in these relationships also allows facilitators to reach out proactively to individuals when they appear to be disengaging and identify how they can be effectively supported.[52]

Thus, the integration of trauma-informed principles into restorative justice practice enhances its transformative potential in addressing trauma and promoting healing. By focusing on safety, trust, choice, collaboration, empowerment and cultural sensitivity, facilitators can better support trauma survivors and contribute to their journey toward healing and resilience. To allow these principles to come to life even more, the next chapter will explain how our association is implementing restorative dialogues in a trauma-informed way.

Notes

1 Benjet et al. (2016); Charuvastra and Cloitre (2008); Johansen et al. (2022).
2 Briere et al. (2016).
3 SAMHSA (2014).
4 See, for example: EFRJ (2021); UNODC (2020).
5 Herman (1997).
6 Van der Kolk (2014).
7 Herman (1997).
8 Herman (1997), p. 62.
9 Herman (1997).
10 Herman (1997).
11 Herman (1997), p. 134.
12 Herman (1997).
13 Herman (1997), p. 133.
14 Herman (1997).
15 UNODC (2020), p .78.
16 Germer and Neff (2015).
17 Van der Kolk (2014).
18 Todahl et al. (2017).
19 Tervalon and Murray-García (1998).
20 Stubbe (2020); Wheeler (2018).

21 Wheeler (2018).
22 Ranjbar et al. (2020).
23 Healthcare Toolbox (2021).
24 Ranjbar et al. (2020).
25 Miyagawa (2020).
26 Herman (1997).
27 Miller and Najavits (2012); National Institute of Justice (2023).
28 Levenson et al. (2021), p. 483.
29 Carter et al. (2022); IOFA and Courtney's House (2018); James (2024).
30 The Information Access Group (2024).
31 Becker (1997); Benson et al. (2011).
32 IOFA and Courtney's House (2018).
33 See more on questions: IACP (2017).
34 More about trauma and memory can be found in the appendix.
35 Van der Kolk (2014).
36 Ford (2023).
37 Cherry (2023).
38 James (2024).
39 Dolezal and Gibson (2022).
40 Brown (2020); Cuncic (2023); Integrative Life Center (2021); Lamia (2011).
41 Gilbert and Procter (2006); Gilligan (2003); Reilly (2023).
42 Brown (2021), p. 25.
43 Dolezal and Gibson (2022).
44 Dolezal and Gibson (2022), p. 7.
45 Dolezal and Gibson (2022), p. 7.
46 Dolezal and Gibson (2022).
47 Brown (2006), p. 49.
48 Germer and Neff (2015).
49 Brown (2020), p. 2.
50 Brown (2006).
51 Brown (2019), p. 5.
52 Dolezal and Gibson (2022).

References

Becker, H. S. (1997). *Outsiders*. Free Press.

Benjet, C., et al. (2016). The epidemiology of traumatic event exposure worldwide: Results from the World Mental Health Survey Consortium. *Psychological Medicine*, 46(2), 327–343. https://doi.org/10.1017/S0033291715001981

Benson, M. L., Alarid, L. F., Burton Velmer, S., & Cullen, F.T. (2011). Reintegration or stigmatization? Offenders' expectations of community reentry. *Journal of Criminal Justice*, 39, 385–393.

Briere, J., Agee, E., & Dietrich, A. (2016). Cumulative trauma and current posttraumatic stress disorder status in general population and inmate samples. *Psychological Trauma: Theory, Research, Practice and Policy*, 8(4), 439–446. https://doi.org/10.1037/tra0000107

Brown, B. (2006). Shame resilience theory: A grounded theory study on women and shame. *Families in Society: The Journal of Contemporary Social Services*, 87(1), 43–52. https://doi.org/10.1606/1044-3894.3483

Brown, B. (2019). *Companion worksheet "I thought it was just me (but it isn't): Making the journey from "what will people think?"*. https://brenebrown.com/resources/itiwjm-making-the-journey-from-what-will-people-think-to-i-am-enough

Brown, B. (2020). *Adding shame, guilt, humiliation, embarrassment, empathy, and self-compassion to the social emotional learning vocabulary*. www.brenebrown.com/daring classrooms

Brown, B. (2021). *"Dare to lead": Read-along workbook*. https://brenebrown.com/resources/dare-to-lead-read-along-workbook

Carter, K., Rutherford, M., & Stevens, C. (2022). *Therapeutic communication for health care administrators*. https://ecampusontario.pressbooks.pub/therapeuticcommunicationforhealthofficeadministrators/

Charuvastra, A., & Cloitre, M. (2008). Social bonds and posttraumatic stress disorder. *Annual Review of Psychology*, 59, 301–328. https://doi.org/10.1146/annurev.psych.58.110405.085650

Cherry, L. (2023). *Trauma informed language guidance*. https://westyorkshiretraumainformed.co.uk/wp-content/uploads/2023/11/West_Yorkshire_Trauma_Informed_Language_Guidance-1.pdf

Cuncic, A. (2023, June 28). *The psychology of shame*. Verywell Mind. www.verywellmind.com/what-is-shame-5115076

Dolezal, L., & Gibson, M. (2022). Beyond a trauma-informed approach and towards shame-sensitive practice. *Humanities and Social Sciences Communications*, 9(214), 1–9. https://doi.org/10.1057/s41599-022-01227-z

European Forum for Restorative Justice (EFRJ). (2021). *Manual on restorative justice values and standards for practice*. www.euforumrj.org/sites/default/files/2021-11/EFRJ_Manual_on_Restorative_Justice_Values_and_Standards_for_Practice.pdf

Ford, R. D. (2023). *Creating safe spaces: The power of trauma-informed language*. https://reggiedford.com/creating-safe-spaces-the-power-of-trauma-informed-language/

Germer, C. K., & Neff, K. D. (2015). Cultivating self-compassion in trauma survivors. In V. M. Follette, J. Briere, D. Rozelle, J. W. Hopper, & D. I. Rome (Eds.), *Mindfulness-oriented interventions for trauma: Integrating contemplative practices* (pp. 43–58). The Guilford Press.

Gilbert, P., & Procter, S. (2006). Compassionate mind training for people with high shame and self-criticism: Overview and pilot study of a group therapy approach. *Clinical Psychology & Psychotherapy*, 13(6), 353–379. https://doi.org/10.1002/cpp.507

Gilligan, J. (2003). Shame, guilt and violence. *Social Research*, 70(4), 1149–1180.

Healthcare Toolbox. (2021). *What is culturally-sensitive trauma-informed care?*www.healthcaretoolbox.org/culturally-sensitive-trauma-informed-care

Herman, J. L. (1997). *Trauma and recovery: The aftermath of violence, from domestic abuse to political terror*. Basic Books.

Integrative Life Center. (2021). *Developing shame resilience*. https://integrativelifecenter.com/mental-health-treatment/shame-resilience

International Association of Chiefs of Police (IACP). (2017). *Successful trauma informed victim interviewing*. www.theiacp.org/sites/default/files/2020-06/Final%20Design%20Successful%20Trauma%20Informed%20Victim%20Interviewing.pdf

International Organization for Adolescents (IOFA) and Courtney's House. (2018). *Trauma-informed language to use when working with survivors of youth sex trafficking. Fact sheet 2018*. https://iofa.org/wp-content/uploads/2017/05/IOFA-Trauma-Informed-Language.pdf

James, D. (2024). *What is trauma informed language?*https://friendsassoc.org/what-is-trauma-informed-language

Johansen, V. A., Milde, A. M., Miodini Nilsen, R., Breivik, K., Øystein Nordanger, D., Morten Stormark, K., & Weisæth, L. (2022). The relationship between perceived social support and PTSD symptoms after exposure to physical assault: An 8 years longitudinal study. *Journal of Interpersonal Violence*, 37(9–10), 7679–7706. https://doi.org/10.1177/0886260520970314

Lamia, M. C. (2011, April 4). Shame: A concealed, contagious, and dangerous emotion. *Psychology Today*. www.psychologytoday.com/us/blog/intense-emotions-and-strong-feelings/201104/shame-concealed-contagious-and-dangerous-emotion

Levenson, J. S., Prescott, D. S., & Willis, G. M. (2021). Trauma-informed treatment practices in criminal justice settings. In E. Jeglic & C. Calkins (Eds.), *Handbook of issues in criminal justice reform in the United States* (pp. 483–502). Springer International Publishing. https://doi.org/10.1007/978-3-030-77565-0_24

Miller, N. A., & Najavits, L. M. (2012). Creating trauma-informed correctional care: A balance of goals and environment. *European Journal of Psychotraumatology*, 3, 1–8. https://doi.org/10.3402/ejpt.v3i0.17246

Miyagawa, L. A. (2020). *Practicing cultural humility when serving immigrant and refugee communities*. https://ethnomed.org/resource/practicing-cultural-humility-when-serving-immigrant-and-refugee-communities

National Institute of Justice. (2023). *Looking beyond recidivism: New research on well-being in prisons and jails from the National Institute of Justice*. https://nij.ojp.gov/topics/articles/looking-beyond-recidivism-new-research-well-being-prisons-and-jails-national

Ranjbar, N., Erb, M., Mohammad, O., & Moreno, F. A. (2020). Trauma-informed care and cultural humility in the mental health care of people from minoritized communities. *Focus*, 18(1), 8–15. https://doi.org/10.1176/appi.focus.20190027

Reilly, M. (2023, July 20). *Shame and anger: Unraveling the dance of emotions*. Counselling Directory. www.counselling-directory.org.uk/memberarticles/shame-and-anger-unraveling-the-dance-of-emotions

Stubbe, D. E. (2020). Practicing cultural competence and cultural humility in the care of diverse patients. *Focus*, 18(1), 49–51. https://doi.org/10.1176/appi.focus.20190041

Substance Abuse and Mental Health Services Administration (SAMHSA). (2014). *SAMHSA's concept of trauma and guidance for a trauma-informed approach*. HHS publication no. (SMA) 14-4884. SAMHSA.

Tervalon, M., & Murray-García, J. (1998). Cultural humility versus cultural competence: A critical distinction in defining physician training outcomes in multicultural education. *Journal of Health Care for the Poor and Underserved*, 9(2), 117–125. http://dx.doi.org/10.1353/hpu.2010.0233

The Information Access Group. (2024). *The importance of using trauma sensitive language*. www.informationaccessgroup.com/news/trauma_sensitive_language.html

Todahl, J., Olson, D., & Walters, E. (2017). Survivor insight: A study of family, friend, and community response to interpersonal violence. *Journal of Aggression, Maltreatment & Trauma*, 26(4), 391–410. https://doi.org/10.1080/10926771.2017.1278732

United Nations Office on Drugs and Crime (UNODC). (2020). *Handbook on restorative justice programmes* (2nd ed.). www.unodc.org/documents/justice-and-prison-reform/20-01146_Handbook_on_Restorative_Justice_Programmes.pdf

Van der Kolk, B. (2014). *The body keeps the score: Mind, brain and body in the transformation of trauma*. Penguin Books.

Wheeler, M. (2018). *Cultural competence and cultural humility: A literature review for understanding and action* (Central Florida Diversity Learning Series). www.tripartners.com/Downloads/Session2/CCC_Humility_032018.pdf

6 Delivering trauma-informed restorative dialogues

Introduction

Restorative dialogues have transformative potential even in the most challenging environments, such as prisons, where conflict and harm often seem insurmountable. By bringing victims and offenders together in a structured and supportive environment, these dialogues aim to address the harm caused by crime through open communication, accountability and mutual understanding. Unlike traditional punitive approaches, restorative dialogues focus on the needs of both the victim and the offender, providing a platform for personal reflection, emotional expression and the possibility of genuine dialogue.

Recognising the profound impact that trauma can have on both victims and offenders, the Swiss programme has been carefully adapted in recent years to incorporate trauma-informed principles. This adaptation has been driven by the understanding that participants in restorative dialogues often carry the weight of significant trauma, which can affect their ability to engage fully and genuinely in the process. Incorporating trauma-informed principles aims to create a safer and more supportive environment in which participants can address the harm experienced and caused by the offence, thereby minimising risk of re-traumatisation. This approach ensures that the programme is sensitive to the emotional and psychological needs of those involved. The Swiss team is also committed to ongoing dialogue and responsiveness to participants' needs and feedback, as well as a continuous learning process to incorporate evidence from trauma research to ensure that interventions are both restorative and sensitive to the complexities of trauma.

This chapter provides a comprehensive overview of the Swiss implementation strategy for restorative dialogues, covering all phases from preparation to aftercare. It begins with key preliminary considerations that need to be made before initiating a programme, and then provides a step-by-step guide through the entire implementation process. The chapter then addresses potential challenges that may arise, incorporating valuable insights and lessons learned from facilitator interviews. Finally, the chapter concludes with a summary reflecting on the key takeaways.

DOI: 10.4324/9781003271611-6

Preliminary considerations before starting a programme

There are two foundational steps that need to be taken before the restorative dialogue programmes begin in prisons. The first involves the selection of facilitators, and the second involves creating a safe environment within the prison for restorative dialogues. Both of these aspects can have a significant impact on the success of the process because they form the bedrock for avoiding more trauma and supporting the recovery of participants. The following section discusses these in more detail.

1. The role of the facilitators

The selection of facilitators is a critical first step in restorative justice because the success of the process depends largely on the personal and professional skills of the facilitator. They play a pivotal role in creating a safe and empowering environment for open, honest and balanced dialogue between participants. This requires a high degree of flexibility to meet the needs and expectations of all participants, skill in recognising and addressing power dynamics, and knowledge of where to get specific support, or at least to direct participants to resources, with specific issues if needed. This requires facilitators who truly embrace their role and are able to guide participants through each step of the process.[1]

The responsibilities of facilitators in restorative dialogues include, but are not limited to:

- *Setting up the programme in prisons*: This requires a clear understanding of the expected behaviour within the prison environment and the ability to communicate and work effectively with prison management. It may also involve completing the necessary process documentation and reporting relevant information to the authorities.
- *Assessing the suitability of the process for victims and offenders*: Facilitators evaluate participants' progress in recovery, consider the impact of trauma and any support received, assess their needs and readiness, understand their expectations and goals, and identify any potential harm that participation may cause.
- *Preparing participants*: Expectations need to be clarified so that participants are fully aware of what restorative dialogues can and cannot achieve. Facilitators also support participants during and between sessions, addressing their specific needs.
- *Facilitating the process*: Facilitators guide participants through the programme and ensure that the group adheres to the established values and ground rules. In addition, facilitators ensure that all voices are heard and adapt the sessions to meet the specific needs of the group.

While professional skills are essential, personal qualities such as compassion and cultural competence are equally important. I once had had a facilitator who was very well trained and had years of experience in the criminal justice system. Yet, this person struggled to empathise with the participants and was perceived as cold and distant as a result. This lack of empathy made it difficult for participants, who needed to feel understood and supported, to fully engage in the restorative process. Unfortunately, despite further training, there was no change in attitude and it was impossible for this facilitator to continue her services because of the impact on the participants. Also, as outlined previously, participants in restorative dialogues often come from different cultural backgrounds, and so cultural diversity among facilitators can foster a sense of safety and reassure participants that they are not alone and that there are individuals who understand the challenges of navigating different cultural contexts. We have had many cases where detainees have shared experiences of being bullied because of their nationality. Unfortunately, at least in our context, there is still a shortage of facilitators from different cultural backgrounds, but where possible, their inclusion greatly enriches the group dynamic.

2. *Creating a safe prison environment*

There are many challenges to creating a safe and comfortable environment within prisons, primarily in respect of locating a suitable room for restorative dialogues to occur and access to the prison estate by victims and facilitators. Prisons were never designed to be warm and welcoming, and the introduction of programmes that welcome non-inmates into the estate were never considered by the original architects. Yet, the intimidating and daunting experience of prisons are not insurmountable if there is a basic willingness on the part of prison management to overcome these conditions. This section discusses access to a suitable space for the dialogues, security measures when entering the prison and the issue of confidentiality.

a) Negotiating access to a suitable room for restorative dialogues

When making arrangements with the prison administration, facilitators should prioritise accessible and comfortable meeting spaces for participants. Often there are not many options and facilitators will need to negotiate access to the premises before the programme begins to ensure the allocated room does not feel too small, too dark or too oppressive. While the room does need to be large enough to allow participants to feel comfortable, our experience has shown that size may not be the most important factor. Rather, it is light and fresh air that can help participants to feel comfortable and safe. Restorative dialogues can be emotionally charged, so if the room is not bright enough, it can add to the heaviness of the emotions in the room. Access to windows can also be important to bring in fresh air, as this can be experienced as both physically and emotionally calming.

We once had difficulty with a proposed room that was too dark and cramped, but we were able to arrange with the prison administration to use the sports hall that was large, airy and bright. Although it was not the most comfortable space, it was better than the other room. Small and dark rooms may be a challenge for some victims, as they may feel that their personal space is being invaded by others or that they cannot see clearly enough what is going on. It is therefore important to discuss the particular circumstances of the venue with the victims in detail, considering what challenges they may face and whether and how these can be addressed. As we run the programme in different prisons, I sometimes explain to victims the strengths and limitations of each facility so that we can decide together which is the most appropriate location for them. This gives victims the flexibility to choose the prison where they feel most comfortable participating, rather than being restricted to one location.

Other physical aspects of the environment should be considered like temperature control. Overly warm rooms can feel stifling, while excessively cold rooms can distract participants. Access to cold water, at least in the form of drinking water, and a hot cup of tea or coffee can also have a calming effect and, in our experience, the prisons in which we work are happy to provide these. The venue must also provide easy access to the toilets. Yet, victims need to be made aware if toilet doors cannot be locked for security reasons. This needs to be checked beforehand and discussed with victims, and arrangements can be made where they are not comfortable with a guard standing outside the door. Often there are lockable toilets at the entrance to the prison, so another option is to provide victims with the opportunity to use these when entering and leaving the secure part of the prison.

It is also important to bear in mind that the further a room is located within the prison, the more sections victims will have to walk through, and this can be uncomfortable for them. To help victims feel more prepared and supported, it may be helpful to take them through a 'mental walkthrough' or to draw a 'visual' picture of the venue, explaining each step and what to expect on the way to the meeting room. In France, victims have the opportunity to visit the prison and see the meeting room once before the programme starts. This is an excellent opportunity to reduce anxiety – meeting offenders is often anxiety inducing enough without worrying about entering a prison, perhaps for the first time, too. If it is possible to negotiate this access in your local prison, area, region or country, that will have a significant impact on your victims.

b) Ensuring security measures are based on trauma-informed practices

When making these initial arrangements, it is also important to determine how victims will access the premises and any required security measures they will have to go through. Facilitators need these details so that they can adequately prepare victims for what to expect and to ensure that the location of the room is suitable for all victims. For example, victims who have been taken hostage or who have suffered any form of abuse may find it very difficult if they have to be patted down for security purposes or if they have to cross many different areas of the prison, where they may also come into contact with other offenders. As such, we recommend asking several specific questions to adequately support victims to prepare and to help prison staff be more trauma-informed:

- What is the dress code for visitors – are there any types of clothing that are not allowed?
- Are there ways of conducting security checks that do not involve physical contact?
- Is it possible to design security measures in a way that does not unduly intimidate or even re-traumatise victims?
- Is it possible for female victims to be screened by female staff?
- What security measures are needed to access the part of the prison where the dialogue is due to take place?
- What parts of the prison do victims have to pass through to get to the venue?
- Whom might they meet along the way?
- Are there many security doors to pass through?

Required security measures also need to be discussed with prison management because they may not be aware of how easily anxiety or other traumatic symptoms can be triggered by their security measures. Prison staff are not used to working with victims, so it is important to educate them about the circumstances and needs of victims who have suffered serious harm so they can help to find ways to make the environment less threatening. Even where processes cannot be changed, prison staff can ensure that their attitudes and interactions are respectful and reassuring while they carry out security checks. Leaders of restorative programmes may sometimes be hesitant to communicate with prison management or security staff when issues arise, fearing that it might jeopardise the continuation of the programme. However, when working from a trauma-informed perspective, the victim's sense of safety must not be compromised.

In our experience, if we explain the problem properly, it is usually met with understanding. For example, in one prison where we ran restorative dialogues for the first time, despite discussing security procedures with the prison governor beforehand, security staff did not follow the agreed-upon instructions and began conducting intimidating and intrusive pat-downs on victims. I tried to stop them immediately, but they said they were in charge of security, not us. I reported this to the prison management, despite the potential repercussions of criticising their staff. The next time, while the security staff did not touch the victims, they treated the group with a dismissive attitude, leaving them feeling unwelcome and triggering unpleasant memories of past interactions with criminal justice professionals. Reporting the issue again to the prison administration was essential to safeguard the victim's well-being and ensure they experienced trauma-informed practices while in the prison. Effective and clear communication about the impact of those practices meant they were receptive to the request and that they reiterated their instructions to the security staff. From this point on, the security checks were conducted in a victim-friendly way. This is why it is so important that restorative justice facilitators understand what happens to individuals who have experienced trauma so that they can explain it to others in simple terms. When staff understand, there is often a very positive attitude towards victims.

c) Confidentiality considerations

The level of confidentiality offered by the venue is another important consideration for all participants. Rooms with mainly glass partitions may provide a greater sense of physical security but may compromise emotional safety, as what is going on in the room is visible to others at all times. Particularly during the storytelling phase, participants may feel even more exposed and inhibited from becoming emotional for fear of being watched from the outside, thereby reducing the quality of the dialogue. For offenders, emotions inside the prison are usually hidden to avoid perceptions of weakness. Addressing this challenge may involve choosing a day and time for the dialogues where there is low foot traffic or using curtains to create privacy, at least where the group sits for the dialogues.

One of the competing needs involves the need for safety and security within the venue (victims often want someone to be there to intervene immediately if necessary) and the need for confidentiality (offenders, who might find it very difficult – if not impossible – to be open and honest with prison staff in the room). This tension requires a solution to be found with the prison management that provides that kind of security and at the same time respects the confidentiality of what happens in the room. Prison authorities will also want updates on the progress of the programme, particularly if there are any difficulties or challenges that need to be addressed. They will also be interested in whether offenders are participating in a respectful and engaged way. As such, it is essential to discuss in advance what information needs to be shared, with whom and when. These agreements need to be communicated to participants before the programme starts to ensure they are fully aware of what information needs to be shared and what can be kept confidential. For example, national law may require disclosure of any crimes for which a prisoner has not been convicted or if there are concerns about the safety of that person or others (fear of harm to self or others).

Preparing participants for restorative dialogues

Preparing victims and offenders to participate in restorative dialogues is crucial for ensuring their safety, well-being and the success of the programme. It is important to remember that restorative dialogues differ from direct victim–offender processes in that participants will not be meeting or interacting with their direct victim or offender, but rather those who are unrelated to their crime.

Effective preparation involves assessing each person's readiness to participate, ensuring their involvement will not compromise their well-being or that of others, and enabling participants to enter the process confidently and without undue anxiety. This phase aims to build trust and rapport between participants and facilitators, while providing them with the information, resources and support they need to make informed decisions about their participation and to actively engage in the restorative process.

In a trauma-informed approach, preparation sessions also focus on creating a safe and supportive environment for participants to express themselves freely if they wish to disclose traumatic experiences. Facilitators discuss coping strategies to deal with potential triggers or challenges that may arise during the meetings and to identify and mitigate any risks or vulnerabilities. As mentioned in Chapter 4, victims and perpetrators are prepared separately for restorative dialogues, so the preparatory activities for each group of participants are discussed separately in the following section.

Preparing victims for participation

Getting to know each other and establishing safety and trust

Relationships are at the heart of trauma-informed approaches, especially in preparing victims for participation in restorative dialogues. Establishing a safe and trusting relationship between facilitators and victims is essential for creating an environment where victims can engage without fear. This process often begins with informal dialogue aimed at building rapport. Rather than immediately delving into their stories, facilitators initiate conversations by exploring how victims heard about the service, their motivations for participation and their expectations. Similarly, victims should also feel encouraged to ask about the facilitators' backgrounds and roles. This approach encourages deeper conversations and cultivates a non-threatening atmosphere. By prioritising victims' needs and attentively addressing their questions and concerns, facilitators create a safe space that fosters trust and confidence.[2]

Providing detailed information about the programme

During the first meeting, it is crucial to provide victims with the full details of the programme. They should understand the objectives of the programme and be given information about the sessions, location, timetable, safety measures and group dynamics. It is imperative that victims understand they are free to choose what to share with the group and that they are not obliged to discuss details of the crime. Additionally, victims should be informed about the availability of support from facilitators during and after the restorative dialogue sessions.

Victims will want to know the types of crime that will be represented in the group, and they should be made aware of specialised groups (e.g. that only include participants involved with gender-based violence or political violence) should they want something more specific. Providing this information and answering questions will enable victims to assess whether restorative dialogues will meet their needs. If a victim feels that this programme is not right for them, it is important to explore alternative avenues of support and discuss possible approaches that are better suited to their needs and preferences.

Listening to the victim's story

Adopting a trauma-informed approach to storytelling requires facilitators to consider various elements to ensure victims feel supported. Facilitators need to remember the impact of memory on storytelling.[3] Since victims may not remember every detail chronologically, they appreciate open-ended, inviting questions rather than detail-oriented ones.[4] Facilitators should maintain a calm and reassuring demeanour, avoiding expressions of shock or disbelief. While sharing the story may be difficult, it is also an important part of the recovery process. Therefore, facilitators need to provide a respectful, empathetic and non-judgemental listening space.[5]

Before delving into the story, facilitators should discuss coping strategies with the victim and enquire about their preferences for emotional support and physical proximity if they become distressed. It is important for facilitators to remain attuned to victims' emotional cues, such as fidgeting, crying, shaking or changes in tone of voice. Active listening, non-verbal cues (e.g. nodding, maintaining eye contact and using verbal affirmations) and patience validate victims' experiences and foster trust.

Addressing feelings of guilt and self-blame is vital. Many trauma survivors struggle with these feelings, which often stem from a desire to regain control.[6] Victims may blame themselves for not reacting differently during traumatic events, unaware of the brain's instinctive survival mechanisms, such as freezing or dissociating. Facilitators play a crucial role in challenging irrational beliefs and promoting self-compassion and self-care.[7] Time management during the process is crucial, with sessions allowing ample time for victims to share their experiences without feeling rushed. Flexibility is key, as emotional discussions may necessitate breaks or rescheduling where the victim feels this is necessary.

Assessing readiness for participation

Assessing readiness for participation requires sensitivity, thoroughness and collaboration. Victims should be actively involved in the assessment process to honour their autonomy. Listening attentively to victims' stories provides valuable insight into their experiences, coping mechanisms and ongoing challenges.[8] Facilitators need to be alert to subtle cues and overt expressions of distress (e.g. trembling, sweating, visible emotional upheaval, avoidance behaviour, dissociation or difficulty in articulating certain aspects of the experience) and create a safe and supportive environment for authentic sharing.

Assessing readiness extends beyond storytelling sessions to consider the victim's broader context, progress in trauma recovery and support networks. Exploring coping strategies, resilience factors and perceptions of growth helps to identify resources for coping with trauma. Facilitators should provide information about additional support resources and explore alternative forms of participation if needed. Ultimately, the goal is to empower victims to make informed, voluntary decisions that facilitate their recovery and participation in restorative justice processes.

Once the preparation process has been completed and victims have made a final decision to participate, it is important that there is an opportunity for the participating victims to get to know each other and the other facilitators before the restorative dialogues begin. This can be done through a Zoom meeting, a face-to-face meeting or it is also possible for the group to meet on the day, prior to the start of the programme. Such a meeting can reduce anxiety before the group meetings start.

Jana's story highlights the importance of thorough preparation with the victim and the transformative potential of restorative dialogues in trauma recovery.

Case study 6.1: Jana's journey

Jana endured years of stalking, including home invasions, by an unknown perpetrator and lived in constant fear. Despite a decade of therapy, the traumatic effects remained, affecting her daily life even after the stalking stopped. Determined to confront her fears and gain insight into the motivations behind such crimes, Jana decided to participate in restorative dialogues. Given her ongoing post-traumatic symptoms, a detailed safety plan was developed with Jana. This plan included weekly meetings with both her therapist and the restorative dialogue group leader. This approach aimed to provide a robust support system, mitigate additional stress and monitor for any signs of re-traumatisation.

The first meeting was particularly challenging for Jana but marked a turning point in her journey. The face-to-face interaction with perpetrators and victims helped to dismantle the horrific images she had imagined. The empathy and support she received was crucial in alleviating her distress. Jana's active participation in the development of the safety plan and her consistent engagement throughout the process demonstrated her commitment to healing. Denying her participation solely because of her symptoms could have deprived her of this important opportunity for recovery. By integrating mental health support and respecting her desire to participate, the process proved to be profoundly beneficial.

Jana's experience highlights the importance of balancing caution with victim empowerment. For victims who exhibit trauma symptoms but express a desire to participate in restorative dialogues, collaborative planning with mental health professionals and tailored support can facilitate meaningful healing and empowerment.

The selection and preparation process for offenders

A trauma-informed approach to offender preparation is essential, as a significant proportion of prisoners have experienced trauma themselves. The prison environment, through its restrictive conditions, threat of violence and lack of autonomy, can exacerbate existing trauma or lead to new trauma, perpetuating cycles of harm and suffering.[9] Many offenders, particularly men, may not disclose their traumatic experiences, often due to feelings of shame. It is therefore imperative that a trauma-informed approach be universally applied to all offenders as a preventative measure.[10]

This approach involves a comprehensive understanding of each individual's experience of trauma and subsequent responses, as well as recognising the structural contexts in which services are delivered. It emphasises the importance of facilitators engaging in self-reflection to ensure the delivery of compassionate and non-judgemental care while advocating for the creation of safe processes. Importantly, adopting a trauma-informed approach does not diminish responsibility and accountability for harmful or offensive behaviour; these aspects remain central.[11] Instead, it prioritises the safety and well-being of offenders throughout the process, potentially increasing their receptiveness to taking responsibility for their actions and addressing the triggers for that behaviour. This, in turn, benefits victims by increasing the likelihood of rehabilitation and reducing the risk of future victimisation.[12]

Raising awareness and providing information sessions

The first step in the selection and preparation process of offenders is to raise awareness about the programme and offer an information session for interested individuals. Various methods, such as distributing leaflets or direct communication from therapists, social workers, probation officers or prison staff, serve to inform prisoners about the opportunity to participate in restorative dialogues. When interested offenders register, they attend a one-hour information session with one or two facilitators. The session aims to provide a basic understanding of restorative justice, its benefits for victims and offenders, and the available approaches, such as direct victim–offender and group processes. Clear communication about the opportunities and limitations of the programmes is essential. Participants are informed that in restorative dialogues they will not meet their own victims and that their participation will not affect their sentencing or release. However, the programme offers the opportunity to hear from victims of similar crimes, ask questions and understand the impact of their actions. After the session, interested individuals complete application forms and proceed to individual interviews with facilitators. Over the years, I have seen several cases of initially resistant offenders who later became passionate supporters of restorative justice.

Conducting individual interviews

The next phase in the preparation process involves conducting individual interviews with each prisoner to understand their motivations for participating in restorative dialogues. As mentioned in Chapter 3, common motivations include seeking insight into the consequences of their crimes, recognising the seriousness of their actions by listening to victims' stories, and offering support to victims by validating their experiences and answering their questions. However, if the sole motivation is to have a positive impact on their sentencing or to seek entertainment outside their cells, participation is deemed inappropriate as it risks further harm to the victims. Victims may perceive a lack of genuine interest in understanding their experience and acknowledging the harm caused, which can be deeply distressing and undermine the effectiveness of the restorative process.

This phase also presents an opportunity to build rapport by treating prisoners with respect and dignity. Facilitators should demonstrate a sincere interest in their lives and acknowledge that offenders, like everyone else, have experienced hardships. Thus, during interviews, practitioners should aim to get a brief overview of each individual's story. It is important to be alert to signs of shifting blame, justifications, denial or minimisation, which should be noted and addressed. Individuals who accept responsibility tend to provide a straightforward account without justification, often expressing guilt and remorse. Additionally, it is important to gauge a person's willingness to share their story with the group, as some may be reluctant due to trust issues within the prison environment. Storytelling is at the heart of the programme, and victims want and need to hear offenders' stories to understand why they reached the point in their lives where they offended and what insights they have gained into their actions since the time of the offence. If reluctance persists, participation in the programme may not be suitable for that person.

After the interviews, facilitators, in collaboration with prison staff, select the offenders who will participate in the upcoming programme. Selection criteria are based on each individual's personal motivation to participate, expressed interest and commitment, as well as the alignment of the crimes committed with those experienced by the victims involved in the programme. This alignment facilitates meaningful dialogue and understanding, and it ensures that participation in the programme adequately addresses the needs and expectations of the offenders involved.

Preparation with the selected group of offenders

Before the offenders meet the victims, there is a preparatory phase with the selected group of offenders. This preparation serves to start establish trust and rapport between the participating offenders and the facilitators. It also ensures cohesive group dynamics and addresses any potential tensions that could hinder the process. Moreover, the preparatory phase sensitises offenders to the needs of victims, offering insights into the profound impact of crime, including trauma and its enduring effects on victims' lives. Key issues such as shame and responsibility are also addressed. Many offenders struggle with feelings of shame, which can prevent them from fully engaging with the group or sharing their story. Through this phase, they gain an understanding of shame, its effect on their lives and constructive strategies for addressing it openly. Additionally, the group discussions encompass respectful and compassionate interactions with victims. Offenders are encouraged to initiate dialogue with victims, overcoming fears of causing distress. They also receive guidance on storytelling and are encouraged to talk not only about the crimes but also about the life experiences they have had as part of their journey to recovery from past trauma.

The preparatory session also provides a space to address any remaining questions or concerns, and to assess the group dynamics to anticipate and mitigate potential challenges. Typically lasting two hours, the session can be extended for groups dealing with particularly sensitive crimes, such as sexual or domestic violence, acts of terrorism or hate crimes. After this preparation, the eight group sessions begin.

James's story serves as an example of the changes that can take place in an offender who was reluctant to attend the information session and then became an advocate for restorative justice.

Case study 6.2: James's initial reluctance

James had already spent 15 years in prison for committing murder while under the influence of drugs and alcohol. This crime occurred during a weekend leave from prison, where he was serving time for various other offences. His chances of leaving prison now seemed bleak, facing not only a standard sentence but also constant re-evaluation of his rehabilitation progress, potentially extending his stay in a secure facility. James felt a deep sense of frustration, having undergone numerous forms of therapy over the past 15 years and believing that repeating the same therapy would not make a difference.

Reluctantly, James attended an information session on restorative dialogues, driven more by frustration and a desire to show cooperation with prison staff than by personal interest. More than 20 offenders attended the session, but James stood out as the most inquisitive, often posing questions in a critical tone, seemingly intent on challenging the restorative justice facilitators and discrediting the programme. However, he found something intriguing about the programme, prompting further questions during the completion of the application form.

I encouraged him to sign up for a face-to-face interview where he could explore his questions in more depth without distraction. James seized the opportunity. It was during this one-to-one interaction that his initial resistance began to crumble. He felt that he was taken seriously, that his concerns were valued, and that he was treated with respect and dignity. As the programme progressed, James's emotional barriers began to break down. Through hours of sharing and storytelling, he unearthed the root causes of his substance abuse, a process that proved excruciatingly painful yet profoundly cathartic. The group enveloped him, and he was deeply moved when a fellow participant, a victim who had lost a loved one to murder, embraced him with compassion. Receiving such empathy, James learned to reciprocate and extend compassion to victims.

Upon completing the programme, James expressed a desire to return and support fellow inmates and new victims through the same process, a request that was granted by the prison governor. Recognising a significant change in his life, his therapists reassessed his situation. He was then transferred to a prison specialising in the rehabilitation of long-term offenders preparing for release. Remarkably, he completed the programme in less than a year and began working outside the prison walls. James is now a free man and a passionate advocate for restorative justice. He shares his experience, emphasising the need for this type of dialogue with students and the media. Though he admits it was the most challenging thing he has ever done, he believes it has brought healing and transformation to himself and others.

Implementation of a trauma-informed approach during the group meetings

The Swiss programme consists of eight sessions, each lasting two hours, delivered in three phases. The first phase focuses on creating a safe space, the second on storytelling and the final phase on programme closure. To reduce participants' anxiety, victims receive an email outlining the main elements of each meeting beforehand and prisoners are briefed at the end of each meeting about the next session. This approach aims to instil a sense of safety, allowing participants to internally prepare and avoid surprises.

1. First phase: community building – creating safety and fostering trust

The initial phase aims to create a safe environment, build trust and cultivate a sense of community within the group while allowing time for participants to get to know each other. In the first meeting, the group collectively identifies the values necessary to ensure safety, respect, openness and honesty. We use a circle process to facilitate controlled and non-threatening communication, equitable participation and attentiveness without fear of interruption or confrontation, which align with trauma-informed principles. The identification of values is achieved by participants responding to the question: "What values do you need us to embody as a group to ensure that you feel safe, respected and able to speak honestly and from the heart?" Each participant responds while holding a feather in the circle until no one has anything more to add. The feather is then passed around the group a final time to confirm each participant agrees that the identified values should guide the group's interactions. If everyone agrees, they sign the list recorded on a flipchart, and this becomes a contract between the participants.

Values tend to be similar across groups and most often include respect, empathy, tolerance, listening, non-judgement, confidentiality, commitment and humour. While humour may seem odd at first, its importance becomes clear as the sessions progress, with shared laughter acting as a source of relief during challenging discussions. In a second circle process, participants also take turns to share their expectations and fears about the programme. Initially, we only addressed this in individual interviews, but we found it beneficial for the group to hear each other's concerns and hopes because this encourages collective responsiveness to each participant's needs. Feedback indicates participants find this process is valuable and victims, in particular, feel it recognises the group's shared humanity and alleviates fears.

During the first meeting, some of the interactions take place in two smaller groups, which means that the entire group of up to 12 participants, including the facilitators, is divided into groups of no more than six. This is particularly appreciated by participants who feel uncomfortable in larger groups. Real-life scenarios are also used to explore the impact of crime and related issues. The flexibility of small groups ensures inclusivity and engagement, with the option of returning to circle methods if a participant feels uncomfortable sharing freely in a larger group.

The next two meetings focus on building trust and familiarity with participants through circle processes, case studies and topical discussions, rather than personal storytelling. This approach allows participants to gauge reactions and build confidence for future storytelling while fostering a comfortable and non-judgemental atmosphere. Participants are encouraged to share personal information at their own pace, and feedback suggests that the structured nature of these sessions helps them to gradually adapt to the group and the programme. Coffee breaks during each session provide opportunities for informal socialising, with facilitators present to monitor participants' comfort levels. By the third session, participants generally seem more relaxed and appreciate these breaks, which are in line with trauma-informed care principles by supporting self-regulation and social bonding, as well as enhancing feelings of safety and belonging.

Each meeting ends with a short circle process followed by reflection, often facilitated by reading a poem or short story. Additionally, participants are reminded of the facilitators' availability for additional support during the week. Offenders can gain access to the facilitators through the prison management or a designated staff member. Flexibility is key in this phase, adapting the programme to address the group's evolving needs, rather than adhering strictly to the topics outlined in the handbook.

2. Second phase: fostering community through storytelling

Restorative justice places significant emphasis on storytelling, recognising its central role in providing victims with a safe and validating platform to share their experiences. Given its centrality, we are often asked why we wait until the fourth meeting to begin storytelling. This serves several purposes:

- *Establishing safety and trust*: The initial meetings focus on creating a safe and respectful environment to build trust and reduce anxiety. This foundation helps participants feel more comfortable and less anxious, making them better prepared for deeper engagement and vulnerability in later storytelling. By sharing other personal experiences beforehand, and observing the group's reactions, both victims and offenders become more comfortable and experience less anxiety.
- *Building community and fostering empathy*: Delaying storytelling allows for the formation of a supportive community among participants, thereby reducing feelings of isolation and shame.[13] This sense of belonging and understanding enhances participants' readiness to share their experiences and receive support from others who can relate to their journey.
- *Maximise impact through connection*: By delaying storytelling, we leverage the evolving relationships within the group to deepen the emotional impact of sharing personal narratives. This heightened connection encourages more profound sharing and mutual support.

This strategy significantly increases the impact on offenders as they empathise with victims' suffering, having come to know and respect them. This preparation also sensitises offenders to consider how their narratives may affect victims, fostering empathetic relationships within the group and minimising the risk of further harm. Before engaging in storytelling, crucial topics such as shame and its profound impact are discussed within the group. Shame, an intensely painful emotion, is often experienced by both victims and offenders. Strategies for dealing with shame include expressing it in an environment where it is met with understanding and empathy and knowing that while it might initially be difficult to talk about, it does become easier once individuals have opened up and shared their experiences.[14]

Participants are asked about their expectations and needs during and after storytelling, fostering a culture of care within the group. After this preparation, the next three meetings are dedicated to storytelling. Victims first share their stories, and after each story, the group can respond by offering support and understanding, or by asking questions. No individual has to respond to a question if they do not feel comfortable. After each story, a break is taken to check in with the storyteller and to allow the group to self-regulate and digest what they have just heard. It is often touching to see how offenders care for victims during these breaks, offering personal words of support they did not feel comfortable sharing with the whole group. Many victims have said how much they appreciate these personal moments of sharing and the empathy.

Following the victims, offenders share their stories, consider the impact of their actions on others and discuss factors contributing to their behaviour, including their upbringing and life trajectories, without justifying their crimes. The narrative approach provides a safe environment for offenders to process their experiences and offending behaviour. Listening to offenders' stories helps victims gain insight into how people come to offend and humanises offenders, while providing opportunities for offenders to support victims and gain insight into the impact of their actions. Such insights can support desistance from crime, fostering a community that listens attentively and validates participants' experiences and suffering.

3. *Third phase: coming to a closure*

Following the emotionally intense storytelling phase, it is important to provide the group with an opportunity to reflect and discuss their experience within the intimate group setting. Often participants have lingering reflections and questions they would like to share, expressing their appreciation for the collective journey and the honesty and vulnerability with which each member shared their experience. Consequently, the seventh meeting is dedicated to this purpose, and at the end, participants are asked if there are any specific issues they would still like to address with the group. During this seventh session, considerations are made regarding the group's interest in meeting some weeks or months later for an informal get-together. However, logistical constraints, such as prisoners leaving or changing prisons, may limit this possibility. At the end of the meetings, participants anonymously complete evaluation forms, enabling them to provide feedback that is vital in shaping future iterations of the programme.

The eighth and final meeting is a celebration of the collective journey. However, given the presence of prison management and services at this closing ceremony, personal details are not shared at this meeting unless individuals choose to share them. Participants share broader reflections on the programme's significance, its impact and any shifts in participants' perspectives. Expectations and fears shared during the first session are revisited, allowing participants to reflect on whether these expectations were met and if fears were validated. All discussions are carried out in a circle process.

In preparation for this closing ceremony, offenders prepare symbolic thank-you gifts for the victims, such as letters or handmade gifts. These are often very meaningful to the victims. For example, one offender made a small angel for a victim of stalking, expressing his hope that she would feel safer at night with the angel in her room. In another group, the victim, who compared her experience to the transformation from a caterpillar to a butterfly, received a beautiful origami butterfly from an inmate. As she had not told the group about this experience yet, tears welled up in her eyes as she expressed how much the butterfly symbolised her journey. These gestures illustrate the empathetic connections fostered among participants through attentive listening. The ceremony includes a shared aperitif, providing an opportunity for personal interactions and farewells between participants. The session culminates in a final circle process and a contemplative story. These stories are usually related to the topics discussed and invite personal reflection or encouragement.

Caring for participants and team members during and after the programme

The ongoing support and well-being of participants and team members is vital to the programme's success. Throughout the eight meetings, participants are assured of continued support from facilitators by phone, email or individual meetings between meetings. The team also remains vigilant for signs of distress among participants, offering proactive support or referrals to therapeutic professionals as needed. For prisoners, accessing support may involve liaising with prison management or social services between meetings, reflecting on the complexities of their situation in a closed environment. Some prisons allow prisoners to contact facilitators by phone or letter, but in other cases, they are required to make an appointment with the facilitators to talk. Providing adequate support to prisoners is a challenge that facilitators face and may be concerned about, and therefore is discussed in the next section.

Following the programme's conclusion, some participants may benefit from additional conversations with facilitators to reflect on their experiences. Informal gatherings of victims and facilitators provide opportunities for shared reflection and programme evaluation, facilitating continuous improvement. Team members, who are exposed to distressing stories throughout the programme, also require support and supervision. It is up to team leaders to actively engage with team members and address any concerns regarding their well-being. These considerations underscore the importance of holistic support for both participants and team members, ensuring the programme's efficacy and sustainability. Chapter 7 is dedicated to this topic, as it is an area that is often forgotten.

Although restorative dialogues tend to progress in a very constructive and positive way, facilitators may still be faced with certain challenges. Being prepared for these is an important next step in delivering an effective, trauma-informed programme. This final part of the chapter draws on the collective wisdom and experience of the facilitators interviewed for this book.

Challenges in implementing restorative dialogues

Interestingly, most facilitators who participated in the interviews took some time to reflect when asked about the challenges they had faced in facilitating their programmes. The prevailing consensus was that, while challenges did exist, they were relatively rare, and the programmes generally evolved in a positive and constructive way. Yet, there are more structural challenges that have no simple solutions, and in recognising the existence of these challenges, it is important to draw on a broader field of practice and experience in an attempt to resolve them.

1. Assessing readiness

The first challenge for facilitators is to assess when the right time has come for a person to be involved in a process such as restorative dialogues. There are no easy answers as to how to ensure this, and an important aspect, particularly with victims, is to make the decision together with the person; otherwise we repeat a structure of disempowerment. If there is uncertainty about an offender's readiness to participate, it is important to facilitate a multi-disciplinary discussion. This may involve their therapists in prison or staff who have intimate knowledge of the offender, including insights into their behaviour and mindset.

2. *Facilitation challenges*

Facilitating dialogue groups of this kind presents a variety of challenges that requires sensitivity, both to the individual participants and to the collective group dynamics. It is a complex undertaking that involves careful planning even before the programme begins, particularly with regard to group dynamics and the composition of both the entire group as well as smaller discussion groups. It is important to think about how to form groups in a way that benefits each individual and to identify which participants could work well together in smaller groups. Especially for the membership of small groups, it may well be that facilitators match the wrong persons and then need to reassess the group's composition.

Managing the expression of emotions is also a challenge for facilitators. They acknowledged that in the end, as facilitators, they tend to find it more difficult than the participants to feel comfortable with certain situations. The challenge is therefore more often about relinquishing control and trusting the group dynamic. It is more about learning "what makes us… more at ease because the group is at ease with what is happening", so the important aspect is that "we don't end up stopping the expression because we, as facilitators, would be more at ease". This can be particularly challenging in moments of frank exchange, where facilitators need to resist the urge to intervene and instead allow the natural flow of dialogue to take place. The key is to create an environment where participants feel comfortable expressing themselves authentically, without undue interference from facilitators. If needed, the use of simple questions or short reflections can help to diffuse tension and bring the group back together. In addition, calling for a short break can provide an opportunity for participants to re-centre themselves before continuing the dialogue.

3. *Challenges related to storytelling*

While the narrative part has proven to be the central aspect of the programme, it is also the most delicate. Listening to the stories is difficult, both for participants and facilitators. This challenge was recognised by the participants and yet they affirmed that it remains a crucial and necessary part of the programme. It is therefore essential to prepare participants adequately for sharing and receiving each other's stories, and to provide ongoing support during and between sessions. As explained in Chapter 3, the victims interviewed agreed that it can be beneficial to hold debriefing sessions between group encounters during the storytelling phase, especially when the stories are emotionally challenging. This debriefing can take place virtually, for example via Zoom, and provides an opportunity to discuss and process what has been heard.

Another challenge raised in this context was how to deal with participants who wanted to read their story rather than tell it spontaneously. While it is understandable that it may be easier to read, facilitators have found that there is a risk that the person reading their story may feel detached from it. This issue was particularly raised in the case of offenders, and the risk of it is illustrated in the following case study.

Case study 6.3: The story that haunted the group

During a restorative dialogue, a prisoner who had committed a gruesome murder read his story to the group verbatim, without making eye contact. For the group, it felt as if he was recounting someone else's experience; there was no emotion or personal connection in his delivery. It was as if he was reading the script of a horror film, devoid of any insight or remorse for his actions.

This lack of emotional engagement was particularly distressing for the victims. The atmosphere in the room became tense and the group discussion that followed was severely hampered. The participants were too shocked to process what they had heard together. As a result, everyone took the story back to their prison cells or homes, where it continued to haunt them.

The prisoner himself realised the impact of his detached delivery when he was back in his cell. The gravity of the situation hit home and he was shaken to the core. He contacted the prison administration to arrange a meeting with the facilitators. During this meeting, he cried and explained how terrible he felt because he realised the pain this must have caused the group, and he wanted to discuss how to address this in the next session.

In the following session, he spoke openly about his feelings and the shock he had caused. This discussion was crucial for the group, as it allowed them to process their feelings and initial shock together. However, this incident also highlighted a significant risk: the ability to hide behind the sheet of paper. The prisoner himself acknowledged this, describing how he had used the script as a shield to distance himself from his actions and their impact on the group.

This case highlights the importance of genuine emotional engagement in restorative dialogues and the potential consequences of its absence. For victims, there is the same risk of detachment, and if they are not fully emotionally present and connected to their story, they may struggle more with the questions or comments they receive from the group after sharing their stories. Therefore, these aspects need to be discussed and explained during the preparation phase. Participants are welcome to bring notes to help them remember aspects that are important to them, but it may be better to encourage them to speak from the heart.

4. Providing support to prisoners

Several facilitators highlighted the challenge of providing adequate support to prisoners throughout the programme. Unlike victims, who can be called or visited throughout the week, participating prisoners cannot be approached as easily by facilitators. As a result, facilitators may have the uneasy feeling that prisoners are struggling with what they are hearing and experiencing throughout the programme without sufficient support. While the situation may vary from one country or prison to another, it is generally more difficult to provide ongoing support to incarcerated participants. As a result, facilitators may have concerns about their well-being and safety, which can be a difficult burden for facilitators.

One approach to addressing this concern is to enquire whether each prisoner has a support person within the prison. This aims to ensure that they have someone to turn to when they need to. Similarly, in our programme we ask about regular meetings with therapists, social workers or prison chaplains. We emphasise the potentially distressing nature of the programme and the importance of having someone to talk to. Throughout the programme, we remind participants to contact the prison administration or staff who can facilitate phone calls or visits with our facilitators between sessions. Past experience has shown that prisoners have taken up this offer. In other countries, facilitators may have access to the prison during the week, allowing them to be present and available at designated times. This clearly eases the challenge of providing ongoing support.

Another strategy we have in place is the careful selection of prisoner groups. Since they all see each other during the information session, we then ask them during the individual interviews if they have seen any prisoners with whom they would not be able to work in the group, and then we try to put together a group where everyone feels comfortable in the presence of the others. As we run groups regularly in the prison, we prioritise attendance based on estimated release dates. Prisoners who are due to be released earlier will attend the current group. Those who are released later receive a letter informing them that they will be attending the next group, ensuring that everyone has the opportunity to attend. Feeling comfortable in the group makes it easier for them to support each other throughout the programme and we have found that it works.

In one of the recent programmes, we were very concerned about one of the prisoners who was very upset after telling his story. First, we asked him if he was in danger of harming himself, which he denied. We then asked his colleagues if any of them would have access to him in the evening when they were locked in their wards, and they said that they were all together and would look after him. The following week we asked the prisoner how it had gone, and he said they had looked after him very well. Thus, if a participant becomes distressed, we take proactive steps to ensure their well-being. We also notify the prison staff if there are any concerns and, in some cases, ask specific members of staff to provide additional support to the individual in need. Despite these efforts, supporting prisoners remains a challenging aspect of the programme. However, by implementing these strategies and remaining vigilant, it is possible to mitigate these challenges and ensure the well-being of all participants.

5. *Comparison among participating victims*

When victims compare their suffering with that of others, additional challenges arise. This can take different forms. Some may begin to minimise the impact of the crime on their lives, feeling that it is nothing compared to the suffering of others in the group. Others, however, may see their suffering as more significant, which in turn diminishes the experiences of other victims. Both situations present their own challenges. Addressing the minimisation of one's suffering is often best done in a group setting, where the feedback and support of the group can validate and encourage individuals in their struggles. On the other hand, addressing the perception of one's suffering as greater than that of others is usually better done through individual conversations between sessions. However, as highlighted by the facilitators who raised this issue, it may still be necessary to address this issue collectively within the group. This ensures that all participants understand the importance of recognising and respecting each person's unique experience, thus preventing any sense of invalidation among victims.

6. *Respecting boundaries*

Another challenge that can arise is the failure of some participants to respect their own or others' boundaries. One expert highlighted the difficulty that can arise in managing individuals who have experienced significant boundary violations in their lives, resulting in a lack of awareness or control over appropriate behaviour in group settings. "It is always a challenge for us to limit that. Sometimes someone will go on and on because they feel they are finally being noticed. They have not experienced boundaries themselves and may unintentionally make others uncomfortable by oversharing or overstepping boundaries."

To address these situations, the facilitator invites the individual to a private conversation between meetings. During this dialogue, the expert gently discusses observations about the individual's feelings and experiences, providing a safe space for exploration and support. This approach aims to provide support while ensuring that the individual does not feel exposed or ashamed in the group setting. Although generally well received, striking the right balance within the group remains a challenge. Facilitators need to encourage natural discussion while establishing and maintaining appropriate boundaries to ensure everyone's dignity and comfort.

7. *Addressing harm caused within the group*

On rare occasions, offenders may – usually unintentionally – harm a victim verbally and such situations can be very challenging to manage. On the one hand, it is crucial to protect the victim and intervene promptly. On the other, there may be legitimate issues to address that could potentially be beneficial to explore. However, the sensitive nature of the situation often means that discussions cannot continue within the group. In such cases, it may be necessary for the offender to leave the group to protect the victim and to send a clear message to others that such behaviour will not be tolerated.

The risk of re-traumatising the victim is a major concern. However, it is important for facilitators to be able to talk to both the victim and the offender separately and to provide support throughout this process. It is also vital that victims are given the opportunity to express any feelings they may have about the exclusion of the offender, or to decide whether they wish to raise the issue within the group and move forward together. Once more, it is about empowering victims throughout such programmes.

8. Dealing with voluntary self-exclusion

Sometimes facilitators encounter situations where a participant chooses to withdraw from the group voluntarily. There are ways to deal with this, either through individual discussions to understand the reasons for their withdrawal or by actively encouraging their inclusion and re-engagement with the group. However, it is vital to respect each individual's pace and recognise that each person is on their own unique journey. As facilitators, we need to embrace this diversity and honour everyone's process. There may be rare occasions when the group needs to say goodbye to a member, but these are uncommon.

9. The significance of language

One expert shared a significant experience that underlined the profound impact of the language used by facilitators. In the first programme she helped to facilitate, she approached a victim after a session and expressed her observation that the victim seemed deeply distressed and still affected by the past crime. However, the victim denied these feelings. The facilitator then referred to the victim's body language as evidence to support her observation, which inadvertently caused the victim distress and anger and led her to question the facilitator's authority to make such claims. Ultimately, the victim requested that the facilitator be removed from the team. This example led to a discussion among the facilitators present at the group interview. They stressed the importance of using trauma-sensitive language, which emphasises inviting individuals to share their experiences and using open-ended questions rather than making assumptions or assertions. Although seemingly simple, this adjustment can significantly change the dynamics of communication.

10. Let go

Ultimately, the experts agreed that the biggest challenge in facilitating restorative dialogues may be to be confident and let go. "The big difficulty, I think, is one that we encounter in any group process, and it's perhaps the question of letting go and trusting that what is at work is sufficient in itself, and that you have to let go of wanting to embrace everything and all the questions."

This quote provides a fitting conclusion to the section on challenges. As the experts affirmed, restorative dialogues are effective in themselves as a means of containing and resolving conflict. The collective wisdom of the group and mutual care mean they are able to overcome many challenges together. While it is important for facilitators to be prepared, it is equally crucial to allow the group dynamic to unfold naturally.

Conclusion

This chapter has emphasised the multifaceted nature of implementing restorative dialogues, underscoring the necessity of a comprehensive, trauma-informed approach to ensure the safety and efficacy of the process. The journey begins with fundamental considerations, including the careful selection of facilitators, an examination of institutional considerations and the thorough preparation of both victims and offenders. This preparation phase is crucial in fostering a safe and trusting environment, enabling participants to approach the dialogue with confidence and openness.

The Swiss programme is carefully structured into three distinct phases, each designed to guide participants through the restorative process. The first phase builds on the trust established during preparation, extending it to the group setting. This foundation enables participants to engage more deeply in the second phase, which is dedicated to sharing their stories. Given the intensity of this phase, the third phase facilitates a gradual stepping back, helping participants find closure and bid farewell. The subsequent follow-up phase is designed to ensure that participants are able to process their experiences and seek additional support if necessary.

The adaptability of restorative dialogues, tailored to the specific needs of the group, is of paramount importance. As one facilitator expressed: "The idea is really to allow people to be as central as possible to their own space, to this space that belongs to them".

Although challenges are less frequent than anticipated, it is essential to be prepared to maintain the integrity and effectiveness of the programme. The relative infrequency of challenges underscores the robustness of the group dynamic and the collective strength and wisdom that participants draw upon. Even experienced facilitators who have accompanied numerous groups concur that each time, they too benefit from the collective wisdom of the group, gaining insights and resilience through each session.

A commitment to trauma-informed practice is an essential component of the success of restorative dialogues, particularly within the prison context where participants are likely to have experienced significant trauma. By continuously adapting our approach based on trauma research and participant feedback, we strive to create restorative interventions that are both effective and sensitive to the complexities of trauma. As previously stated, the objective of this chapter is to provide a comprehensive overview of our strategies while also encouraging further discourse among restorative justice facilitators. By disseminating knowledge and best practices, it is possible to develop services that support the recovery and empowerment of all participants, thereby fostering a restorative process that is safe and transformative.

Nevertheless, guiding these groups through their journey remains a challenging task. Therefore, it is imperative that restorative justice services prioritise the well-being of facilitators, and that they recognise and mitigate the risks of secondary traumatisation. This concern will be explored in greater detail in the next chapter.

Notes

1 Bolitho (2015); Lanni (2021); UNODC (2020).
2 Canaff et al. (2023); SAKI (2015).
3 More about memory is found in the appendix.
4 IACP (2017); Office of Justice Programs (2024).
5 Herman (1997); Van der Kolk (2014).
6 Manda (2019); Rico (2020).
7 Manda (2019).
8 Jaeger et al. (2014).
9 Miller and Najavits (2012).
10 Benedict (2014); Miller and Najavits (2012); Pringer and Wagner (2020).
11 Scott and Jenney (2023).
12 Miller and Najavits (2012).
13 Brown (2006); van der Merwe and Gobodo-Madikizela (2008).
14 Brown (2006).

References

Benedict, A. (2014). *Using trauma-informed practices to enhance safety and security in women's correctional facilities.* www.ojp.gov/ncjrs/virtual-library/abstracts/using-trauma-informed-practices-enhance-safety-and-security-womens

Bolitho, J. (2015). Putting justice needs first: A case study of best practice in restorative justice. *Restorative Justice*, 3(2), 256–281. https://doi.org/10.1080/20504721.2015.1069531

Brown, B. (2006). Shame resilience theory: A grounded theory study on women and shame. *Families in Society*, 87(1), 43–52.

Canaff, R., Lonsway, K. A., & Archambault, J. (2023). *Trauma-informed interviewing and the criminal sexual assault case: Where investigative technique meets evidentiary value.* https://evawintl.org/wp-content/uploads/2020-02_TB-Trauma-Informed-Interviewing-and-the-Criminal-SA-Case-Technique-Meets-Evidentiary-Value.pdf

Herman, J. L. (1997). *Trauma and recovery: The aftermath of violence, from domestic abuse to political terror*. Basic Books.

International Association of Chiefs of Police (IACP). (2017). *Successful trauma informed victim interviewing.* www.theiacp.org/sites/default/files/2020-06/Final%20Design%20Successful%20Trauma%20Informed%20Victim%20Interviewing.pdf

Jaeger, J., Lindblom, K. M., Parker-Guilbert, K., & Zoellner, L. A. (2014). Trauma narratives: It's what you say, not how you say it. *Psychological Trauma: Theory, Research, Practice and Policy*, 6(5), 473–481. https://doi.org/10.1037/a0035239

Lanni, A. (2021). Taking restorative justice seriously. *Buffalo Law Review*, 69(3), 635–681.

Manda, C. B. (2019). *Re-authoring life narratives after trauma: A holistic narrative model of care*. AOSIS.

Miller, N. A., & Najavits, L. M. (2012). Creating trauma-informed correctional care: A balance of goals and environment. *European Journal of Psychotraumatology*, 3, 1–8. https://doi.org/10.3402/ejpt.v3i0.17246

Office of Justice Programs. (2024). *Trauma-informed victim interviewing*. www.ovcttac.gov/taskforceguide/eguide/5-building-strong-cases/53-victim-interview-preparation/trauma-informed-victim-interviewing

Pringer, S. M., & Wagner, N. J. (2020). Use of trauma-informed care with incarcerated offenders. *Journal of Addictions & Offender Counseling*, 41, 52–64. https://doi.org/10.1002/jaoc.12075

Rico, A. (2020, December 10). *It really wasn't your fault: How understanding the brain's response to trauma can lessen victim-blaming and self-blame*. U. S. Army. www.army.mil/article/241611/it_really_wasnt_your_fault_how_understanding_the_brains_response_to_trauma_can_lessen_victim_blaming_and_self_blame

Scott, K. L., & Jenney, A. (2023). Safe not soft: Trauma- and violence-informed practice with perpetrators as a means of increasing safety. *Journal of Aggression, Maltreatment & Trauma*, 32(7–8), 1088–1107. https://doi.org/10.1080/10926771.2022.2052389

Sexual Assault Kit Initiative (SAKI). (2015). *Trauma-informed communication*. https://sakitta.org/toolkit/docs/Trauma-Informed-Communication-Pamphlet.pdf

United Nation Office on Drugs and Crime (UNODC). (2020). *Handbook on restorative justice programmes* (2nd ed.). www.unodc.org/documents/justice-and-prison-reform/20-01146_Handbook_on_Restorative_Justice_Programmes.pdf

Van der Kolk, B. (2014). *The body keeps the score: Mind, brain and body in the transformation of trauma*. Penguin Books.

Van der Merwe, C., & Gobodo-Madikizela, P. (2008). *Narrating our healing: Perspectives on working through trauma*. Cambridge Scholars Publishing.

7. Preventing and addressing secondary trauma

Introduction

Imagine the emotional toll on a therapist who listens empathetically to distressing stories on a daily basis, or on a first responder who is confronted with acute human suffering. Similarly, restorative justice facilitators are exposed to the deeply painful and often traumatic experiences shared in restorative dialogues. Although they do not experience the trauma directly, their repeated exposure to these raw, emotional narratives can lead to secondary trauma – a profound psychological distress that is often overlooked.

For restorative justice practitioners, secondary trauma is a pervasive problem that requires urgent attention. Facilitators risk absorbing the trauma of those they support, which can manifest over time in symptoms such as anxiety, depression and sleep disturbances. Addressing this risk is essential to maintaining the well-being of practitioners and the integrity of the restorative justice process.

At present, this potential risk appears to be given minimal consideration in the context of restorative justice. A search of the literature on this issue for restorative justice practitioners yielded no results, suggesting that it remains under-researched. This gap may be due to the historical focus of restorative justice on minor offences. However, as the field has expanded to include serious crimes, practitioners are increasingly exposed to traumatic narratives. Recognising and mitigating secondary trauma is therefore crucial.

This chapter provides an introductory exploration of secondary trauma, drawing on literature, insights from colleagues, real-life case studies and the author's experience of leading an organisation of volunteer practitioners working with cases of serious harm. It begins by highlighting the prevalence of secondary trauma and the urgent need for awareness and proactive intervention. The chapter then examines risk factors and signs to help practitioners identify and address the issue. It also provides practical strategies and tools for self-care and organisational support, adapted from other helping professions to fit the restorative justice context.

The chapter, therefore, represents a preliminary exploration of the topic and highlights the need for further research and broader discussion among restorative justice practitioners and scholars. Ultimately, it is a call for practitioners

DOI: 10.4324/9781003271611-7

and organisations to acknowledge the reality of secondary trauma and take steps to mitigate it, ensuring that those who provide care are also cared for. To better understand the implications of secondary trauma, the following section clarifies key terms with specific meanings and relevance to practitioners.

Clarifying key concepts

The terms burnout, compassion fatigue, secondary traumatic stress (STS) and vicarious trauma are frequently used in discussions about the emotional toll that working with trauma survivors can take on professionals. Although these terms are often used interchangeably, they describe distinct experiences.[1] This section clarifies these terms, highlights their differences and the specific risks they pose.

1. Burnout

Burnout is often discussed alongside compassion fatigue, STS and vicarious trauma, but it is primarily rooted in organisational and workplace challenges rather than direct exposure to traumatic material. According to Maslach and Jackson's definition, burnout is characterised as "a syndrome of emotional exhaustion, depersonalization, and reduced personal accomplishment that can occur among individuals who work with people in some capacity".[2] More recent definitions describe burnout as a state of emotional, mental and physical exhaustion caused by prolonged stress.[3] Unlike STS and vicarious trauma, burnout is more closely linked to workplace conditions,[4] yet it remains a significant risk for helping professionals,[5] including restorative justice practitioners.

2. Compassion fatigue or empathic strain

Compassion fatigue, sometimes equated with STS and PTSD, refers to the emotional and physical exhaustion that occurs when professionals empathise deeply with their clients. This can lead to symptoms similar to those experienced by clients, making it more difficult to connect with and support them.[6] Compassion fatigue is characterised by the profound emotional and physical erosion that occurs when professionals are unable to recharge and regenerate,[7] affecting not only their work with clients but also their relationships with colleagues and loved ones.[8] Research suggests that the most empathetic and caring professionals are often the most vulnerable to compassion fatigue.[9]

However, some experts argue that the term 'compassion fatigue' can be misleading. True compassion, defined by warmth and a desire to help others without absorbing their suffering, is inherently rewarding and can protect against burnout. As Miller notes, research shows that compassion activates the brain's reward centre (the nucleus accumbens), suggesting that it is an energising rather than a fatiguing emotion.[10] Consequently, terms such as 'empathic strain' or 'empathic distress' may better describe the negative effects of overwhelming empathy, where the boundaries between self and other become blurred.[11] Unlike empathy, which can lead to distress, compassion promotes resilience by fostering care without absorbing the pain of others.[12]

3. Secondary traumatic stress

Secondary traumatic stress (STS) can be difficult to define because it overlaps with terms such as 'compassion fatigue' or 'vicarious trauma'. Figley introduced compassion fatigue as a less stigmatising term for STS and defined STS as "a set of observable reactions to working with the traumatized and mirrors the symptoms of post-traumatic stress disorder (PTSD)".[13] STS occurs when individuals develop PTSD-like symptoms after hearing or witnessing others' traumatic events. Those affected by STS may re-experience personal trauma, experience heightened arousal and avoidance behaviours, and notice changes in memory, perception and self-efficacy.[14]

STS also results from "from helping or wanting to help a traumatized or suffering person".[15] This emphasises that the stress is not only due to the intensity of the trauma but also to the feelings of helplessness and overwhelm experienced by the helper – similar to the feelings experienced by the trauma survivor.[16] Unlike vicarious trauma, which develops gradually, STS is characterised by the sudden onset of PTSD-like symptoms resulting from indirect trauma exposure.[17]

4. Vicarious trauma

Vicarious trauma results from repeated exposure to the suffering of others, affecting both the body and the mind and leading to profound and lasting changes over time. Unlike the more temporary distress of STS, vicarious trauma gradually infiltrates one's emotions, relationships and well-being.[18] It refers to profound negative

Table 7.1 Key concepts of secondary trauma

Concept	*Definition*	*Main characteristics*	*Key differences*
Burnout	Emotional, mental and physical exhaustion from prolonged workplace stress.	Linked to organisational issues and work environment challenges.	Arises from workplace conditions, not exposure to traumatic material.
Compassion fatigue/empathic strain	Emotional and physical exhaustion from deep empathy with clients.	Symptoms similar to PTSD; it is debatable whether it is truly about 'compassion'.	Involves empathy – some argue that compassion is a protective factor.
Secondary traumatic stress (STS)	PTSD-like symptoms from exposure to traumatic material.	Sudden onset of PTSD symptoms, similar to PTSD.	Immediate reaction to traumatic material; no gradual process.
Vicarious trauma	Gradual, profound change from repeated exposure to trauma narratives.	Affects beliefs about self, relationships and the world.	Long-term cognitive shifts rather than immediate symptoms.

changes in a professional's inner world as a result of their empathetic connection to a client's trauma and their commitment to help.[19] Thus, it is "empathy that creates the greatest risk and vulnerability to vicarious trauma".[20]

Unlike STS, which involves immediate PTSD-like symptoms, vicarious trauma leads to lasting cognitive changes that disrupt fundamental beliefs about self, relationships and the world.[21] While these changes can be deeply challenging, they are not necessarily pathological and may be a normal response to repeated exposure to trauma.[22] However, recognising and addressing vicarious trauma is crucial to mitigating its negative effects.

To visualise the above content in a simple way, Table 7.1 summarises the main characteristics and key differences of the concepts.

In the remainder of this chapter, the term 'secondary trauma' will be used as an umbrella term.

Relevance of these concepts to restorative dialogues

All of the concepts described above are highly relevant to the work of restorative justice facilitators and highlight significant risks, particularly for those facilitating restorative dialogues in cases of serious harm. The cumulative effect of hearing multiple traumatic narratives can have a profound impact on a practitioner's well-being. From both personal experience and conversations with colleagues, I know the toll this work can take – feelings of helplessness, the strong desire to alleviate the pain of others, and the risk of over-identifying with clients are all too real. How real these risks are also becomes visible when looking at research that outlines the prevalence of secondary trauma among helping professionals.

The prevalence of secondary trauma

A review of the growing body of literature written for mental health workers and other professionals who work with trauma survivors reveals that the phenomenon of secondary trauma is a tangible and substantial risk. While methodologies across studies vary in terms of design, measurement focus and participant demographics,[23] an estimated average suggests that approximately 50% of helping professionals may experience secondary trauma at some point in their careers.[24] The range and severity of symptoms may vary considerably, and not all individuals affected by secondary trauma meet the criteria for PTSD. Nevertheless, PTSD UK (2024) indicates that 34% of victim support workers in the UK meet the diagnostic criteria for PTSD due to secondary trauma,[25] which is a notable figure in comparison to approximately 4% in the general population.[26]

This underlines the need to recognise that anyone exposed to the suffering and narratives of traumatised clients is at risk of developing secondary trauma.[27] These statistics are as relevant to restorative justice practitioners as they are to any other helping professionals. It is therefore essential to take these figures seriously and understand the profound impact of secondary trauma on the quality of interactions and relationships, both professionally and personally.

The need of addressing secondary trauma in restorative justice

In restorative processes, such as in restorative dialogues, in which practitioners engage with victims, offenders and their families or communities, they frequently encounter narratives that can have a profound effect on them. As Remen (2006) poignantly observed, "The expectation that we can be immersed in suffering and loss daily and not be touched by it is as unrealistic as expecting to be able to walk through water without getting wet".[28] Being touched by the suffering is not per se harmful; on the contrary, being fully present with clients, listening attentively, is a key element in facilitating restorative processes. However, the cumulative exposure to pain and suffering can deeply affect restorative justice practitioners.

It is thus not surprising that, over the years, I have heard numerous restorative justice practitioners describe sleepless nights haunted by the images of particular cases. Many struggle to leave their work behind as even at home, the traumatic stories echo through their minds, affecting their interactions with family and friends. Their experiences mirror my own.

What is surprising, however, is that the issue does not seem to be receiving much attention. In a research study I conducted a few years ago, experienced restorative justice practitioners expressed concerns about the absence of self-care structures and mechanisms to prevent secondary trauma within the field and their own services.[29] This gap in support is worrying because failure to address these concerns can lead to negative outcomes for both practitioners and the clients they serve.[30] Like other helping professions, restorative justice organisations must, therefore, prioritise the implementation of strategies to prevent and mitigate secondary trauma.[31]

To be truly trauma-informed, as this book advocates, organisations need to extend trauma-informed care beyond their clients to their staff. In this context, a trauma-informed approach provides a vital framework for managing the emotional impact of work, promoting overall well-being and reducing the risk of secondary trauma.

To illustrate the real and significant risks posed by secondary trauma, the following two real-life case studies highlight its profound impact on restorative justice practitioners. These cases serve as a tangible reminder of the importance of understanding and addressing secondary trauma, particularly for those facilitating restorative dialogues.

Case study 7.1: Pauline's suffering

Pauline, a restorative justice facilitator, found herself increasingly affected by the traumatic narratives she encountered during restorative dialogue sessions. As she absorbed the stories of victims and offenders, she began to experience intrusive thoughts and vivid memories of the trauma narratives outside of work. These experiences shared by her clients weighed heavily on her and left her feeling overwhelmed with intense feelings of despair and helplessness. She had a strong desire to help her clients but did not know how. In addition, Pauline began to remember her own traumatic childhood experiences. Over time, her own history and suffering seemed to blur with the narratives of the participants in the restorative dialogues. She began to have nightmares, reliving her own trauma as well as that of her clients.

Pauline's husband noticed her distress, and her personal relationships began to suffer. She struggled to connect emotionally with her husband and children and found it difficult to participate fully in family activities or conversations. Not only her husband but also Pauline's colleagues felt that she was not well and asked her about it. At first, Pauline did not feel comfortable talking about it. She felt that it would be an admission of failure and that she could no longer work as a restorative justice facilitator, a job she loved.

However, gentle encouragement from her colleagues and the reassurance that feeling these things was normal and could happen to anyone encouraged Pauline to open up to her colleagues. She also sought professional help. Months later, after several therapy sessions and feeling well equipped with new tools to face her work, Pauline returned to work as a facilitator. It had not been an easy experience for her, but she felt that the support and understanding she received had not only helped her to learn how to deal with these traumatic stories in her work but had also furthered her personal healing. For this to happen, however, it was necessary to have caring colleagues who were there for Pauline, who recognised the signs and were able to show her that these feelings and experiences were normal. By normalising them, they opened the door for Pauline to seek help and begin to heal.

While Pauline, with the necessary support, had the chance to return to the work she loved, Robert did not, as his story reveals.

Case study 7.2: Robert's sleepless nights

Robert had been employed in a senior role in law enforcement for over two decades when he started volunteering as a restorative justice practitioner. Following his training, he began co-facilitating restorative dialogues with great enthusiasm and dedication. He was highly regarded as a facilitator by both participants and the team, and initially appeared to flourish in his new role. However, over time, he began experiencing nightmares and an increasing number of symptoms indicating a sleep disorder. He was haunted by the images shared by the victims of serious crimes and found it increasingly difficult to sleep.

However, since he loved his new role, he did not want to give it up. Robert also had difficulty understanding how it could affect him so badly, given his decades of experience in law enforcement. He then came to realise that, although he had been working with serious crimes, he had only been able to gain insight into the offender's perspective rather than that of the victims. Now these victims' stories were having a profound impact on his life that he was reluctant to acknowledge.

Robert continued to work in this capacity until he reached a point where he felt he could no longer cope. He eventually sought professional help, but by then, his symptoms were so severe that the therapist advised him to cease his volunteer work. It took him years to recover, and the team mourned his loss deeply and felt guilty. Nevertheless, the incident served as a valuable reminder to the team to be vigilant of each other's well-being and to communicate openly about the potential impact of the work on their mental health. It was crucial for them to be transparent with each other and to seek help when needed, as well as to check in with each other about their emotional well-being.

These real-life case studies show that secondary trauma can affect anyone, regardless of their professional experience. Pauline faced a new challenge when she began working with clients who had suffered or caused serious harm. In contrast, Robert brought decades of experience to the field but had not been exposed to traumatic stories in the same way. Both cases highlight the crucial role that managers or colleagues play in preventing and dealing with secondary trauma. In Pauline's case, her colleagues recognised the signs and encouraged her to seek help, enabling her to return to the job she loved. In Robert's case, however, his colleagues were oblivious to his suffering. When he finally sought help from a therapist, they decided that the best course of action was for him to step down from his role as a volunteer facilitator.

These examples highlight the importance for restorative justice organisations – whether working with employed or volunteer facilitators – to be well trained in the prevention of secondary trauma. Where prevention is not possible, early identification and prompt intervention are essential. The following sections outline the risk factors for secondary trauma and provide strategies for prevention and intervention.

Risk factors for secondary trauma

Identifying potential risk factors is the first step in preventing secondary trauma. Trauma experts and organisations, such as the Tend Academy, OVC, NetCE, STS – Secondary Trauma Consortium, the Cannabis Health Evaluation Partnership, and Miller, highlight four main categories that can increase vulnerability.[32]

1. Personal factors

Personal factors include experiences and characteristics that increase an individual's vulnerability to secondary trauma, including:

- *Previous trauma*: Previous adverse childhood experiences (ACES) or traumatic events.
- *Current life stressors*: Experiencing personal crises, such as coping with a family emergency, caring for someone with significant needs or a recent bereavement within the last year.
- *Personality traits*: Tendency towards social isolation, difficulty expressing emotions, increased anxiety or avoidance of stress.
- *Level of experience*: Younger age or limited work experience.
- *Coping strategies*: Defensive or inadequate coping mechanisms and lack of a sense of coherence (feeling in control, finding meaning in work).

2. *Work environment factors*

Working conditions can significantly influence the risk of secondary trauma, with key factors including:

- *Lack of support*: Inadequate preparation, orientation, training, supervision and support structures, including peer support.
- *Exposure to trauma*: High volume and frequency of trauma cases, leading to increased vulnerability.
- *Job satisfaction*: Low levels of job satisfaction and negative experiences of supervision.
- *Stress and workload*: High levels of stress, excessive workload, role strain, bureaucratic barriers and interpersonal tensions among staff or colleagues.
- *Resource constraints*: Inadequate resources, feelings of powerlessness or lack of control over one's work environment.
- *Ethical conflicts*: Dilemmas such as insufficient time or resources to provide adequate care to clients, or conflicts between maintaining client confidentiality and the duty to report potential harm.

3. *Socio-cultural factors*

Socio-cultural factors, including race, culture, gender and sexual identity, can have a significant impact on the risk of secondary trauma:

- *Influence perceptions*: These factors shape individuals' experiences, perspectives, coping mechanisms and responses to traumatic content.
- *Systemic inequalities*: Inequalities related to race, ethnicity and sexual orientation can increase vulnerability, particularly for professionals from marginalised or minority groups who may face additional stressors such as discrimination or lack of representation.
- *Cultural beliefs*: Cultural beliefs and societal attitudes towards trauma and mental health can discourage individuals from seeking support and increase their vulnerability.

- *Gender-specific risks*: Research suggests that women working with high caseloads of sexual abuse survivors may be more vulnerable to secondary trauma due to the intense emotional involvement required in these cases.[33]

4. Community and contextual factors

Community and contextual factors, including social support networks and environmental influences outside the workplace, have a significant impact on the risk of secondary trauma.

- *Social support*: Lack of social support, both inside and outside the workplace, can lead to feelings of isolation, loneliness and alienation.
- *Access to resources*: Communities with limited access to mental health services or support groups face greater challenges in managing the psychological impact of their work.
- *Cultural norms*: Cultural and societal norms around trauma and mental health can affect the willingness of professionals to seek help, potentially preventing them from disclosing their struggles and increasing their vulnerability.

Some of these risk factors are evident in the two case studies. For example, Pauline had a personal history of trauma and a tendency to withdraw in moments of distress, which led her to delay talking about her suffering. She was also regularly exposed to a high volume of traumatic stories, which further increased her risk.

Robert also struggled to express his feelings and experiences. He believed that, given his years of experience in law enforcement, he should be able to cope with the demands of his job. This attitude may have been influenced by his generation, where seeking help for mental health problems was uncommon and often stigmatised. As a result, the barrier to seeking help was probably higher for him.

This is a pattern I have observed in other facilitators. Many have spent years in the helping professions and feel that their experience should enable them to deal with these challenges independently. Others come from professions such as law enforcement, where the need for mental health support has sometimes been seen as a sign of weakness.[34] Although perceptions are slowly changing in these professions too, some facilitators still struggle to acknowledge their need for support. It is therefore crucial for restorative justice organisations to address these challenges openly, to normalise the experience of being deeply affected by the traumatic stories of others, and to provide support in a way that feels natural and accessible, rather than something reserved for those who are 'unable to cope'.

However, according to the responses I received from interviewees during my research on trauma-informed approaches in restorative justice,[35] many of them mentioned that there were still no support structures in place to address secondary trauma within their restorative justice organisations or contexts. Therefore, the problem is not just that some facilitators may find it difficult to ask for help, but that there seems to be a lack of provision within restorative justice organisations to monitor and address the risks of secondary trauma.

Another risk factor is that many restorative justice organisations are severely under-resourced, both financially and in terms of staff. Practitioners are often under pressure to deal with as many cases as possible to secure the necessary funding. This pressure can lead organisations to neglect the personal well-being of facilitators, resulting in insufficient opportunities for supervision or peer support. Without effective processes for discussing clients' traumatic experiences, practitioners may struggle to process their own emotions, increasing their vulnerability to secondary trauma. This is of particular concern for restorative justice practitioners who facilitate restorative dialogues, as they are at significant risk from repeated exposure to trauma narratives.

Therefore, it is important to be aware of these risks, to communicate openly about them within restorative justice organisations and teams, and to normalise these discussions. The next section explores how secondary trauma can affect individuals.

The signs and impact of secondary trauma

Secondary trauma can affect individuals in many ways and to varying degrees. The effects can be emotional, cognitive, physical or related to personal relationships and professional life. Table 7.2 outlines the impact of secondary trauma as identified by organisations such as SAMHSA, Health Canada, OVC, NetCE, and secondary trauma experts Miller and Bercier.[36]

The impact of secondary trauma on individuals is very broad and can permeate many different aspects of their lives, as Table 7.2 shows. Emotionally, they may struggle with overwhelming feelings of sadness, anxiety and even despair, which can undermine their sense of confidence and hope. Cognitively, secondary trauma can alter their worldview, leading to increased suspicion, loss of trust and intrusive thoughts that disrupt their daily functioning. Physically, the toll manifests itself in chronic fatigue, sleep disturbance and other somatic symptoms that compound the emotional distress. Relationally, the trauma can create barriers in personal relationships, leading to social withdrawal, loss of empathy and challenges in maintaining close relationships. Professionally, these effects can diminish a practitioner's ability to provide quality care, leading to burnout, absenteeism and even the decision to leave the field altogether.

Many of these manifestations mirror those experienced by individuals exposed to primary trauma. While the symptoms of secondary trauma may be less intense, they still have a profound effect on the individual, causing significant distress and suffering. Given the pervasive harm that secondary trauma can cause at multiple levels, it is crucial to recognise early warning signs to prevent its development and allow for timely intervention. For this to happen, it is vital to develop both individual and organisational strategies to prevent and address secondary trauma, as discussed below.

Table 7.2 The impact of secondary trauma

Emotional impact	*Cognitive impact*	*Physical impact*	*Relational impact*	*Professional impact*
Distressing, intense emotions including sadness or grief, depression, anxiety, dread and horror, fear, rage or shame Loss of confidence in abilities and frustration with limitations Numbing or avoidance Defensiveness Hopelessness, despair, generalised despair Reduced self-confidence Cynicism	Cognitive shifts (e.g. chronic suspicion of others, heightened sense of vulnerability, extreme sense of helplessness, loss of personal control and freedom) Disrupted cognitive schemas Intrusive images, nightmares, flashbacks Loss of trust in others and institutions Changes in views of self, identity, society and the world Change in spirituality, belief systems Altered sensory experiences (e.g. symptoms of dissociation)	Somatic reactions (e.g. somatic pain, sleep difficulties, headaches, gastrointestinal distress) Chronic fatigue Exhaustion Physical illness Sleep disturbance Increased forgetfulness about important matters Substance abuse, compulsive eating	Disruptions in personal relationships (e.g. increased stress, difficulties related with trust and intimacy) Inability to be emotionally close to others Social withdrawal Disconnection from loved ones Loss of empathy Decreased sense of personal safety and safety of significant others The world becomes a frightening place Hypervigilance	Distracted, inattentive, forgetful, overwhelmed Poor decision-making Professional withdrawal/isolation Absenteeism Impairment of daily functioning in professional role Lack of motivation Decreased ability to provide high-quality care to clients Challenge of maintaining professional boundaries between personal and professional life Over-identification with or distancing from clients Damage or compromise to the client relationship Burnout Leave work/field

Individual strategies for preventing and addressing secondary trauma

A review of guidelines and documents from specialist organisations such as the British Medical Association, Phoenix Australia, Risk and Resilience, the NCTSN, the Visible Project, NetCE and Health Canada reveals numerous strategies for individuals to prevent and address secondary trauma.[37] Three areas that emerge repeatedly are Awareness, Balance and Connection, sometimes referred to as the ABC of addressing secondary trauma. A fourth area that is mentioned frequently is reflective practice. This section explores these in more detail.

1. Awareness: self-awareness and monitoring

Self-awareness is the starting point for recognising and addressing secondary trauma. Self-awareness involves recognising personal risk factors and becoming attuned to the early signs of secondary trauma. This process involves self-reflection and self-assessment, where individuals actively observe their internal experiences and behaviours.[38]

The importance of this practice is illustrated by Pauline and Robert's experiences. For Pauline, the increasing intrusion of traumatic memories and the emotional strain of her work went unnoticed until her well-being was significantly compromised. Similarly, Robert's initial lack of awareness of how the victims' narratives were affecting him led to serious consequences. This highlights the importance for restorative justice practitioners to engage in deliberate self-reflection and self-assessment, actively monitoring their internal experiences, emotions and behaviours.

To be effective, self-awareness must be coupled with a clear understanding of the potential signs and symptoms of secondary trauma. By learning what to look out for, as Pauline and Robert eventually did, practitioners can better identify when their well-being is at risk. This knowledge enables them to monitor their well-being and intervene in a timely manner if necessary.

Monitoring is the ongoing process of regularly checking in with oneself. Practical tools such as self-assessment scales (e.g. ProQOL) or personalised questionnaires can help to track personal well-being. Pauline's return to work after receiving professional help and support from her colleagues highlights the importance of such a proactive approach. By remaining aware of any changes in their well-being, practitioners can take action before secondary trauma affects their ability to carry out their role effectively, preventing situations like Robert's where the trauma became overwhelming.

The following sections present some personalised self-assessment tools that can assist in this process of self-awareness and monitoring.

Step 1: Evaluate general well-being

Detecting early warning signs can be challenging, as these signs are not always obvious to the individual, as Pauline and Robert's cases illustrate. However, as observed in Pauline's situation, loved ones or colleagues may be able to recognise these signs before the affected person does. One of the common signs of secondary trauma is the feeling of helplessness and overwhelm – the feeling that one cannot do anything about a particular situation or suffering,[39] which also was one of Pauline's experiences. This echoes the feelings of primary trauma, where trauma survivors also often feel helpless, powerless and overwhelmed.[40] However, as illustrated in Figure 7.1, secondary trauma can manifest in many different ways, affecting emotional, cognitive, physical, relational or professional well-being. Since every person is different, it is important to learn how to recognise

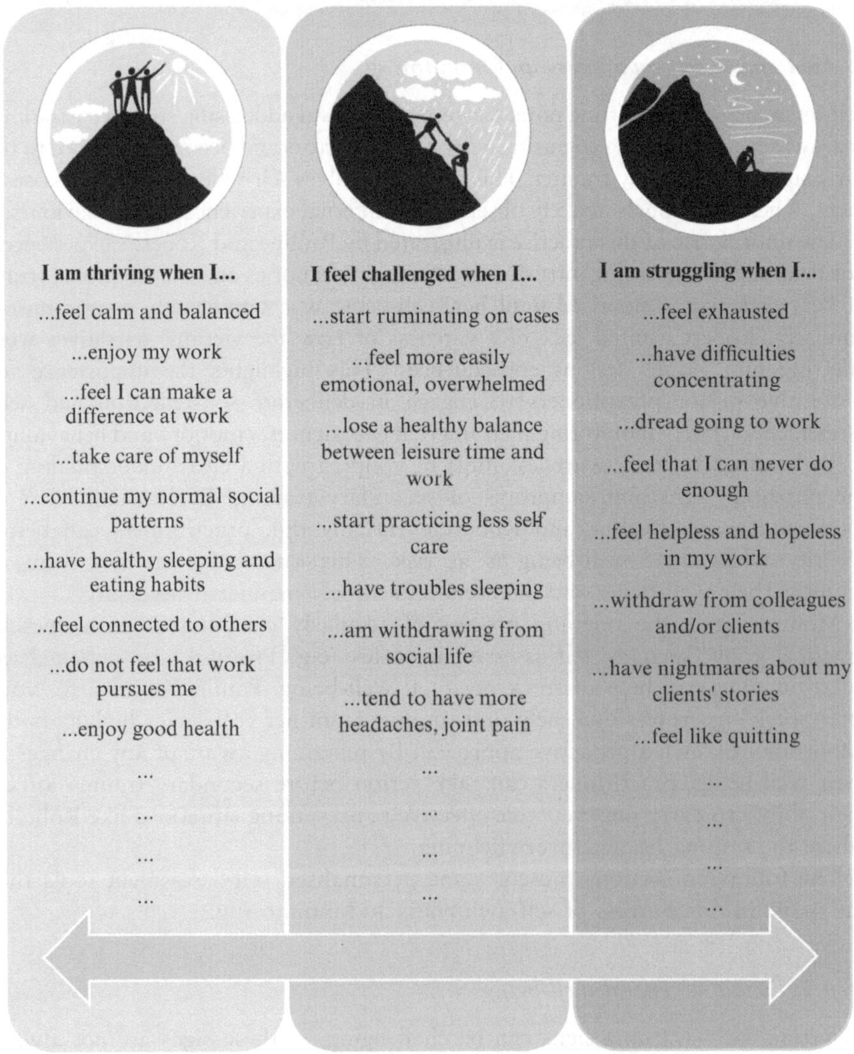

Figure 7.1 The personal traffic light
Note: This figure was inspired by the "Stress Continuum Model" adapted by The National Fallen Firefighters Foundation (2013), Plumbly (2022) and Mathieu (2023). All images by Julia Bakay 2024.

one's personal warning signs and symptoms. The following two tools may assist in learning to detect these signs and also help in monitoring them.

One possible approach is to assess one's general well-being first rather than immediately looking for early warning signs. A possibility for doing so is to observe whether one is thriving, feeling challenged or deeply struggling. These three stages can be thought of as traffic lights:

- *Green*: The person feels that they are thriving, feeling good with no significant symptoms of stress.
- *Yellow*: The individual feels challenged, noticing some warning signs, such as maybe ruminating on cases or having trouble sleeping, but is still managing. However, this still indicates that something is going on and that it would be important to slow down and analyse what is happening and how this can be addressed.
- *Red*: The same as with the traffic light, red indicates the need to stop. The person is struggling deeply and experiencing strong symptoms in one or more areas, maybe feeling exhausted or dreading going to work. Such a situation needs immediate attention and professional support.

By undertaking regular assessments of one's position on this continuum, it is possible to adopt a proactive approach in response to any indications that a person may be moving from the green to the yellow or red zone.

Step 2: Identify personal warning signs

Once an individual has recognised that they are in the yellow or red zone with the personal traffic light system, the next step is to use the tool presented in Figure 7.2. This tool is designed to assist in the identification of specific symptoms and their impact on overall well-being. The primary objective is to identify the early warning signs when an individual is in the yellow zone and to take prompt action to prevent a progression to the red zone.

The tool in Figure 7.2 can be used by first reflecting on the questions and thinking about your current emotional and physical state and behaviour. After reflecting on the questions, review the associated signs of secondary trauma that may correlate with the identified experiences. Based on the insights gained from the questions and the symptoms identified, decide what steps you need to take. This may include seeking support from a colleague, adjusting workload or implementing specific coping strategies.

As Pauline and Robert's experiences illustrate, early identification of signs of secondary trauma is crucial for restorative justice practitioners to prevent its escalation. While the personal traffic light system provides a quick assessment of overall well-being, the personal warning signs tool provides a more detailed assessment when distress signals emerge. Thus, to ensure that a practitioner's well-being is consistently maintained and promoted, well-being monitoring should be an ongoing practice rather than a one-off activity.

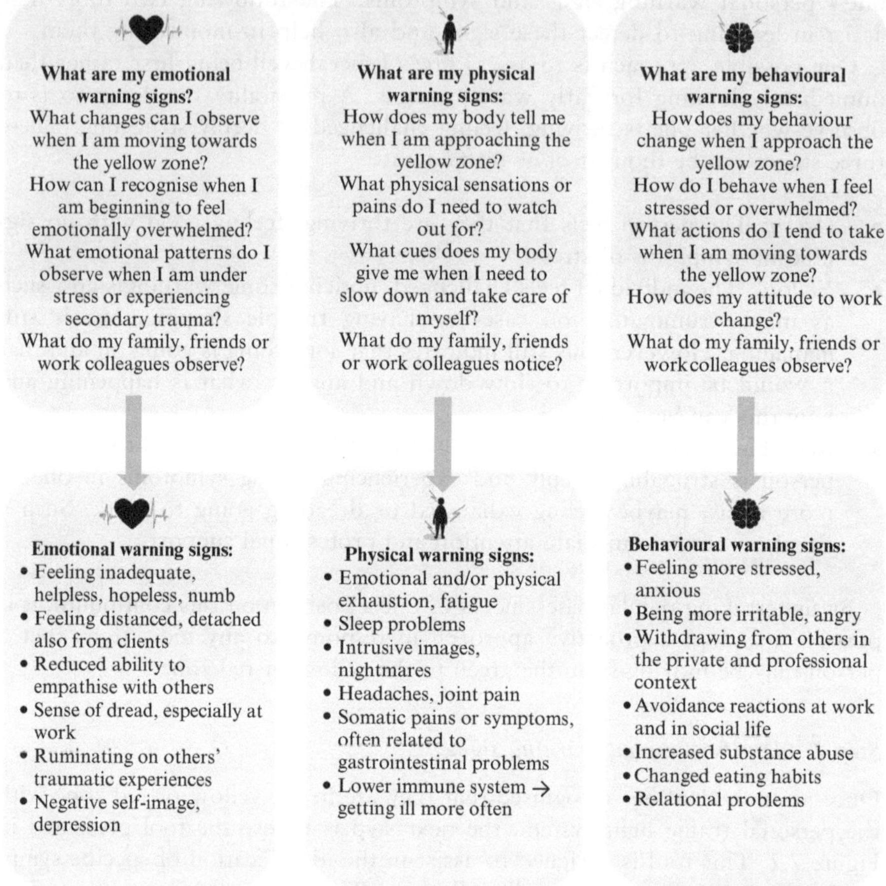

Figure 7.2 Understanding personal warning signs
Note: The warning signs and questions in this figure have been developed based on Mathieu (2017) and Plumbly (2022). All images created by Julia Bakay 2024.

To support this ongoing process and take proactive steps in preventing secondary trauma, the development of a personal self-care plan is essential. A well-designed self-care plan provides a structured approach to maintaining mental, emotional and physical health, helping practitioners to proactively address potential stressors and build resilience over time.

2. *Developing a personal self-care plan*

For restorative justice practitioners working with trauma survivors, developing a personal self-care plan is vital. Although many practitioners know this, it often proves challenging to go through with the plan. For some, there seems to be simply no time to spend on self-care; for others, it may even feel like a selfish act. However, as well as improving personal well-being, it also increases effectiveness at work and promotes healthy relationships with colleagues and clients. Otherwise, the risk is that practitioners do not have the emotional, psychological and even physical energy to serve their clients well and to be fully present when accompanying them through their suffering and process.

Thus, the aim of a personal self-care plan is to help create a healthy balance between private life and work. Because self-care is deeply individual, each person must determine what self-care means to them and how best to apply it in their daily lives. Thus, "[m]any experts in the field emphasize the importance of developing one's own self-care plan".[41]

When developing a self-care plan, it can be useful to consider the six areas mentioned in Figure 7.3.

The six areas illustrated in Figure 7.3 contribute to overall balance and well-being. Possible activities in each area are:[42]

- *Emotional self-care*: Activities that help manage and nurture emotions, such as journaling, mindfulness, therapy, creative outlets or engaging in joyful activities.
- *Physical self-care*: Regular exercise, a balanced diet, adequate rest, hydration, good hygiene and routine medical check-ups are essential for maintaining physical health.

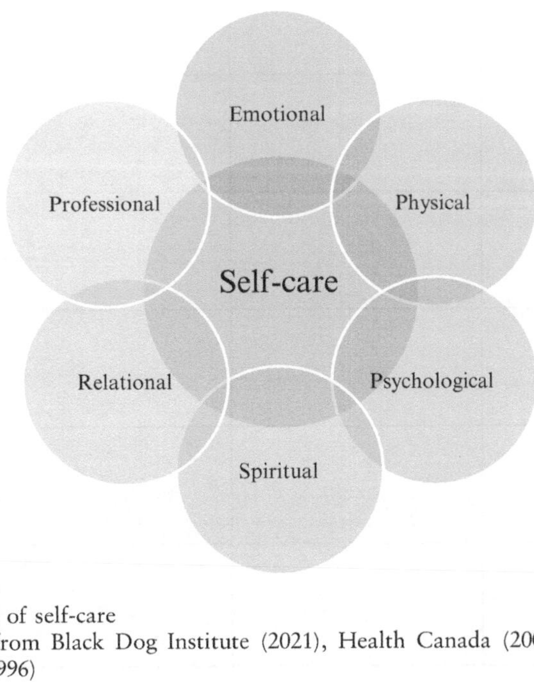

Figure 7.3 Areas of self-care
Note: Adapted from Black Dog Institute (2021), Health Canada (2001) and Saakvitne and Pearlman (1996)

- *Mental self-care*: Support cognitive and mental well-being by managing stress, setting goals, learning new skills and challenging negative thought patterns.
- *Spiritual self-care*: Cultivate a sense of purpose and connection through prayer, meditation, spending time in nature or engaging in acts of service that resonate with personal beliefs.
- *Relational self-care*: Cultivate healthy relationships by spending time with loved ones, setting boundaries and participating in community activities.
- *Professional self-care*: Maintain work–life balance, set boundaries, seek support through supervision or mentorship, and engage in ongoing professional development.

Step 1: Brainstorming

The first step in developing a self-care plan is to identify specific actions for each area. This first step should be seen as a free 'brainstorming' step, where the practitioner lists all the possible activities that come to mind without evaluating them. A format similar to Table 7.3 can be used for this purpose.

Table 7.3 Brainstorming for self-care plan

Area of self-care	*Things I need or like to do to stay healthy*	*Things I already do*	*Things I would like to do*
Emotional			
Physical			
Psychological			
Spiritual			
Relational			
Professional			

Step 2: Reality check

For a self-care plan to be effective, it is important to set realistic, achievable goals based on the current situation, personal preferences and time available. Therefore, after brainstorming ideas, it is important to do a 'reality check'. The following considerations may be useful in assessing options and developing a realistic self-care plan to which to commit.

KEY STEPS TO CREATE AN EFFECTIVE SELF-CARE PLAN

- *Be realistic*: Evaluate the daily or weekly schedule and set achievable goals that fit within that timeframe.
- *Choose enjoyable activities*: Choose activities that are meaningful or enjoyable to ensure long-term adherence.
- *Integrate self-care into the daily routine*: Prioritise self-care by scheduling it like any other essential task, recognising its importance to overall well-being.
- *Share the plan*: Sharing the plan with trusted people can provide accountability and support for sticking to it.
- *Evaluate regularly*: Evaluate the self-care plan every six months and make adjustments as needed to reflect changing circumstances.[43]

In addition, it may be useful to consider the questions in Figure 7.4 about possible barriers and coping strategies before committing to something that may not be realistic.[44]

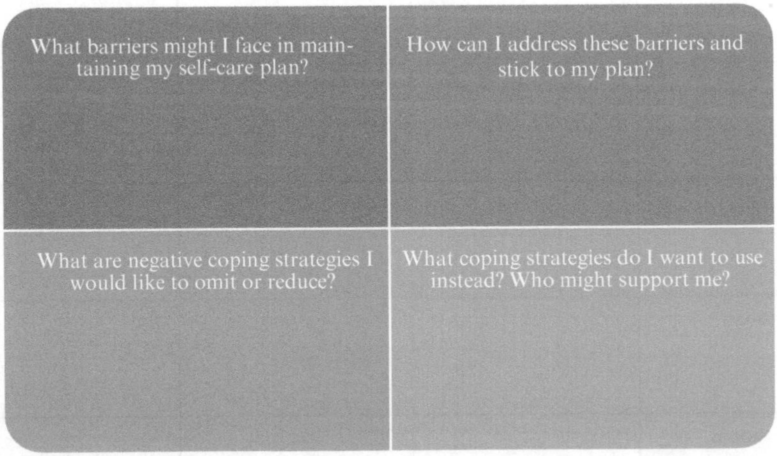

Figure 7.4 Barriers and coping strategies
Source: Adapted from Butler (2024)

Step 3: Make a commitment

With these previous considerations in mind, it is time to identify which actions are most important to you and decide what you can commit to on a daily, weekly or monthly basis.[45] A tool like the Personal Self-Care Commitment tool shown in Table 7.4 can be useful for this.

As nice and easy as it may sound, many restorative justice practitioners will know how difficult it is to stick to a self-care plan. Especially when working in small organisations where workloads and stress levels are high, it is easy to skip the well-intentioned self-care plan because one is simply too tired to think about and follow it. However, especially when working with trauma survivors and being exposed to many trauma narratives, as practitioners facilitating restorative dialogues are, there is a high risk that not following a self-care plan can have a detrimental effect on the practitioner's well-being, as in the case of Pauline and Robert. Therefore, as in Step 2, it may be useful to share the plan with a family member, friend or colleague who will check in regularly to see how the plan is going.

Table 7.4 Personal self-care commitment

Area of self-care	*What I can commit to on a daily basis*	*What I can commit to on a weekly basis*	*What I can commit to on a monthly basis*
Emotional			
Physical			
Psychological			
Spiritual			
Relational			
Professional			

Table 7.5 Emergency self-care plan[46]

Top 5 helpful strategies	*Top 5 strategies, places or people to avoid*	*Support people I can contact*
1.	1.	1.
2.	2.	2.
3.	3.	3.
4.	4.	4.
5.	5.	5.

Source: Adapted from Black Dog Institute (2021)

Step 4: Have an emergency self-care plan

There are times in life when circumstances simply become overwhelming. From personal experience, I can remember times when I was working more than full time, dealing with multiple cases of serious harm while also dealing with family emergencies. The same was true for colleagues, who mentioned that they felt much more vulnerable to clients' trauma narratives when they were going through personal difficulties. At such times, it is a challenge to remind oneself of the need for personal self-care. Moreover, these are the moments when the risk of developing signs of secondary trauma is highest. Therefore, an important fourth step is to have an emergency self-care plan that includes both strategies that are helpful and unhelpful in such moments, as well as support people to contact. They need to be aware that they are on this list.

Step 5: Develop rituals

The saying 'Old habits die hard' holds much truth, even when it comes to self-care. In addition to creating a formal self-care plan, incorporating small daily rituals into one's routine can be very beneficial. Over time, these rituals can become a natural part of the day rather than feeling like an extra task or burden. For practitioners working with trauma survivors, establishing clear boundaries between work and personal life is essential but challenging. Both Pauline and Robert described how these boundaries had blurred and they had taken the trauma narratives home with them. Developing consistent rituals for leaving work can therefore help maintain this distinction, enabling practitioners to transition from the demands of their work to their private lives without carrying the emotional burden of their work.

NetCE (2016) proposes some rituals and reflection questions that can be useful:[47]

- Walking or cycling home from work through a pleasant neighbourhood or park.
- Reading an engaging and relaxing novel while taking public transport home instead of driving your own car.
- Changing out of work clothes and putting them away as soon as you get home.

- Taking a five- or ten-minute period of silence or meditation before leaving work or immediately after arriving home to help you switch off from work, traumatic material and other work-related stress.
- Doing some form of exercise.
- Closing or locking your office or door at work in a conscious way, symbolically shifting your attention away from work matters and any traumatic images or distress you have encountered during the day.

Questions for reflection:

- Is there anything you do that helps you leave your work at work?
- Do you allow yourself a transition period between work and home?
- Do you have a ritual that you follow at the end of your working day? If not, experiment for the next week by trying a ritual, reflecting on it and its effect on you. If it was not helpful or did not have the intended effect, change it. Talk to friends and colleagues and find out about any rituals they have that they would recommend. Keep experimenting until you find something that works for you.

While many self-care practices are solitary activities, it is crucial to remember the importance of relationships – highlighted by the 'C' in the ABC of secondary trauma management: connection.

3. Connection: create a support network

The importance of relationships and community has been emphasised throughout this book. Not surprisingly, feeling connected to others and part of a community is one of the key factors highlighted by expert organisations for preventing and addressing secondary trauma. As the Headington Institute (n.d.) notes: "Maintaining nurturing relationships and meaningful contact with family, friends, and colleagues is one of the best things we can recommend to help address vicarious trauma".[48] However, the kind of connection needed goes beyond casual interactions. In moments of distress, what is needed is a 'true community' – a network of people who know each other well, share similar values, and provide support in both good times and challenges.[49]

Bercier's research (2013) underscores the central role of social support for those working with trauma survivors.[50] Building a network of colleagues, mentors, friends and therapists who understand the challenges of this work can provide essential validation, empathy and practical guidance. It is also crucial to extend this network beyond professional circles to include people who are not associated with the field. Healthy connections serve both as a primary shield against the effects of trauma and as a pathway to recovery.

Engaging in low-impact debriefing with peers is essential for mutual support, and maintaining strong connections outside the workplace builds resilience. If Pauline and Robert's organisations or teams had done this, their suffering might have been recognised earlier by their colleagues. This practice is therefore essential for restorative justice practitioners and highly recommended for teams facilitating restorative dialogues, as they often know each other well and there is usually a high level of trust. Nevertheless, it requires open and focused communication that helps to break the silence and isolation while increasing validation and hope.[51] Regular contact with friends and family outside of work also helps to counteract the isolation often associated with trauma work.[52]

Connection is not limited to relationships with other people; it also includes a deeper connection to that which nourishes and grounds an individual's sense of meaning and purpose. This may be belief in God, spirituality, nature or a broader connection to humanity. Maintaining this spiritual connection is crucial to preventing and addressing the loss of meaning and hope often associated with vicarious trauma. Transforming secondary trauma therefore involves discovering and regularly engaging in activities or practices that bring a sense of awe, joy, wonder, meaning or hope.[53]

Pauline and Robert's experiences highlight the critical importance of connection in dealing with secondary trauma. Both practitioners struggled with the effects of secondary trauma and their suffering went unrecognised for too long, largely because they lacked the necessary support networks and meaningful connections that could have provided early intervention. To prevent similar outcomes, it is essential for restorative justice practitioners to actively cultivate a 'true community' – a network of trusted colleagues, mentors and friends who understand the unique challenges of trauma work and can offer both emotional and practical support. By embedding these connections in daily life and engaging in activities that promote well-being, practitioners can better protect themselves from the effects of secondary trauma and maintain their ability to effectively support others.

4. Reflective practice

Reflective practice emerged as an additional component in the prevention and management of secondary trauma in several of the guidelines reviewed. On the one hand, reflective practice can help to increase self-awareness of the signs of secondary trauma and enable timely action, and, on the other hand, it can help to deal with the distressing situations and trauma narratives that restorative justice practitioners are exposed to.

Reflective practice thus should be an ongoing process for practitioners. One tool proposed by Risk and Resilience (2024)[54] for engaging in regular reflective practice is Gibb's reflective cycle (1998),[55] which has been presented in Chapter 4. The process and questions proposed in that chapter could be extended by the following questions:

1 Description

- What signs of stress, if any, did you observe in yourself during or after the situation?

- Were there any signs that you might have been affected by the emotional weight of the case or story?

2 Feelings

- How did the situation affect your emotional and psychological well-being?
- In reflecting on your feelings, have you noticed any of your personal warning symptoms of secondary trauma in this situation?

3 Evaluation

- Have you noticed any patterns in your emotional responses that might indicate secondary trauma?
- How did your feelings of stress or emotional distress affect your professional reaction in the situation?

4 Analysis

- What factors contributed to any signs of secondary trauma you experienced?
- Were there any aspects of the case that were particularly triggering?

5 Conclusion

- What has this experience taught you about your own vulnerability to secondary trauma?
- What might help you recognise possible signs of secondary trauma in future situations?

6 Action plan

- What (additional) steps will you take to monitor and manage secondary trauma in the future?
- Are there any actions you should incorporate into your self-care practices – or would it be good to seek support from others?

According to Miller (2022), reflective practice also involves consciously acknowledging and processing the emotions that arise in the course of work, not just afterwards.[56] It is inevitable that working with trauma survivors will evoke strong emotions. However, Miller states that these feelings are not harmful in themselves and do not lead to secondary trauma. What is much more harmful is to try to avoid these feelings or to try to inhibit their intensity. The energy this takes is what causes harm. On the other hand, allowing these feelings to emerge and dealing with them consciously can be beneficial for practitioners.[57]

The following steps and recommendations, which can be very useful for restorative justice practitioners, are based on Miller's CE-CERT model (components for enhancing clinician engagement and reducing trauma).[58]

1. Experiential engagement

This first step involves acknowledging and allowing the feelings that arise from working with trauma survivors. Suppressing these feelings can lead to empathetic strain (compassion fatigue), as it takes considerable energy to inhibit them. Instead, by consciously engaging with these emotions, practitioners can experience and release them naturally. Reflecting on these experiences requires three key skills:

- *Intentionality*: Consciously acknowledging the feelings that arise, rather than avoiding or suppressing them, allows practitioners to process and release these emotions.
- *Consciously acknowledge the experience*: Identifying and labelling emotions as they arise during work helps to shift from a reactive to a responsive mode, which improves emotional regulation.
- *Non-reactivity*: Trusting the natural process of emotions and allowing them to run their course helps prevent becoming stuck in a cycle of rumination.

2. Reducing rumination

After listening to traumatic stories, such as is the case during restorative dialogues, it can be difficult to 'leave work at work'. This can lead to rumination, where negative thoughts and images replay in the mind, affecting emotional regulation and mood. Strategies for reducing rumination include:

- *Acknowledgement*: Recognising when rumination is occurring is the first step. Distinguishing between rumination and problem-solving is essential, as rumination exacerbates emotional distress.
- *Focused engagement*: Redirecting thoughts to purposeful activities such as exercise, hobbies or meditation can interrupt rumination and promote emotional balance.
- *Social engagement*: Engaging in conversation with others helps break the cycle of rumination and fosters a supportive environment.
- *Action-oriented thinking*: Shifting the focus from passive re-experiencing to concrete, action-oriented thinking helps counteract feelings of helplessness and promotes problem-solving.

3. Conscious narrative

Creating a coherent narrative about work experiences is essential for emotional regulation and maintaining a positive outlook. Reflecting on experiences through narrative helps to make sense of them and find meaning. This process can be broken down into three parts:

- *Antecedent narrative*: Reflecting on one's beliefs, past experiences and confidence levels before embarking on challenging work helps to maintain a positive outlook and prepares practitioners for the task ahead.
- *Concurrent narrative*: During challenging restorative meetings, maintaining a problem-solving mindset and recognising opportunities for growth promotes resilience and skill development.
- *Consolidation narrative*: After difficult sessions, reflection through supervision or self-reflection helps practitioners process their emotional reactions, integrate insights and strengthen their narrative of professional growth.

As well as providing helpful suggestions, Miller's reflective model also highlights that practitioners ultimately need others to support them through difficult times. Although self-awareness, monitoring and self-care are important, it is not possible to deal with secondary trauma in isolation. Just as trauma survivors need the support of a community, so too do practitioners. This is what organisational strategies are about.

Organisational strategies for preventing and addressing secondary trauma

Practitioners do not develop secondary trauma in isolation; rather, it emerges as a result of their work, their care and their deep involvement with clients. Consequently, addressing and preventing secondary trauma cannot be the sole responsibility of individuals; organisations have an ethical duty to support their staff.[59]

Smaller restorative justice organisations may initially be reluctant to embrace this thought, questioning where they will find the necessary resources. However, as renowned trauma experts such as Cozolino, Herman, Treisman, and Van der Kolk have pointed out,[60] it is relationships that play a central role in trauma recovery – and they do not come at any extra cost. Consequently, the emphasis on relationships, belonging and community, woven throughout the book, extends beyond the work with clients. Supportive relationships and a sense of community are as relevant to those at risk of secondary trauma as they are to primary trauma survivors. Treisman (2017) affirms that "relationships are the most powerful mental health intervention known to mankind".[61] Consequently, the following proposals for organisational strategies to prevent and address secondary trauma focus considerably on relational aspects. These suggestions can also be applied to organisations working with volunteers.

The following strategies are informed by recommendations from several respected sources, including toolkits and guidelines by Bercier, CTIPP, Fetzner and Chelius, Headington Institute, ISCRR, ITTIC, the Office of the U.S. Surgeon General, OVC, and Risk and Resilience.[62] They are also shaped by years of personal experience running a small volunteer restorative justice organisation and feedback from colleagues who have experienced secondary trauma in this field. The strategies outlined in the toolkits and guidelines have been adapted to suit restorative justice organisations. Based on these sources, the chapter focuses on the four areas of organisational strategies for preventing and responding to secondary trauma illustrated in Figure 7.5.

Although supportive leadership is at the top of this pyramid, to illustrate the need for top-down guidance on organisational support, the suggestions start at the bottom, laying the foundations with supportive relationships and a trauma-informed environment. At the centre are the resources and training that inform the whole framework. To provide more detail, each aspect is discussed individually in the following section.

1. Cultivate supportive relationships

Fostering supportive relationships within restorative justice organisations is essential for preventing and addressing secondary trauma among both paid practitioners and volunteers. Strong, supportive relationships between colleagues are essential due to the sensitive and demanding nature of the work. Such relationships can provide emotional validation, resilience and a safe space to process difficult emotions. This culture of mutual support promotes practitioners' well-being and sustained engagement. For example, Pauline's story shows how gentle encouragement and support from her colleagues enabled her to open up about her struggles and seek professional help, ultimately enabling her to return to work with renewed strength.

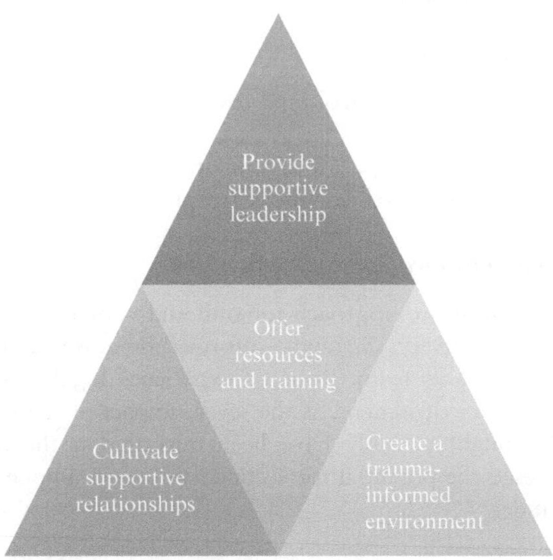

Figure 7.5 Organisational care pyramid

Some ideas of how to foster supportive relationships:

a Invest in relationship building

- *Team-building activities*: Offer regular workshops, social events or annual retreats to strengthen bonds between team members.
- *Mentoring programmes*: Pair experienced facilitators with newer members to foster connections and share knowledge.
- *Open communication*: Schedule regular one-on-one meetings that focus on personal well-being rather than performance.

b Encourage peer support

- *Peer support groups*: Organise regular meetings for facilitators to discuss challenges and offer mutual support.
- *Buddy system*: Pair facilitators to provide ongoing support and check-ins for each other. In Robert's case, if a peer support system had been in place, his increasing struggle with nightmares might have been identified earlier, potentially preventing the escalation of his symptoms.

c Encourage conflict resolution

- *Provide conflict resolution training*: Equip all facilitators with skills to manage conflict constructively.
- *Clear protocols*: Establish procedures for resolving conflict in accordance with restorative values.
- *Open dialogue*: Encourage constructive feedback and view conflict as an opportunity for growth.

d Emphasise collaboration

- *Team collaboration*: Encourage teamwork through joint projects and initiatives.
- *Regular team meetings*: Meet regularly, facilitate brainstorming, provide updates and foster collaborative problem-solving.

2. Create a trauma-informed environment

Adopting a trauma-informed approach for staff and volunteers is as important as applying it to service delivery. A trauma-informed organisation must address the trauma-related needs of its team. Robert's experience highlights the importance of a trauma-informed environment, as the severe impact of the victims' stories on his mental health might possibly have been mitigated if the organisation had proactively addressed the potential for secondary trauma among its staff.

Key steps include:

- *Cultivate a trauma-informed culture*: Involve the team in defining how trauma-informed principles apply to their work environment, with a focus on creating a safe, trustworthy and inclusive space where everyone feels valued and supported.

- *Normalise discussions about trauma*: Openly discuss the risks, signs and symptoms of primary and secondary trauma, starting at the interview stage. Pauline's initial reluctance to speak out highlights the need to normalise these discussions, making it clear that such experiences are not a sign of failure.
- *Identify and minimise triggers*: Help facilitators to identify and minimise exposure to situations that may trigger secondary trauma.
- *Hold regular debriefing sessions*: Integrate debriefing into routine practice to provide a space for emotional expression and resilience building.
- *Maintain a balanced workload*: Diversify tasks to reduce exposure to traumatic cases and increase job satisfaction.
- *Embrace cultural humility*: Embrace and celebrate cultural diversity, fostering an inclusive environment where cultural competence is a priority.

3. Offer resources and training

Providing resources and training is essential to equip staff and volunteers with the tools to prevent and manage secondary trauma. Affordable options include:

- *Work with local institutions*: Partner with universities or non-profit organisations to offer workshops and seminars.
- *Use online resources*: Use webinars, training videos and other digital tools for accessible training. For example, trauma-awareness training could have helped Robert understand the impact of victim narratives on his well-being, potentially leading him to seek help sooner.
- *Peer-to-peer training*: Encourage experienced facilitators to share their expertise with newer members. Pauline's journey back to work after therapy illustrates the value of equipping facilitators with tools and strategies for dealing with trauma, which can be effectively shared through peer-to-peer training.
- *Skill-building opportunities*: Support attendance at workshops or conferences on relevant topics, with knowledge shared within the team.
- *Organise information*: Collect and distribute accessible resources on trauma and its prevention.

4. Provide supportive, trauma-informed leadership

Leadership plays a central role in creating a supportive, trauma-informed organisational culture. In both Pauline and Robert's cases, leadership attuned to the signs of secondary trauma could have played a crucial role in providing timely support and intervention. Key practices include:

- *Trauma-informed decision-making*: Approaching all decisions and interactions with an awareness of the impact of trauma.
- *Modelling values*: Demonstrate the organisation's values,[63] as well as the trauma-informed principles of safety, trust, choice, collaboration, empowerment and cultural humility, in all actions.[64] If the organisation has not

yet defined its values, it should do so through a collaborative team process involving everyone in the organisation.
- *Acknowledge trauma*: Foster a culture where the discussion of trauma is encouraged and non-judgemental.
- *Open door policy*: Actively listen to practitioners' concerns and provide a safe space for expression.
- *Reflective supervision*: Focus supervision on well-being, skill development and resilience, separate from performance evaluation. Adopt a trauma-informed supervision format.[65]
- *Compassionate exits*: Ensure that staff who have been affected by trauma are supported so that they can leave the organisation with dignity and feel valued. Robert's difficult decision to stop volunteering due to severe trauma symptoms highlights the importance of a compassionate exit process, which could have helped him transition out of his role with more support and less guilt.

In conclusion, a trauma-informed approach and strong, supportive relationships are crucial to preventing and addressing secondary trauma in restorative justice organisations. As Pauline's recovery and Robert's struggle demonstrate, ensuring that facilitators feel supported by a caring community enhances their well-being and effectiveness. However, while working with trauma survivors can be challenging, it can also lead to positive personal growth for the practitioners involved.

Compassion satisfaction and vicarious resiliency

Working with trauma survivors, while challenging, offers significant potential for positive outcomes for practitioners. One such outcome is compassion satisfaction, which refers to the pleasure and fulfilment derived from helping others. Many professionals are drawn to their work by empathy and a desire to help and this satisfaction fosters a positive work experience and continued commitment.[66] In restorative justice, witnessing the positive impact of one's work and the gratitude of clients can be incredibly empowering.

Compassion satisfaction contributes to psychological well-being and job satisfaction, helping to reduce the distress associated with working with trauma survivors.[67] Factors that promote compassion satisfaction include secure attachment styles, self-compassion and a sense of common humanity – recognising the shared experiences of others and oneself. A balanced relationship with personal emotions and a strong sense of vocation also serve as protective factors against burnout.[68] It is therefore crucial to promote self-compassion among restorative justice practitioners and to provide training in this area, as it protects against empathic strain (compassion fatigue). Self-compassion and supportive colleagues also played a significant role in Pauline's recovery from secondary trauma.

Another positive outcome is vicarious resilience – the personal growth that professionals experience by observing the resilience of their clients.[69] This phenomenon can enhance the ability to cope with stress and trauma in both personal and professional life.[70] Secure attachments and supportive relationships, including supervision and peer supervision, play a critical role in fostering vicarious resilience. Other factors include education, self-care, task-oriented coping, spirituality and strong family support. Working with trauma survivors can lead to greater empathy, greater social activism, increased self-esteem and a greater sense of hope that individuals can overcome traumatic experiences.[71] However, Robert's case illustrates the need for early identification and support to prevent secondary trauma and ensure that vicarious resilience remains a positive outcome.

Recognising the impact of this work on facilitators and taking steps to prevent and address secondary trauma is essential. With the right support and strong relationships, the work can be both satisfying and enriching.

Conclusion

Secondary trauma is a critical but underexplored issue in the field of restorative justice. This chapter has highlighted the profound impact that facilitating restorative processes can have on practitioners, especially when they are regularly exposed to emotionally intense and traumatic narratives, as is the case when facilitating restorative dialogues following serious harm. The cases of Pauline and Robert are a stark reminder of the many ways in which secondary trauma can manifest itself, and underline the importance of recognising its symptoms early and taking proactive steps to address it.

The well-being of restorative justice practitioners is not only a personal concern but also a professional necessity. Practitioners must prioritise their mental and emotional health by seeking support, engaging in consistent self-care and setting boundaries to protect their emotional resources. However, the responsibility for addressing secondary trauma does not rest solely on the shoulders of individual practitioners. Restorative justice organisations need to take an active role in creating supportive environments that reduce the risks associated with secondary trauma.

It is imperative that restorative justice organisations adopt trauma-informed approaches that include regular trauma-awareness training, accessible mental health resources, and a culture that encourages open dialogue about the emotional challenges inherent in this work. By implementing these strategies, organisations can ensure that practitioners remain resilient and effective, ultimately enhancing the effectiveness of the restorative justice processes.

There is also an urgent need for further research in this area. While secondary trauma has been recognised in other helping professions, it has not been sufficiently explored within restorative justice. There is a significant gap in the literature regarding the specific impact of secondary trauma on restorative justice practitioners, and the development of tailored protocols and tools is essential. Research should focus on creating evidence-based strategies that organisations can adopt to better support their practitioners.

The call to action is clear: both practitioners and organisations need to work together to recognise and address the risks of secondary trauma. By fostering a culture of well-being and implementing comprehensive support systems, restorative justice organisations can ensure that their practitioners remain healthy, resilient and able to facilitate the profound, transformative work that restorative justice promises. The future of restorative justice depends not only on the care of those who have experienced harm but also on the care of those who work tirelessly to facilitate healing.

Notes

1 Mathieu (2021); Miller (2022).
2 Maslach and Jackson (1984), p. 134.
3 WCSAP (2019).
4 Bercier (2013); Jenkins and Baird (2002).
5 Rauvola et al. (2019).
6 Figley (1995).
7 Mathieu (2012).
8 Mathieu (2021).
9 Mathieu (2012).
10 Miller (2022); Klimecki and Singer (2012).
11 Singer and Klimecki (2014).
12 Miller (2022).
13 Figley (2012), p. 4.
14 NCTSN (2022).
15 Figley (1995), p. 10.
16 Miller (2022).
17 NCTSN (2022).
18 Health Canada (2001).
19 Pearlman and Saakvitne (1995); Saakvitne et al. (2000).
20 Health Canada (2001), p. 12.
21 Rauvola et al. (2019).
22 Bercier (2013).
23 Miller (2022).
24 Miller (2022); Ogińska-Bulik et al. (2021); OVC (2024).
25 PTSD UK (2024).
26 Koenen et al. (2017).
27 Bercier (2013); Bride (2007).
28 Remen (2006), p. 52.
29 Christen-Schneider and Pycroft (2021).
30 Filteau (2017).
31 Pearlman and Mac Ian (1995).
32 All information on risk factors is based on: Tend Academy (2024); OVC (2024); NetCE (2016); Secondary Trauma Consortium (2018); Cannabis Health Evaluation Partnership (2023); Miller (2022).
33 Brady et al. (1999).
34 Clamp (2023).
35 Christen-Schneider and Pycroft (2021).

36 Table developed based on: SAMHSA (2014); Health Canada (2001); OVC (2024); NetCE (2016); Bercier (2013); Miller (2022).
37 British Medical Association (2024); Phoenix Australia (2024); Risk and Resilience (2024); NCTSN (2022); Visible Project (2019); NetCE (2016); Health Canada (2001).
38 British Medical Association (2024); NCTSN (2022); NetCE (2016); Phoenix Australia (2024); Visible Project (2019).
39 Miller (2022).
40 Herman (1997); Van der Kolk (2014).
41 NetCE (2016), p. 44,
42 Black Dog Institute (2021); Saakvitne and Pearlman (1996).
43 Key considerations based on Mosunic (2023).
44 Butler (2024).
45 Broughton (2022).
46 Black Dog Institute (2021).
47 NetCE (2016), p. 19.
48 Headington Institute (n.d.), p. 31.
49 Headington Institute (n.d.).
50 Bercier (2013).
51 Health Canada (2001).
52 WCSAP (2019).
53 Headington Institute (n.d.).
54 Risk and Resilience (2024).
55 Gibbs (1988).
56 Miller (2022).
57 Miller and Sprang (2017).
58 Miller (2022); Miller and Sprang (2017).
59 Cozolino (2006); Figley (1995); Miller (2022); OVC (2024).
60 Cozolino (2006); Herman (1997); Treisman (2017); Van der Kolk (2014).
61 Treisman (2017).
62 Bercier (2013); CTIPP (2023); Fetzner and Chelius (n.d.); Headington Institute (n.d.); ISCRR (2023); ITTIC (2021); Office of the U.S. General Surgeon (2022); OVC (2024); Risk and Resilience (2024).
63 More on organisational values can be found in Fetzner and Chelius (n.d.).
64 More on the trauma-informed approach and the principles can be found in Chapter 5.
65 PCAR (2020).
66 Buceta et al. (2019); Lightbody (2020).
67 Buceta et al. (2019).
68 Buceta et al. (2019).
69 Hernandez-Wolfe (2018).
70 NetCE (2016).
71 Kerig (2019); NetCE (2016); Reynolds (2020).

References

Bercier, M. L. (2013). *Interventions that help the helpers: A systematic review and meta-analysis of interventions targeting compassion fatigue, secondary traumatic stress and vicarious traumatization in mental health workers* [Doctoral dissertation, Loyola University Chicago]. https://ecommons.luc.edu/luc_diss/503/

Black Dog Institute. (2021). *Importance of self-care planning*. www.blackdoginstitute.org.au/wp-content/uploads/2021/11/Importance-of-selfcare-planning.pdf

Brady, J. L., Guy, J. D., Poelstra, P. L., & Brokaw, B. F. (1999). Vicarious traumatization, spirituality and the treatment of sexual abuse survivors: A national survey of women psychotherapists. *Professional Psychology, Research and Practice*, 30, 386–393.

Bride, B. (2007). Prevalence of secondary traumatic stress among social workers. *Social Work*, 25(1), 63–70.

British Medical Association. (2024). *Vicarious trauma: signs and strategies for coping*. www.bma.org.uk/advice-and-support/your-wellbeing/vicarious-trauma/vicarious-trauma-signs-and-strategies-for-coping

Broughton, T. (2022, February 16). *Self-care planner*. Let's talk mental healthhttps://centreself.com.au/resources/

Buceta Toro, M. I., Bermejo Higuera, J. C., & Villacieros Durban, M. (2019). Elementos potenciadores de la satisfacción por compasión en profesionales sociosanitarios. *Anales de Psicología/Annals of Psychology*, 35(2), 323–331. https://doi.org/10.6018/analesps.35.2.345101

Butler, L. D. (2024). *Developing your self-care plan*. https://socialwork.buffalo.edu/resources/self-care-starter-kit/developing-your-self-care-plan.html

Campaign for Trauma-Informed Policy and Practice (CTIPP). (2023). *Trauma-informed workplaces: Concepts, strategies, and tactics to build workplaces that support well-being*. www.ctipp.org/post/toolkit-trauma-informed-workplaces

Cannabis Health Evaluation and Research Partnership. (2023). *Empathic strain*. https://decyde.ca/wp-content/uploads/2023/11/Empathic-Strain-GP_11_2023.pdf

Christen-Schneider, C., & Pycroft, A. (2021). An exploration of trauma-informed practices in restorative justice: A phenomenological study. *The International Journal of Restorative Justice*, 4(2), 229–252. https://doi.org/10.5553/TIJRJ.000075

Clamp, K. (2023). *A restorative framework for transforming police practice*. IIRP Presidential Paper Series, 9. https://store.iirp.edu/a-restorative-framework-for-transforming-police-practice

Cozolino, L. (2006). *The neuroscience of human relationships: Attachment and the developing social brain*. W.W. Norton & Company.

Fetzner, A., & Chelius, L. (n.d.). *Creating a trauma-informed workplace: A toolkit to support planning and implementation*. CCALAC. https://ccalac.org/wordpress/wp-content/uploads/origins-CCALAC-organizational-toolkit-WEB.pdf

Figley, C. R. (1995). *Compassion fatigue: Coping with secondary traumatic stress disorder in those who treat the traumatized* (1st ed.). Routledge.

Filteau, C. (2017). Living with vicarious trauma. *First Light on Trauma*, 38–42. https://ccvt.org/_docs/publications/first_light/First_Light_Winter_2017.pdf

Gibbs, G. (1998). *Learning by doing: A guide to teaching and learning*. Further Educational Unit.

Headington Institute. (n.d.). *Understanding & addressing vicarious trauma: Reading course*. www.headington-institute.org/blog/resource/understanding-vt-reading-course

Health Canada. (2001). *Guidebook on vicarious trauma: Recommended solutions for anti-violence workers*. Public Health Agency of Canada.

Herman, J. L. (1997). *Trauma and recovery: The aftermath of violence, from domestic abuse to political terror*. Basic Books.

Hernandez-Wolfe, P. (2018). Vicarious resilience: A comprehensive review. *Revista de Estudios Sociales*, 66, 9–17.

Institute for Safety, Compensation and Recovery Research (ISCRR). (2023). *Vicarious trauma in the workplace: Prevention and intervention strategies*. https://research.iscrr.

com.au/__data/assets/pdf_file/0019/3411064/342_ER_Vicarious-trauma-prevention-FINAL-15.06.2023.pdf

Institute on Trauma and Trauma-Informed Care (ITTIC). (2021). *Trauma-informed organizational change manual*. Buffalo Center for Social Research.

Jenkins, S. R., & Baird, S. (2002). Secondary traumatic stress and vicarious trauma: A validational study. *Journal of Traumatic Stress*, 15, 423–432.

Kerig, P. K. (2019) Enhancing resilience among providers of trauma-informed care: A curriculum for protection against secondary traumatic stress among non-mental health professionals. *Journal of Aggression, Maltreatment & Trauma*, 28(5), 613–630.

Koenen, K. C., Ratanatharathorn, A., Ng, L., McLaughlin, K. A., Bromet, E. J., Stein, D. J., Karam, E. G., Meron Ruscio, A., Benjet, C., Scott, K., Atwoli, L., Petukhova, M., Lim, C. C. W., Aguilar-Gaxiola, S., Al-Hamzawi, A., Alonso, J., Bunting, B., Ciutan, M., de Girolamo, G., Degenhardt, L., … Kessler, R. C. (2017). Posttraumatic stress disorder in the World Mental Health Surveys. *Psychological Medicine*, 47(13), 2260–2274. https://doi.org/10.1017/S0033291717000708

Lightbody, M. (2020, October 29). *Compassion satisfaction and compassion fatigue: Helpful tips for our frontline workers*. Department of Psychiatry and Behavioral Sciences. The University of Texas Health Science Center at Houston.

Maslach, C., & Jackson, S. E. (1984). Burnout in organizational settings. *Applied Social Psychology Annual*, 5, 133–153.

Mathieu, F. (2012). *The compassion fatigue workbook: Creative tools for transforming compassion fatigue and vicarious traumatization*. Taylor & Francis.

Mathieu, F. (2017). *Warning signs of secondary trauma and compassion fatigue*. Tend. www.tendacademy.ca/warning-signs-of-vicarious-traumasecondary-traumatic-stress-and-compassion-fatigue

Mathieu, F. (2021). *Why it is time to stop using "compassion fatigue"*. Tend. www.tendacademy.ca/stop-using-compassion-fatigue

Mathieu, F. (2023). *Identifying your warning signs*. Tend. https://tendtoolkit.com/

Miller, B. C. (2022). *Reducing secondary traumatic stress: Skills for sustaining a career in the helping professions*. Routledge.

Miller, B., & Sprang, G. (2017). A components-based practice and supervision model for reducing compassion fatigue by affecting clinician experience. *Traumatology*, 23(2), 153–164. https://doi.org/10.1037/trm0000058

Mosunic, C. (2023). *How to create a self-care plan personalized to your needs*. Calm. www.calm.com/blog/self-care-plan

NetCE. (2016). *Vicarious trauma and resilience*. www.netce.com/courseoverview.php?courseid=2635

Office for Victims of Crime (OVC). (2024). *The Vicarious Trauma Toolkit*. https://ovc.ojp.gov/program/vtt/what-is-the-vt-org

Office of the U.S. General Surgeon. (2022). *The U.S. Surgeon General's framework for workplace mental health & well-Being*. www.hhs.gov/surgeongeneral/priorities/workplace-well-being/index.html

Ogińska-Bulik, N., Gurowiec, P. J., Michalska, P., & Kędra, E. (2021). Prevalence and predictors of secondary traumatic stress symptoms in health care professionals working with trauma victims: A cross-sectional study. *PLOS ONE* 16(2), Article e0247596. https://doi.org/10.1371/journal.pone.0247596

Pearlman, L. A., & Mac Ian, P. S. (1995). Vicarious traumatization: An empirical study of the effects of trauma work on trauma therapists. *Professional Psychology: Research and Practice*, 26(6), 558–565. https://doi.org/10.1037/0735-7028.26.6.558

Pearlman, L. A., & Saakvitne, K. W. (1995). *Trauma and the therapist: Countertransference and vicarious traumatization in psychotherapy with incest survivors*. W. W. Norton.

Pennsylvania Coalition Against Rape (PCAR). (2020). *A guide to trauma-informed supervision*. https://pcar.org/sites/default/files/resource-pdfs/trauma_informed_supervision_guide_508.pdf

Phoenix Australia. (2024). *Vicarious trauma*. https://training.phoenixaustralia.org/offerings/vt-2022

Plumbly, C. (2022). *Vicarious trauma: What it is and how to prevent it*. Dr Paula Redmond. https://drpaularedmond.com/vicarious-trauma-what-it-is-and-how-to-prevent-it

PTSD UK. (2024). *Causes: Secondary trauma from work*. www.ptsduk.org/secondary-trauma-in-occupations

Rauvola, R. S., Vega, D. M., & Lavigne, K. N. (2019). Compassion fatigue, secondary traumatic stress, and vicarious traumatization: A qualitative review and research agenda. *Occupational Health Science*, 3, 297–336. https://doi.org/10.1007/s41542-019-00045-1

Remen, R. N. (2006). *Kitchen table wisdom: Stories that heal (*10th anniversary ed.). Riverhead Books.)

Reynolds, A. (2020). *Exploring vicarious resilience among practitioners working with clients who have experienced traumatic events* [Doctoral dissertation, CUNY Graduate Center]. CUNY Academic Works. https://academicworks.cuny.edu/gc_etds/3529

Risk and Resilience. (2024). *Vicarious trauma: A toolkit for organisations and individuals*. www.risk-and-resilience.co.uk/resources.html

Saakvitne, K. W., Gamble, S. G., Pearlman, L. A., & Lev, B. T. (2000). *Risking connection: A training curriculum for working with survivors of childhood abuse*. Sidran Foundation and Press.

Saakvitne, K. W., & Pearlman, L. A. (1996). *Transforming the pain: A workbook on vicarious traumatization*. Norton.

Secondary Traumatic Stress Consortium (STS). (2018). *Assessing contributing factors*. https://stsconsortium.com

Singer, T., & Klimecki, O. M. (2014). Empathy and compassion. *Current Biology*, 24 (18), R875–R878. https://doi.org/10.1016/j.cub.2014.06.054

Substance Abuse and Mental Health Services Administration (SAMHSA). (2014). *SAMHSA's concept of trauma and guidance for a trauma-informed approach*. HHS Publication no. (SMA) 14-4884. Substance Abuse and Mental Health Services Administration.

Tend Academy. (2024). *Contributing factors: Identifying work-related stress*. https://tendtoolkit.com/contributing-factors-strategy

The National Fallen Firefighters Foundation. (2013). *Stress first aid for firefighters and emergency medical services personnel*. Homeland Security.

Treisman, K. (2017,November). *Good relationships are the key to healing trauma* [Video]. TED. www.ted.com/talks/karen_treisman_good_relationships_are_the_key_to_healing_trauma

Van der Kolk, B. (2014). *The body keeps the score: Mind, brain and body in the transformation of trauma*. Penguin Books.

Visible Project. (2019). *Vicarious (secondary) trauma and self-care resource*. https://visibleproject.org.uk/wp-content/uploads/2019/05/Visible-vicarious-trauma-web.pdf

Washington Coalition of Sexual Assault Programs (WCSAP). (2019). *Addressing compassion fatigue & vicarious trauma: What is my responsibility?*www.wcsap.org/sites/default/files/uploads/resources_publications/advocacy_station/Advocacy_Station_Compassion_Fatigue.pdf

8 Final reflections and recommendations

Introduction

The restorative dialogue group gathers in a circle for the last time, ready to share their final reflections and say goodbye. "My expectations that restorative justice would be helpful for everyone involved were fully met", says one of the victims. Another adds: "Years after the murder of my daughter, this programme has finally helped me to confront feelings that I had suppressed for a long time". An offender reflects: "This experience helped me to mature and understand the pain that victims go through. It has allowed me to see the situation from a new perspective and I am grateful for the opportunity to complete my personal self-reflection". Another offender chimes in: "I would never have believed it, but this has become like a family to me and I will miss you all".[1]

The group nods in agreement, echoing the unexpected bond of belonging, safety and trust that has formed. What began as a gathering of individuals has become a close-knit community. Together they have shared moments of laughter and tears, struggled to find the right words, and engaged in deep, authentic dialogue that transcends their differences. It is in this dialogue – and the sense of community it fosters – that the true power of restorative dialogues lies.

As this group's journey draws to a close, so too does this book's exploration of trauma-informed restorative dialogues. This final chapter reflects on three key themes discussed throughout the book – dialogue, community and trauma-informed practice. It also addresses common questions that practitioners and service providers may have when initiating restorative dialogues. Finally, the chapter identifies gaps in current research and offers considerations for the future development of restorative dialogues, before concluding with some final remarks.

Final reflections on the key concepts presented in this book

The themes of dialogue, community and trauma-informed practice have run like a thread through this book. Therefore, each of them deserves a final word of reflection.

DOI: 10.4324/9781003271611-8

The centrality of dialogue

The concept of dialogue, as explored in the introductory chapter, is the cornerstone of restorative dialogues. It embodies the essence of these encounters – where the focus shifts from confrontation to genuine exchange, mutual understanding and empathy. As the Greek word '*dialogos*' suggests, dialogue is a process that engages both heart and mind, creating a space where participants can share their experiences and listen deeply to each other.[2] It is through this intentional, empathic exchange that restoration and recovery begin to take shape.

As highlighted in Chapter 4, such dialogue cannot develop within a rigid programme structure. It requires flexibility that allows participants the freedom to identify and explore what they need to discuss. This flexibility also requires that the group is given sufficient time to engage in these conversations. For practitioners, this means being prepared to adapt the programme and schedule to the needs of the group. More importantly, it requires the courage to relinquish control and trust the process. As discussed in Chapter 6, this is one of the greatest challenges for facilitators. However, by letting go, facilitators empower participants to regain some of the power and control they may have lost as a result of the harm suffered or their imprisonment. This empowerment enables the group to work through their pain, guilt, shame and initial mistrust together. The result is the formation of a community – a community capable of supporting each other in the face of adversity.

The power of community

The role of community also resonates throughout this book. As discussed in Chapter 3, both victims and offenders have highlighted the significance of belonging and connection as key factors in the effectiveness of restorative dialogues. It is this essence of community – characterised by connection, understanding and mutual support, and based on a shared narrative[3] – that fundamentally shapes their experience.

In restorative dialogues, community serves as a powerful catalyst for healing and transformation. It is not just about being in the same room with others; it is about creating a space where participants can make deep, authentic connections and engage in meaningful dialogue. The power of community lies in its ability to offer validation and empathy, to break down the isolation that often accompanies both trauma and incarceration, and to foster a sense of belonging. As Cozolino (2006) insightfully observes, "We need each other and our stories to discover ourselves, regulate our emotions, and heal from traumatic injuries".[4] This interconnectedness is not only beneficial but essential for meaningful recovery.

Trauma isolates individuals and creates distance between them and others. However, as Herman (1997) points out, healing cannot occur in isolation; it requires "*healing relationships*".[5] Victims need the opportunity to share their experiences within a compassionate, non-judgemental community that understands the impact of trauma on their lives.[6] In restorative dialogues, the co-constructed community provides this supportive environment necessary for participants to feel seen, heard and validated. This space is essential for *all* participants in need of healing as they work towards recovery and change.

The power of community is particularly evident in the dynamics of small group interaction, where individuals find that their experiences are shared and their struggles are understood. As Block (2008) emphasises, the small group setting allows participants to realise that they are not alone, fostering a deep sense of belonging and connectedness.[7] This awareness – that they are part of a larger whole that understands and shares their concerns – is a cornerstone of restorative dialogues, as interviewees pointed out. For victims, the isolation that often accompanies trauma is alleviated by the support and shared experiences within the community. For offenders, who may face increased isolation due to incarceration, the emergence of a supportive community provides a crucial opportunity for connection and understanding in their own path of recovery.[8]

Ultimately, the power of community in restorative dialogues lies in its ability to create a space where barriers of isolation and 'otherness' can be broken down, fostering a collective sense of belonging and 'togetherness'.[9] This sense of community transforms the dialogue into a powerful force for change, enabling participants to confront their pain, build mutual understanding and move towards recovery together.

The need for a trauma-informed approach – for all

The third key theme in this book is the importance of a trauma-informed approach to restorative dialogues – not only for victims and offenders but also for facilitators. While this topic has been explored in depth throughout, this section will highlight the key benefits and considerations. As highlighted in Chapter 4, trauma is a pervasive experience that can affect anyone, making a trauma-informed approach essential in the context of restorative dialogues. Trauma does not discriminate; it can affect any participant, which is why a trauma-informed approach is essential. This approach promotes healing and prevents further harm or re-traumatisation by ensuring that restorative dialogues are always conducted with sensitivity and care.

For victims, a trauma-informed approach creates a sense of emotional and psychological safety, enabling them to participate more fully. Victims often struggle to express their feelings, particularly when dealing with shame and self-blame.[10] As explored in Chapter 5, facilitators who are attuned to these challenges can provide crucial support in helping victims deal with these painful feelings. This is critical as shame, in particular, can be a significant barrier to recovery and can exacerbate PTSD symptoms.[11] Addressing shame in a supportive environment can thus greatly aid recovery by breaking the silence and isolation that trauma often brings.[12]

A trauma-informed approach is equally important for offenders. By recognising the trauma that may have influenced their harmful behaviour,[13] facilitators can guide offenders towards meaningful accountability. Understanding their actions in the context of their trauma does not excuse their behaviour, but it can foster genuine remorse and a commitment to change. Addressing underlying trauma can help to break the cycle of violence and reduce the likelihood of reoffending as offenders gain deeper insight into their actions and their impact.[14]

For facilitators, trauma-informed training equips them to manage the emotional intensity that often accompanies restorative dialogues. They can create a supportive environment that encourages honest communication while being sensitive to participants' triggers and vulnerabilities. Furthermore, trauma-informed practices provide facilitators with tools to manage their own emotional responses, thereby reducing the risk of secondary trauma. As mentioned in Chapter 7, a shared understanding of trauma within the facilitation team promotes mutual support and resilience.

Without a trauma-informed approach, there is an increased risk of re-traumatising participants, especially victims. Conversely, when trauma is acknowledged and respected, participants are more likely to trust the process and engage deeply – essential for the open and honest communication that restorative dialogues require. Thus, a trauma-informed approach is not only beneficial but fundamental to creating a process that is safe, effective and transformative for all involved.

It is important to remember, however, that restorative justice is not inherently trauma-informed. Facilitators need to acquire specific knowledge about trauma and its effects to truly integrate a trauma-informed approach into their practice.

By carefully considering these three essential elements – dialogue, community and trauma-informed practice – practitioners can lay a solid foundation for a safe and effective restorative dialogue programme. However, many questions may still arise for those interested in developing and implementing such dialogues. The following section addresses some of these basic questions.

Common questions concerning the implementation of restorative dialogues

For services or individual practitioners who desire to start implementing restorative dialogues for the first time, there may be many questions that arise. Some of these common questions will be addressed in this section.

1. How to initiate restorative dialogues?

A structured and multidisciplinary approach is recommended when starting to develop or implement restorative dialogues. Ideally, there should be a collaboration with both victim services and the prison system to receive input on important considerations but also to receive feedback on programme proposals. Additionally, it can be very useful to get input from adult education specialists. Equally important is the involvement of victims and offenders at the planning stage. Their perspectives are invaluable in shaping a programme that feels safe and meaningful to all participants.

Working with colleagues who have experience of running restorative dialogues is highly beneficial. Learning from their challenges and successes can provide insights and practical solutions to help avoid common pitfalls.

Understanding the specific context in which restorative dialogues will be implemented is also essential. Factors such as whether victims are permitted or not to enter a prison, scheduling constraints and the time available need to be taken into account. For example, in Switzerland sessions may last two hours, while in France they can last three hours. Programmes should be designed with these logistical considerations in mind and tailored to the constraints and opportunities of the local environment.

Programmes should not be static; ongoing evaluation is key to their success. Regular feedback from participants – collected through anonymous forms, in-session feedback sessions and follow-up meetings – is essential for continuous improvement. While logistical challenges may limit opportunities for feedback from offenders, efforts should be made to gather their insights wherever possible.

Transparency about the pilot status of new programmes and openness to feedback from participants fosters trust and commitment. Participants should be informed that the programme is in development and that their input is crucial to its refinement. This approach has been well received in Switzerland and contributes to the evolution of the programme.

Finally, facilitator training is of paramount importance, as highlighted in Chapter 4. Facilitators need to be well versed not only in the specifics of the programme, but also in basic areas of knowledge such as victimology, criminology and trauma. This comprehensive training is necessary to effectively manage the intense and emotionally charged nature of restorative dialogues.

2. *At what stage should the dialogues be offered?*

Restorative dialogues can be offered to victims and offenders at any time, as long as both parties are willing and ready to participate. While these dialogues are often offered to offenders after sentencing, this is not the only option. Although many programmes are run in prison, there are other approaches.

For example, the Belgian programme has successfully facilitated restorative dialogues outside prison, either after offenders have completed their sentence or for those who have never been imprisoned. This approach can be particularly beneficial for victims who may have considerable fear or anxiety about entering a prison environment. Recognising these benefits, some organisations, including ours, are exploring the possibility of offering restorative dialogues in non-prison settings.

While post-conviction programmes are common, restorative dialogues can also be offered prior to sentencing. However, this presents particular challenges. For example, as discussed in Chapter 3, one interviewee expressed that he would not have attended the programme if he had known that one of the offenders involved had not yet been sentenced: "My feeling was, I'm getting abused again! Because my fear is okay, you're going to use those days in front of the judge ... and I don't want to be part of that process". Such concerns need to be taken seriously.

In the spring of 2024, the Swiss RJ Forum conducted a pilot programme on restorative dialogues during pre-trial detention. Given the complexity of pre-trial dialogues, the facilitators took special care to prepare the participants. Victims were informed that the programme involved offenders in pre-trial detention who admitted some or all of the charges against them and were willing to discuss their actions. Only victims who had previously participated in restorative dialogues and expressed an interest in re-engagement were invited to participate. This selection process was designed to reduce the risk of unfulfilled expectations, particularly for victims seeking detailed information from offenders.

Offenders were also fully informed of the pilot nature of the programme, and their concerns about confidentiality and the potential impact on their sentencing were carefully addressed. Some offenders chose not to participate, citing concerns that their involvement might affect their legal outcome. Those who did participate received additional preparation, including discussions about expectations of openness and the importance of acknowledging the harm they had caused.

Confidentiality was emphasised throughout the programme, particularly in the initial meetings. As a result, the programme was well received by both victims and offenders. Victims reported that the openness of pre-sentence offenders was comparable to that of sentenced offenders in previous dialogues. Offenders expressed that the experience had a positive impact on their attitudes towards their crimes and recommended that restorative dialogues should be offered regularly during custody. Concerns about confidentiality dissipated as the programme progressed.

The provision of restorative dialogues during pre-trial detention is therefore feasible, but requires careful preparation and consideration of the particular challenges involved. However, with appropriate measures in place, such programmes can be as effective and meaningful as those conducted after sentencing.

3. *How are interested individuals referred to restorative dialogues?*

Despite growing interest in restorative justice among legal professionals, referrals to restorative justice services, particularly for restorative dialogues, remain limited. Most referrals focus on direct victim–offender dialogues, as many services are unaware of the potential of group dialogues. As a result, many victims learn about restorative dialogues on their own or by word of mouth. With many programmes offered in prisons, it is easier for incarcerated offenders to access information than for victims.

In Switzerland, the referral process for victims to restorative justice, and in particular to restorative dialogues, is particularly underdeveloped. While some victim services recognise the value of restorative approaches and provide information to those who express an interest, many do not. This is often due to a lack of awareness, fear or scepticism about restorative justice. Another challenge is that victims often seek support in the immediate aftermath of a crime, prioritising psychological, financial or legal support over restorative processes. At this early stage, they may not be receptive to the idea of restorative justice. However, when victims return to these services at a later stage, they may be more open to receiving information about restorative options.

Even in countries with more established restorative justice services, there is still some concern, particularly among victim services, about the potential impact on victims. In Switzerland, a critical issue is the need to effectively disseminate information about restorative dialogues to a wider audience of victims. As in other countries, much of this information is still spread informally by word of mouth, highlighting the urgent need to improve referral systems. Ensuring that victims and other interested parties have access to comprehensive and timely information is essential if they are to make informed choices about restorative justice services.

4. Who has access to restorative dialogues?

Any interested victim or offender should have access to restorative dialogues. There are no strict criteria for participation in restorative dialogues; however, an individual's suitability for the programme is assessed during an interview. A key factor is the nature of the offences to be addressed in the group. The aim is to ensure that participants have similar experiences of victimisation or offending, which promotes deeper understanding and empathy. As a result, people who have been involved in crimes such as sexual violence, domestic violence or terrorism may not be suitable for groups that focus on other types of crime. Instead, they may be better suited to groups specifically designed for these types of offences.

5. Should community members be included?

As discussed in Chapter 2, some restorative dialogue programmes, particularly in France and Belgium, include community members in group meetings. These individuals represent the wider community or society within these dialogues. Their role is to provide a supportive presence, to listen without judgement, to offer recognition and validation, and to support the group emotionally and psychologically through their process. Importantly, these community members do not have a professional role but are volunteers.

While including community members in restorative dialogues is not mandatory, it provides an opportunity to demonstrate to participants that the wider community cares about them and is willing to listen and support them. Victims who have participated in programmes with community members shared their experiences during the interviews. One victim particularly appreciated the presence of these individuals, emphasising that they were volunteers who gave their time and attention, which touched him deeply. He felt that their willingness to participate without compensation as representatives of the wider community or society played a significant role in his experience. Another interviewee acknowledged that while the presence of community members can be helpful, she did not see them as a crucial part of the programme. She mentioned that their role was not always clearly understood by the group. However, she appreciated being heard and validated by members of the wider community and felt that their presence could be particularly important for victims who felt that their own community of care was distant or unsupportive.

Ultimately, the decision to involve community members is up to the organisation or facilitators running the restorative dialogues. Sometimes the decision may depend on logistical considerations, such as the size of groups allowed into the prison and any restrictions on who can participate. In some cases, prisons may only allow victims and facilitators to be present. Where there are no restrictions, it may be worthwhile to try facilitating programmes with and without community members and to evaluate their significance with the programme participants.

6. *What about including family members in restorative dialogues?*

During the interviews, a group of three victims as well as a group of three facilitators discussed the potential benefits of including family members in restorative dialogues. They explored whether the presence of family members could support victims and offenders by allowing them to experience the process together and benefit from sharing with each other. It was suggested that family members of victims might gain a deeper understanding of the victim's suffering, enabling them to provide better support afterwards. For offenders, involving their families could promote understanding, help to identify factors behind the offending behaviour and support the offender's rehabilitation, particularly on release from prison. This could be particularly valuable for offenders who have lost contact with their families.

Facilitators recognised these potential benefits, but also highlighted significant challenges. A major concern was the additional logistical effort required to prepare and support family members throughout the process, similar to the preparation of victims and offenders. This could strain the capacity of the facilitators and challenge the sustainability of the programme. In addition, expanding the group to include more participants could dilute the effectiveness of the small group dynamic that is central to the process.[15]

Another challenge is the potential impact on group dynamics and the sense of safety within the dialogues. The core aim of restorative dialogues is to create a safe space where victims and offenders can openly discuss their experiences. The presence of family members can threaten this safety, particularly if victims or offenders have experienced harm at the hands of family members. For victims, family reactions may have been distressing, possibly involving blame or lack of understanding. Similarly, offenders may have strained relationships with their families as a result of past harm. These dynamics suggest that widening the circle to include family members could involve potential risks.

Given these concerns, the facilitators discussed alternative ways of involving participants' communities of care without directly involving family members in the dialogues. One suggestion was to set up separate groups for the relatives – one for the families of the victims and the other for the families of the offenders. These groups would allow family members to share experiences and offer mutual support. For victims' families, these meetings could include education about trauma and its effects, potentially leading to greater understanding and support for the victim within their community. For offenders' families, such groups could address issues of shame and stigma and help them to find ways to support their loved ones while in prison and after release.

Another suggestion was to offer victims and offenders the opportunity to engage in individual family processes after participating in restorative dialogues. These processes could address issues that arise during the dialogues and require further discussion with family members. In Switzerland, for example, our organisation, the Swiss RJ Forum, has been offering 'Re-entry Circles' to long-term prisoners and their families since 2022, focusing on the impact of the offence and imprisonment on family relationships. This approach has been well received, particularly by relatives.[16] Similarly, victims may find it valuable to involve their families in processing their experiences and reactions. However, the feasibility of such services depends largely on the availability of facilitators and adequate funding. In Switzerland, as in many other countries, funding is a major challenge. Many restorative justice services continue to rely on volunteers due to insufficient support from the state or other sources, such as prison or victim services. As a result, the provision of these services often depends on the availability of trained volunteer facilitators.

Therefore, while including family members in restorative dialogues could offer certain benefits, the potential challenges and risks suggest that alternative approaches, such as separate support groups or individual family processes, may be more viable. These options could provide meaningful support while maintaining the integrity and safety of restorative dialogues.

7. *Are there alternatives to restorative dialogues for widening access to restorative justice?*

As discussed in Chapter 1, the Council of Europe Recommendation Concerning Restorative Justice in Criminal Matters emphasises that restorative justice should be "a generally available service".[17] However, as outlined in Chapter 2, direct processes between victims and offenders are not always possible due to the voluntary nature of these encounters and various other factors. While restorative dialogues can widen access to restorative justice when direct processes are not feasible, they may not be suitable for everyone.

For some individuals, the group format may not be ideal, as they may feel uncomfortable in a group setting. Others may find it difficult to commit to multiple sessions because of work or other commitments, or because they live far from the nearest available programme. These challenges have been common in our service, highlighting the need to develop alternative processes to make restorative justice more accessible to a wider range of individuals.

One alternative approach, implemented by the Swiss RJ Forum and considered by other facilitators, is the one-to-one dialogue between unrelated victims and offenders. In this format, the two parties engage in direct dialogue without a group, with facilitators present to guide the process. Prior to the meeting, both parties go through a preparation phase to learn about each other's expectations, questions and issues they wish to discuss. While one-to-one dialogue may not address all of the participants' questions or needs, it offers a way to engage in a restorative process within existing boundaries. This approach provides a way for clients who cannot participate in direct or group dialogues to still be involved in a restorative process.

While one-to-one dialogues between unrelated victims and offenders are a valuable alternative when direct processes are not feasible, they are only one option. To truly widen access to restorative justice, it is essential to continue to explore and develop creative processes that meet the diverse needs of all individuals who wish to participate in a restorative process, even when direct victim–offender encounters are not possible. Therefore, there is still a need for more research and development in this area.

Areas for future research

While this book has explored many important aspects of implementing restorative dialogues, much remains to be learned, developed and researched. There is still a lack of comprehensive research on the approach of restorative dialogue programmes. For example, although Prison Fellowship International's 'Sycamore Tree Project'® has been researched,[18] there is a noticeable gap in research evaluating the wider range of restorative dialogue programmes worldwide.

Some key areas for further research include:

- *Participant satisfaction and recommendations*: How satisfied are victims and offenders with restorative dialogues? What changes would they suggest to improve the effectiveness of these programmes?
- *Long-term effects*: What are the long-term effects of restorative dialogues on the recovery, desistance, empowerment and social reintegration of both victims and offenders?
- *Best practices in different contexts*: What are the best practices in different social and cultural contexts? Are there universal principles that should be applied to all programmes?
- *Effectiveness of victim-centred, trauma-informed approaches*: Are restorative dialogues that give priority to victim-centred and trauma-informed practices

more effective? If so, how do these approaches improve outcomes? If not, what might explain this?

- *Comparative effectiveness of different restorative models*: How do restorative dialogues compare with other restorative justice models, such as victim–offender dialogue or conferencing, in terms of outcomes for victims and offenders? Are there particular contexts in which one model is more effective than others?
- *Training and competence of facilitators*: What impact does the training and experience level of facilitators have on the outcomes of restorative dialogues? What specific skills or areas of knowledge are most important for facilitators to be able to lead these processes effectively?
- *Ethical considerations and safeguards*: What ethical challenges arise in restorative dialogues, particularly in cases involving serious harm or power imbalances? What safeguards are needed to protect vulnerable participants and to ensure that the process remains fair and constructive?
- *Measuring success beyond satisfaction*: Beyond participant satisfaction, what other metrics can be used to measure the success of restorative dialogues? For example, how can we assess changes in participants' mental health, behaviour or relationships over time?
- *Cultural adaptations and sensitivities*: How do restorative dialogues need to be adapted to be culturally sensitive in different contexts? What are the challenges of implementing these dialogues in multicultural or multi-ethnic settings, and how can facilitators effectively navigate cultural differences?

Further research is essential for the continued development, expansion and recognition of restorative dialogues. It is crucial to promote collaboration between practitioners, researchers and experts from different fields such as psychology, social work, law enforcement and mental health. Integrating these interdisciplinary perspectives can enrich understanding, inform best practice and help to create more effective and supportive processes for all participants.

Conclusion

Restorative dialogues are more than just an alternative when direct encounters between victims and offenders are not possible; they represent a powerful mechanism for healing, understanding and transformation. Their true strength lies in creating a safe space where victims and offenders can share their feelings, suffering and experiences openly, finding mutual support and understanding – a space where the weight of suffering and isolation is eased through collective empathy.

Restorative dialogues challenge the traditional foundations of justice by emphasising community, authentic dialogue and the possibility of change. These dialogues remind us that justice is not only about punishment but also about restoration – the restoration of dignity, trust and the human spirit.

Although not yet as widely implemented as other restorative justice practices, restorative dialogues hold significant potential for expanding access to restorative justice, facilitating the recovery of victims and supporting the rehabilitation of offenders.

Incorporating a trauma-informed approach is not merely beneficial; it is essential. It recognises the pervasive impact of trauma and the need for the justice system to evolve to meet the needs of the most vulnerable. By embedding trauma-informed practices within restorative dialogues and broader justice processes, it is possible to redefine how justice is understood and delivered. This can transform not only the lives of victims and offenders but also the fabric of our communities, paving the way for a more compassionate and resilient society as those affected by trauma are given a chance to heal.

This book calls for the wider adoption of trauma-informed restorative justice practices that go beyond restorative dialogues. The aim is to provide safe and effective services for all participants – victims, offenders and practitioners alike – while preventing secondary trauma among those who facilitate these processes. Achieving this requires ongoing training, policy development and a collective commitment to uphold the principles of trauma-informed care in all aspects of restorative justice.

Ultimately, this book serves as both a resource and a call to action for practitioners, policy makers and researchers. By adopting a trauma-informed approach to restorative justice, we can create more inclusive, compassionate and effective practices that honour the experiences and needs of all involved. In doing so, we are taking meaningful steps towards a justice system that is truly restorative in every sense of the word.

Notes

1 Comments from participants of the Swiss RJ Forum's programme in restorative dialogues.
2 New World Encyclopedia (n.d.).
3 Lowe (2021).
4 Cozolino (2006), p. 307.
5 Herman (1997), p. 133.
6 Todahl, et al. (2017).
7 Block (2008).
8 McNeill et al. (2012).
9 Lowe (2021).
10 Dolezal and Gibson (2022).
11 Taylor (2015).
12 Brown (2006).
13 Godsoe (2022).
14 MacNair (2015); Miller and Najavits (2012).
15 Block (2008).
16 See Stoll et al. (2023).
17 Council of Europe (2018).
18 See, for example: Feasy and Williams (2009).

References

Block, P. (2008). *Community: Restoring the possible*. Berrett-Koehler.

Brown, B. (2006). Shame resilience theory: A grounded theory study on women and shame. *Families in Society: The Journal of Contemporary Social Services*, 87(1), 43–52. https://doi.org/10.1606/1044-3894.3483

Council of Europe. (2018). *Recommendation CM/Rec(2018)8 of the Committee of Ministers to member States concerning restorative justice in criminal matters*. https://search.coe.int/cm?i=09000016808e35f3

Cozolino, L. (2006). *The neuroscience of human relationships: Attachment and the developing social brain*. W.W Norton & Company.

Dolezal, L., & Gibson, M. (2022). Beyond a trauma-informed approach and towards shame-sensitive practice. *Humanities and Social Sciences Communications*, 9(214), 1–9. https://doi.org/10.1057/s41599-022-01227-z

Feasy, S., & Williams, P. (2009). *An evaluation of the Sycamore Tree Programme: Based on an analysis of Crime Pics II Data*. Sheffield Hallam University.

Godsoe, C. (2022). The victim/offender overlap and criminal system reform. *Brooklyn Law Review*, 87(4), 1319–1350.

Herman, J. L. (1997). *Trauma and recovery: The aftermath of violence, from domestic abuse to political terror*. Basic Books.

Lowe, T. (2021, February 26). *What is 'community' and why is it important?*Centre for Public Impact. www.centreforpublicimpact.org/insights/what-is-community-and-why-is-it-important

MacNair, R. (2015). Causing trauma as a form of trauma. *Peace and Conflict: Journal of Peace Psychology*, 21(3), 313–321.

McNeill, F., Farrall, S., Lightowler, C., & Maruna, S. (2012) *How and why people stop offending: Discovering desistance*. www.iriss.org.uk/resources/insights/how-why-people-stop-offending-discovering-desistance

Miller, N. A., & Najavits, L. M. (2012). Creating trauma-informed correctional care: A balance of goals and environment. *European Journal of Psychotraumatology*, 3, 1–8. https://doi.org/10.3402/ejpt.v3i0.17246

New World Encyclopedia. (n.d.). Dialogue. In *New world encyclopedia*. www.newworldencyclopedia.org/entry/Dialogue

Stoll, A., Campistol, C., & Christen-Schneider, C. (2023). « Dialoguer avec ses proches » en détention. *Jusletter*, 4. https://doi.org/10.38023/1bc48a38-794a-40be-b6d2-7d214434ab58

Taylor, T.F. (2015). The influence of shame on posttrauma disorders: Have we failed to see the obvious? *European Journal of Psychotraumatology*, 6(1). http://dx.doi.org/10.3402/ejpt.v6.28847

Todahl, J., Olson, D., & Walters, E. (2017). Survivor insight: A study of family, friend, and community response to interpersonal violence. *Journal of Aggression, Maltreatment & Trauma*, 26(4), 391–410. https://doi.org/10.1080/10926771.2017.1278732

Appendix: Trauma and its effects on brain and body

Introduction

This appendix provides a concise overview of trauma and its effects on the brain and body, and offers essential insights for practitioners to understand the rationale behind trauma-informed practice. The chapter covers definitions and types of trauma, the physiological and psychological effects on individuals, and the complex responses triggered by traumatic experiences. By explaining the underlying neurobiological mechanisms and their impact on behaviour and relationships, the appendix aims to equip practitioners with the basic knowledge needed to apply trauma-informed approaches effectively.

What is trauma?

The Greek word '*trauma*' means 'wound'. Trauma refers to a psychological wound caused by events or experiences that overwhelm an individual's ability to cope,[1] resulting in "lasting adverse effects on the individual's functioning and physical, social, emotional, or spiritual well-being".[2] Trauma can result from a wide range of experiences, from 'capital T' trauma – such as life-threatening situations like natural disasters, violent crime or serious accidents[3] – to 'small T' trauma, which involves non-life-threatening events such as interpersonal conflict, bullying, infidelity, or prolonged stressors such as divorce or financial difficulties.[4] Both types of trauma can significantly disrupt an individual's sense of safety, self and stability, with 'capital T' trauma often leading to a deep sense of powerlessness and lack of control.

According to the Substance Abuse and Mental Health Services Administration (SAMHSA), trauma can result from an "event, series of events, or set of circumstances that is experienced by an individual as physically or emotionally harmful or threatening".[5] However, as Maté (2022) explains, "trauma is not what happens to you but what happens inside you".[6] This means that the true nature of trauma lies in its internal impact on an individual (how it affects them) rather than the external event itself (what happened).[7] Each person has a unique point at which fear becomes trauma, disrupting their thoughts, feelings and the way they process sensory information.[8]

Trauma is shaped by many factors, including a person's personality, past experiences, social support and available resources.[9] How a person perceives an event, the meaning they attach to it and their ability to process it all determine how deeply the trauma affects them.[10]

Trauma is characterised by three core elements:

1. It was unexpected.
2. The person was unprepared.
3. There is nothing the person could do to stop it from happening.[11]

These elements often lead to what Van der Kolk (2014) calls a state of 'speechless horror', where the experience feels too overwhelming to be put into words. He explains that the essence of trauma lies in its overwhelming, unbelievable and unbearable nature.[12] This can create a profound sense of helplessness and terror, triggering what Herman (1997) calls 'responses of catastrophe'.[13]

Therefore, trauma can profoundly alter an individual's sense of self, relationships and worldview. It can cause both immediate and long-term psychological distress; however, the impact varies from one individual to another. While some may find ways to integrate the experience into their lives, others may feel that the trauma is still ongoing, even years later.[14] Thus, trauma is a very subjective experience: what may be non-threatening for one person can be traumatic for another.[15]

Recovery from trauma is possible, although it can be a complex and non-linear process. With appropriate support and care, individuals can transform their experience, moving from survival to growth and resilience. As with physical wounds, psychological wounds from trauma have the potential to heal, although some scars may remain. Healing involves acknowledging the trauma, allowing oneself to feel its effects and finding ways to reintegrate the experience into one's life story.

Types and causes of trauma

There are many types of trauma, including:

Acute/single-event trauma

This type involves a single traumatic event, sometimes referred to as 'simple' trauma – a term that can underestimate its impact. Even a single event, such as a natural disaster, accident, serious illness or witnessing a traumatic incident, can cause severe and lasting psychological harm. Its impact may be just as significant as chronic or complex trauma, depending on personal risk and protective factors.[16]

Chronic trauma

Chronic trauma results from repeated or ongoing exposure to traumatic conditions, such as prolonged abuse, persistent bullying, domestic violence or living in a war zone. It may also arise from repeated medical procedures linked to chronic illness. Chronic trauma can affect individuals at any stage of life, from childhood to adulthood, and often leads to long-term psychological consequences.[17]

Complex trauma

Complex trauma has several unique characteristics that distinguish it from other types of trauma. It often begins in early childhood, during critical developmental stages. Not only does it threaten physical safety, but it also disrupts a child's emotional and psychological development.[18] Unlike other types of trauma, which may or may not be perpetrated by another person, complex trauma is interpersonal and is often perpetrated by a caregiver, creating a deep sense of betrayal. This creates profound issues with trust, attachment, relationships and self-perception, leading to feelings of shame, low self-esteem, anger and defiant behaviour.[19] While adults may respond to trauma with a fight-or-flight response, children, whose survival depends on their caregivers, are more likely to dissociate to mentally 'escape' from the trauma.[20] Due to its wide-ranging effects, complex trauma is often not fully captured by a diagnosis of PTSD.[21] Common causes include various forms of abuse, neglect and exposure to domestic violence.[22]

Perpetration-induced traumatic stress (PITS)

PITS describes the trauma that can be experienced by individuals who have committed acts of violence, such as in military combat or abuse. First identified in Vietnam War veterans, research has shown that those involved in killing or violence can experience severe PTSD symptoms, along with feelings of shame and guilt. However, more research is needed in this area to better understand its full implications.[23]

Collective trauma

Collective trauma affects groups or societies through events such as mass violence, war, terrorism, pandemics or natural disasters. It can also include historical and racial trauma. According to Erikson (1976), collective trauma damages the social fabric, weakening community ties and affecting social cohesion, norms and values.[24] It can undermine trust in society and disrupt the individual's sense of security, belonging and meaning. Unlike individual trauma, which creates personal vulnerability, collective trauma creates a sense of widespread insecurity.[25] As Walecki (2022) notes, "individual trauma says, 'I am not safe,' collective trauma says, 'no one is.'"[26]

Collective trauma can persist beyond the lifetimes of those directly affected, with narratives evolving across generations and potentially leading to destructive trauma dynamics.[27] Recent global events, such as the Covid-19 pandemic, have introduced new forms of 'cascading' or 'cumulative' collective trauma, where multiple successive traumas have a compounding effect.[28]

Responses to trauma

The 6 F's

When a person experiences a traumatic event, the body's primary goal is to protect itself by perceiving a threat, responding to it and returning the body to a balanced state as quickly as possible.[29] This can be done through a series of instinctive survival responses, often referred to as the 6 F's: Friend, Fight, Flight, Freeze, Flop and Faint, as illustrated in Figure A.1.[30]

The brain and body's responses to threat are not conscious decisions, but instinctive responses triggered by the amygdala – the brain's 'fear centre' – which rapidly assesses danger based on sensory input and past experience. It is therefore important not to judge or blame a person for their instinctive reactions.[31]

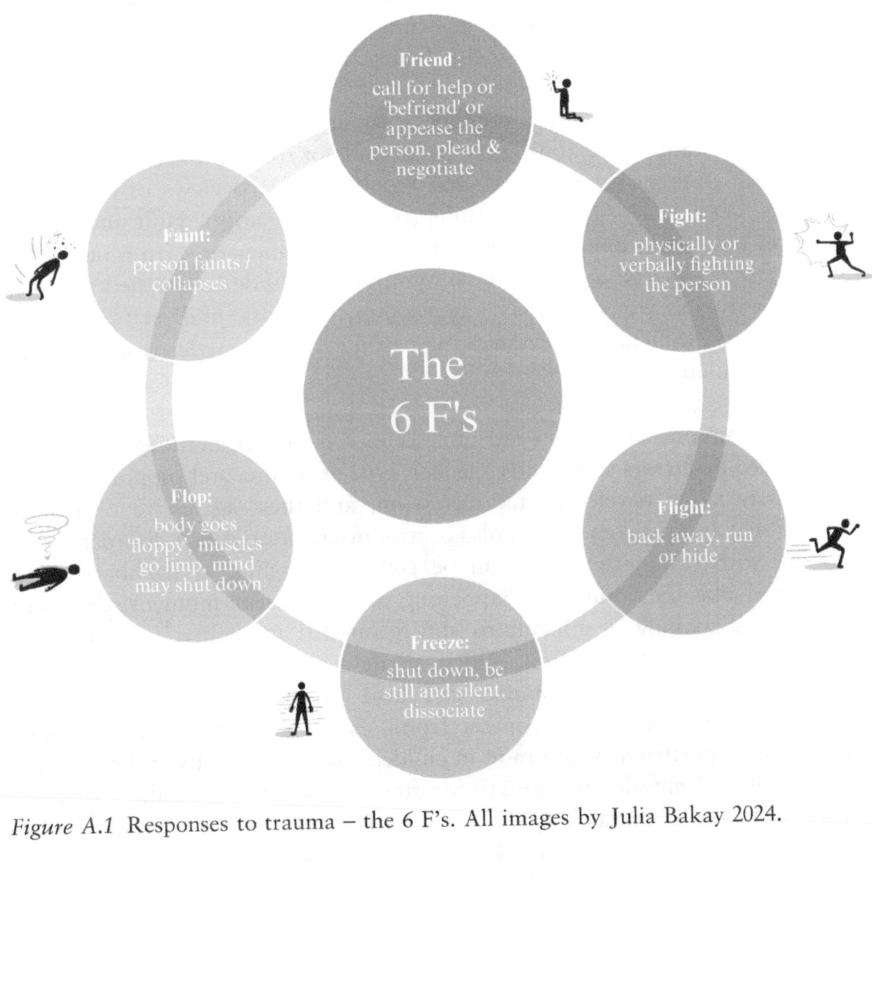

Figure A.1 Responses to trauma – the 6 F's. All images by Julia Bakay 2024.

How do traumatic stress or PTSD develop?

When the adaptive responses of the brain and body to a threat are overwhelmed or ineffective, and an individual's ability to cope is exceeded, the stress response can become prolonged and lead to traumatic stress. This transition from normal stress to traumatic stress is characterised by an inability to return to a balanced state. Stress hormones remain elevated, causing serious disruptions in the body's systems and leading to ongoing stress responses that interfere with normal functioning. Key factors that increase the risk of traumatic stress include the intensity of the stressor, the individual's age, previous traumatic experiences and lack of social support.[32]

Traumatic stress can develop into PTSD when the symptoms last for more than a month and significantly interfere with the person's daily life and the person exhibits at least one or two symptoms of each of the four categories defined in the DSM-V manual.[33]

1 *Intrusion*: Unwanted and intrusive thoughts and memories of the traumatic event, which may manifest as nightmares or flashbacks (involving any of the five senses, particularly smell). It may feel as if the trauma is recurring or ongoing.
2 *Avoidance*: Efforts to avoid reminders, thoughts or feelings associated with the trauma. Substance abuse may be an attempt to suppress these memories.
3 *Negative changes in cognitions and mood*: Distorted views of oneself and others, persistent negative emotions (such as fear, anger, guilt and shame), loss of interest in daily activities and a sense of alienation from others.
4 *Changes in arousal and reactivity*: Symptoms include heightened alertness, irritability, angry outbursts, aggression, reckless and self-destructive behaviour, difficulty concentrating, exaggerated startle responses and sleep problems.[34]

Trauma symptoms in children and adolescents can differ from those in adults and are influenced by factors such as age, gender, type of trauma and support. Younger children may show developmental regression, and their aggressive or irritable behaviour may be mistaken for impulse control or attention deficit disorders.[35]

Coping with traumatic stress can be very challenging, as flashbacks often make it feel like the trauma is happening in the present moment, disrupting daily life and making it difficult to stay grounded in reality.[36] Another significant challenge is dissociation, which, while a natural coping mechanism to distance oneself from the trauma, can lead to memory lapses, emotional numbing, and a sense of detachment from oneself and one's surroundings.[37] Dissociation is particularly common in children and can negatively impact their development and emotional regulation, often persisting into adulthood. However, dissociation is treatable.[38]

The impact of trauma

Traumatic stress leaves deep marks on the brain, body, memory and relationships, profoundly altering each of these areas. The following sections explore how these impacts manifest and the different ways in which trauma can affect individuals.

Effects on the brain

Trauma, and particularly chronic traumatic stress, can cause both chemical and structural changes in the brain that profoundly affect its functioning.[39] Key areas such as the prefrontal cortex, hippocampus and amygdala are particularly affected by these changes and play a crucial role in stress responses. Figure A.2 illustrates their normal functions in the absence of trauma.[40]

As shown in Figure A.2, these three brain areas – the prefrontal cortex, hippocampus and amygdala – are essential for regulating emotions, behaviour, rational thought and learning. Trauma can profoundly disrupt the functioning of these areas, impairing their ability to perform these critical tasks effectively.

Prefrontal cortex: Traumatic stress can reduce the volume, activity and connectivity of the prefrontal cortex, the brain's rational centre. As this area

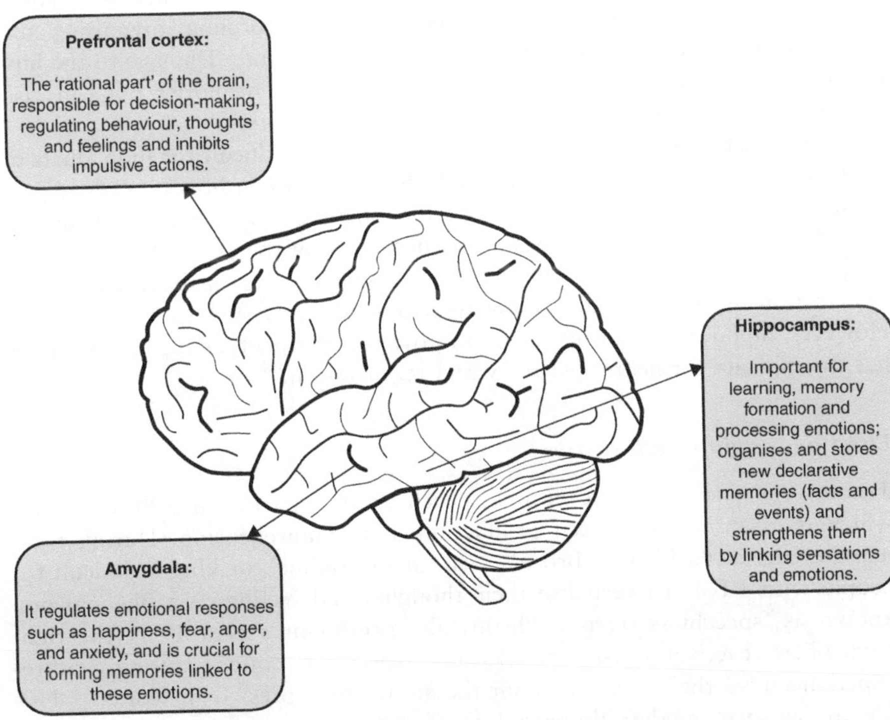

Figure A.2 Normal functioning of prefrontal cortex, amygdala and hippocampus

becomes less active, the brain shifts to survival responses driven by the amygdala. This impairs the ability to regulate behaviour, fear and emotions, affecting concentration, rational thinking, decision-making and impulse control. As a result, people may react in an impulsive rather than a thoughtful way. A less active prefrontal cortex also makes it more difficult to process traumatic experiences rationally, as it becomes harder to override the danger signals sent by the amygdala, even in the face of perceived threats. Trauma can also increase the risk of substance abuse as a coping mechanism.[41]

The amygdala: Trauma can cause the amygdala to become overactive and enlarged, triggering stress responses even to perceived threats.[42] This means that neutral stimuli (such as sounds, smells, images or touch), when associated with past trauma, can evoke fear, leading to fight-or-flight reactions and prolonged stress responses that increase post-traumatic symptoms. When the prefrontal cortex is impaired, people may react with 'survival instincts', leading to heightened reactions such as being easily startled, becoming irritable or freezing. An overactive amygdala not only increases emotional responses but also affects the hippocampus, as these two regions are closely connected. The amygdala's influence on the hippocampus can make fear-related memories more vivid and persistent.[43]

The hippocampus: Trauma can cause the hippocampus to shrink, making it difficult to remember important details or events, which can increase anxiety and stress.[44] This affects the hippocampus's role in forming, organising and retrieving memories, as well as regulating stress hormones. Damage to the hippocampus not only disrupts the ability to form new memories but can also increase stress hormone levels, further impairing memory.[45]

Trauma's effect on the hippocampus also makes it difficult for individuals to distinguish between past and present, which can lead to flashbacks – where past memories are experienced as if they were happening now. This reactivates the amygdala, triggering fear responses and perpetuating the cycle of trauma.[46] In addition, a smaller hippocampus can cause survivors to misinterpret neutral information as threatening, leading to increased aggression or withdrawal.[47] However, hippocampal shrinkage is not always permanent, as the hippocampus has the capacity for neural plasticity and regeneration.[48]

Effect on certain speech centres

Trauma can also affect the brain's speech centres, particularly Broca's area, which is essential for speech production and comprehension. During traumatic events or flashbacks, Broca's area can go 'offline', making it difficult for people with PTSD to verbalise their thoughts and feelings – a phenomenon known as 'speechless terror'. Meanwhile, Brodmann's area 19 in the right hemisphere reactivates visual and sensory aspects of trauma, causing vivid re-experiencing of the trauma without the ability to express it in words.[49] This impairment also hinders the encoding of conscious memories and the development of a coherent narrative, which is essential for trauma processing and psychological healing.[50] As a result, survivors may find it difficult to talk about their trauma, often feeling disconnected from their emotions or describing the experience as if it had happened to someone else.[51]

Effects on the body

Trauma can have significant effects on the immune, cardiovascular, digestive and reproductive systems, as well as on metabolism and neural function. Prolonged stress leads to increased levels of stress hormones such as adrenaline and cortisol, which can strain the cardiovascular system, disrupt digestion and impair reproductive functions.[52] These hormones also suppress protein production, weakening the immune system and increasing susceptibility to disease. The body's constant state of heightened alert due to these hormonal changes can lead to metabolic disorders and a range of physical health problems, highlighting the strong link between chronic stress, such as traumatic stress, and disease.[53]

Effects on the memory

As illustrated by the effects of trauma on the amygdala and hippocampus, trauma significantly impacts memory by disrupting the way experiences are encoded, stored and retrieved. Memory can be categorised into explicit (conscious and generally verbally accessible) and implicit (unconscious and situationally triggered) types, each with its own subtypes and neural underpinnings.[54]

Explicit memory includes:

- *Declarative (semantic) memory*: This involves the recall of factual information and is often less emotionally charged. Trauma can impair the formation and integration of these memories, leading to difficulties in organising and recalling coherent facts.
- *Episodic (autobiographical) memory*: This type includes personal experiences and their emotional context. Trauma fragments or shuts down these memories, making them vivid but disconnected, mixing past and present experiences. This fragmentation can result in flashbacks where past traumas are relived as if they were happening now, perpetuating ongoing distress.[55]

Implicit memory includes:

- *Emotional memory*: This memory stores the emotions experienced during events. Trauma can intensify these memories, making them highly responsive to triggers such as sounds or smells, which can evoke intense emotional responses without a clear context.
- *Procedural memory*: This type deals with habits and skills. Trauma can alter procedural memories, affecting automatic responses and behaviours. These changes often manifest as heightened survival instincts or maladaptive behaviours that affect the way individuals interact with their environment.[56]

Traumatic memories are a powerful form of implicit memory, often triggered by high levels of cortisol released during extreme stress, which "affect the function of the hippocampus and impede consolidation of explicit memory".[57] Trauma disrupts the brain's normal pathways for processing and integrating memories, making it difficult to distinguish between past and present events. During trauma, the release of cortisol impairs the formation of explicit, conscious memories, while adrenaline enhances implicit memories, leading to intrusive sensations or images that seem to appear out of nowhere. This disruption makes it difficult for individuals to switch between implicit and explicit types of memory, preventing the integration of traumatic experiences into a coherent narrative and causing ongoing distress, as if the trauma were constantly being replayed in the present.[58]

The impact on relationships

Trauma can also have a profound effect on an individual's ability to form and maintain healthy relationships. Some of the ways in which trauma can manifest itself in relationships include:

Altered thought processes and trust issues:

- Trauma can fundamentally change the way individuals view themselves, others and the world, often leading to trust issues. For example, a person who has experienced betrayal may find it difficult to trust or let others in for fear of harm or disappointment.[59]
- Survivors may develop rigid, negative beliefs about relationships, expecting rejection or abandonment and avoiding intimacy to protect themselves.[60]

Hypervigilance and emotional reactions:

- Trauma often activates the amygdala, keeping the individual in a state of hyperarousal, which can cause disproportionate reactions to perceived threats in relationships. These responses may cause others to get frustrated or angry.[61]
- Shame-based responses are common, where trauma survivors may feel unworthy or flawed, making them prone to defensive reactions, hiding their true selves, or using addictive behaviours to cope.[62]

Avoidance behaviours:

- Avoidance is a common response to trauma; individuals may avoid people, places or conversations that trigger distressing memories. While this may initially reduce anxiety, over time it can lead to increased isolation and difficulty maintaining emotional connections.[63]
- Avoidance can take several forms, such as avoiding emotionally charged conversations in intimate relationships or avoiding places that evoke trauma.[64]

Attachment styles:

- Trauma, particularly in childhood, can significantly influence adult attachment styles. Insecure attachment styles (anxious, dismissive-avoidant, fearful-avoidant) often present unique challenges in relationships, such as fear of abandonment, difficulty with emotional intimacy or mistrust of partners. These patterns are not conscious choices but are shaped by early life experiences.[65]

Trauma re-enactment:

- Trauma survivors may unconsciously seek out relationships that mirror their traumatic experiences, a phenomenon known as trauma re-enactment. This can lead to repeated involvement in unhealthy relationships, such as those that involve emotional or physical harm.[66]
- Trauma bonding can lead individuals to feel attracted to partners who are inconsistent or abusive, reinforcing dysfunctional patterns and making it difficult to leave unhealthy relationships.[67]

Communication challenges:

- Trauma can affect communication styles, making it difficult for survivors to express emotions or engage constructively in conflict resolution. They may re-enact communication patterns learned in childhood, such as aggression or passivity, which can lead to misunderstandings and conflict in relationships.[68]

Impact on emotional regulation and mental health:

- Trauma can disrupt the development of emotional intelligence, impairing the ability to manage emotions, empathise and communicate effectively in relationships.[69]
- There is a notable association between trauma and mental health conditions such as anxiety and depression, which can further complicate interpersonal relationships.[70]

Trust issues and isolation:

- Trauma can lead to social isolation, as survivors may have experienced significant betrayal, feel misunderstood or fear being a burden to others. Trauma survivors often have difficulty forming or relying on supportive relationships due to trust issues or fear of rejection.[71]
- The difficulty trauma survivors have in sharing their feelings and experiences can also lead to isolation.[72]

Summary of symptoms

As the previous section has illustrated, trauma impacts individuals in many different ways. Figure A.3 summarises some of the common symptoms:

Emotional

- Intense emotions, such as fear, anxiety, anger, or sadness, often without clear triggers or seemingly disproportionate
- Feelings of numbness, detachment, dissociation, emotional shutdown or overwhelm (hyper- or hypoarousal)
- Guilt, shame, or feeling undeserving of safety or love, mood swings, irritability

Physical

- Chronic fatigue or pain, headaches, digestive or cardiovascular problems, muscle tension, weakened immune system
- Sleep disturbances (e.g., insomnia, nightmares) and changes in appetite (may lead to eating disorders) or sexual activity
- Heightened startle responses, sweating, heart palpitations (often as part of hyperarousal or anxiety)

Cognitive

- Problems with memory, concentration, rational thinking and decision-making
- Persistent worry or negative thoughts, such as self-blame, fear of recurrence, or feelings of helplessness and powerlessness
- Cognitive distortions (e.g. viewing the world as entirely dangerous or oneself as permanently damaged)

Behavioural

- Avoidance of people, places or activities that remind them of the trauma, withdrawal from social or intimate situations
- Increased use of substances like alcohol or drugs as a coping mechanism, engaging in high-risk behaviours
- Angry outbursts, argumentativeness, difficulty communication emotions, potentially leading to strained relationships

Existential

- Questioning of life's meaning, purpose, personal beliefs
- Questions such as "why me?"
- Feelings of hopelessness or cynicism
- Loss of faith in others or humanity; increased reliance on spiritual practices as a coping mechanism

Figure A.3 Common trauma symptoms
Source: Adapted from SAMHSA (2014).

Conclusion

Understanding trauma and its pervasive effects on the brain, body and relationships is essential for restorative justice practitioners to understand the rationale behind trauma-informed practices and to implement them effectively. Trauma is a complex and deeply personal experience that can significantly alter an individual's emotional, cognitive and physiological functioning. Recognising the different types of trauma and the unique ways in which trauma manifests allows practitioners to approach individuals with greater understanding and allows them to provide support tailored to their specific needs. By acknowledging both the immediate and long-term effects of trauma, practitioners can better understand and respond to the common reactions of trauma survivors without taking potentially harsh reactions personally. This knowledge forms the basis for promoting a safe and supportive environment for all those affected by trauma.

Notes

1 Herman (1997).
2 SAMHSA (2014), p. 7.
3 American Psychological Association (2024).
4 Barbash (2017).
5 SAMHSA (2014), p. 7.
6 Maté (2022).
7 Maté (2022).
8 Cozolino (2010).
9 SAMHSA (2014).
10 Klinic Community Health Centre (2013).
11 Klinic Community Health Centre (2013).
12 Van der Kolk (2014).
13 Herman (1997).
14 Klinic Community Health Centre (2013).
15 SAMHSA (2014).
16 SAMHSA (2014).
17 Columbia Center for EMDR Therapy (n.d.); SAMHSA (2014), p. 7.
18 Ford et al. (2015); NCTSN (2003).
19 Ford et al. (2015); NCTSN (2003).
20 Cozolino (2010).
21 Cruz et al. (2022); Ford et al. (2015); NCTSN (2003).
22 Cruz et al. (2022).
23 MacNair (2002, 2015).
24 Erikson (1976).
25 Veerman and Ganzevoort (2001).
26 Walecki (2022).
27 Hirschberger (2018).
28 Harvard School of Public Health (2022).
29 Cozolino (2006).
30 Based on: Rape Crisis England and Wales (2022); Van der Kolk (2014).
31 Cozolino (2006).
32 Richter-Levin and Sandi (2021); Van der Kolk (2014).
33 American Psychiatric Association (2013).
34 American Psychiatric Association (2013).

35 Arnsten et al. (2015).
36 Cozolino (2010); Van der Kolk (2014).
37 Van der Kolk (2014).
38 Beacon House (2020); Choi et al. (2017).
39 Arnsten et al. (2015).
40 Based on: Arnsten et al. (2015); Guy-Evans (2023a, 2023b).
41 Arnsten et al. (2015); McAdam (2022); Van der Kolk (2014).
42 Cozolino (2006).
43 Guy-Evans (2023b); Van der Kolk (2014).
44 Cozolino (2006); Rousseau (2023).
45 Rousseau (2023).
46 McAdam (2022); Van der Kolk (2014).
47 Cozolino (2006); Van der Kolk (2000).
48 Bremner (2006); Van der Kolk (2000).
49 Van der Kolk (2014).
50 Cozolino (2010).
51 Van der Kolk (2014).
52 To understand the effect of trauma on the body it is important to understand the role of the hypothalamic-pituitary-adrenal (HPA) axis, which is a complex system that regulates the body's stress response by controlling the release of stress hormones. For further reading see, for example: Chu et al. (2024); Sheng et al. (2021).
53 Chu et al. (2024); Cozolino (2006); Sheng et al. (2021).
54 Blueknot Foundation (2018); Government of Canada (2023); Levine (2015).
55 Blueknot Foundation (2018); Iffland and Neuner (2016); Levine (2015); NICABM (2017).
56 Blueknot Foundation (2018); Levine (2015); NICABM (2017).
57 Blueknot Foundation (2018), p. 52
58 Blueknot Foundation (2018); Levine (2015); NICABM (2017); Van der Kolk (2014).
59 Gupta (2023).
60 Greenberg (2019).
61 Gupta (2023).
62 Greenberg (2019).
63 SAMHSA (2014).
64 SAMHSA (2014).
65 Lebow (2021).
66 Lebow (2021).
67 Greenberg (2019).
68 Lebow (2021).
69 Lebow (2021).
70 Lebow (2021).
71 SAMHSA (2014).
72 Gupta (2023).

References

American Psychiatric Association. (2013). *Diagnostic and statistical manual of mental disorders: DSM-5^{TM}* (5th ed.). American Psychiatric Publishing. https://doi.org/10.1176/appi.books.9780890425596

American Psychological Association. (2024). *Trauma*. www.apa.org/topics/trauma

Arnsten, A. F., Raskind, M. A., Taylor, F. B., & Connor, D. F. (2015). The effects of stress exposure on prefrontal cortex: Translating basic research into successful treatments for post-traumatic stress disorder. *Neurobiology of Stress*, 1, 89–99. https://doi.org/10.1016/j.ynstr.2014.10.002

Barbash, E. (2017, March 13). *Different types of trauma: Small 't' versus large 'T'*. Psychology Today. www.psychologytoday.com/us/blog/trauma-and-hope/201703/different-types-trauma-small-t-versus-large-t

Beacon House. (2020). *Dissociation in children and teens*. https://beaconhouse.org.uk/wp-content/uploads/2020/02/Dissociation-in-Children-Teens-Resource_compressed.pdf

Blueknot Foundation. (2018). *Talking about trauma: Guide to conversations and screening for health and other service providers*. Blue Knot Foundation.

Bremner, D. J. (2006). Traumatic stress: Effects on the brain. *Dialogues in Clinical Neuroscience*, 8(4), 445–461.

Choi, K. R., Seng, J. S., Briggs, E. C., Munro-Kramer, M. L., Graham-Bermann, S. A., Lee, R. C., & Ford, J. D. (2017). The dissociative subtype of posttraumatic stress disorder (PTSD) among adolescents: Co-occurring PTSD, depersonalization/derealization, and other dissociation symptoms. *Journal of the American Academy of Child and Adolescent Psychiatry*, 56(12), 1062–1072. https://doi.org/10.1016/j.jaac.2017.09.425

Chu, B., Marwaha, K., Sanvictores, T., Awosika, A. O., & Ayers, D. (2024, May 7). *Physiology, stress reaction*. www.ncbi.nlm.nih.gov/books/NBK541120

Columbia Center for EMDR Therapy. (n.d.) *What's the difference between chronic trauma and complex trauma?*www.columbiaemdr.com/single-post/what-s-the-difference-between-chronic-trauma-and-complex-trauma

Cozolino, L. (2006). *The neuroscience of human relationships: Attachment and the developing social brain*. W. W Norton & Company.

Cozolino, L. (2010). *The neuroscience of psychotherapy: Healing the social brain* (2nd ed.). W. W. Norton & Company.

Cruz, D., Lichten, M., Berg, K., & George, P. (2022). Developmental trauma: Conceptual framework, associated risks and comorbidities, and evaluation and treatment. *Frontiers in Psychiatry*, 13, Article 800687. https://doi.org/10.3389/fpsyt.2022.800687

Erikson, K. (1976). *Everything in its path*. Simon & Schuster.

Ford, J. D., Grasso, D. J., Elhai, J. D., & Courtois, C. A. (2015). Understanding psychological trauma and posttraumatic stress disorder (PTSD). In J. D. Ford, D. J. Grasso, J. D. Elhai & C. A. Courtois, *Posttraumatic stress disorder* (2nd ed., pp. 1–42). Academic Press.

Government of Canada. (2023). *Part III – How trauma affects memory and recall*. www.justice.gc.ca/eng/rp-pr/jr/trauma/p4.html

Greenberg, M. (2019, August 13). *How traumas create negative patterns in relationships*. Psychology Today. www.psychologytoday.com/us/blog/the-mindful-self-express/201908/how-traumas-create-negative-patterns-in-relationships

Gupta, S. (2023, August 24). *How trauma can affect your relationship*. Verywell Mind. www.verywellmind.com/how-trauma-impacts-relationships-6745693

Guy-Evans, O. (2023a). *Hippocampus Anatomy, Function, Location and Damage*. SimplyPsychology. www.simplypsychology.org/hippocampus.html.

Guy-Evans, O. (2023b). *Amygdala: What it is & its functions*. SimplyPsychology. www.simplypsychology.org/amygdala.html

Harvard School of Public Health. (2022, November 1). *The mental health toll of cascading collective trauma*. www.hsph.harvard.edu/news/hsph-in-the-news/the-mental-health-toll-of-cascading-collective-trauma/

Herman, J. L. (1997). *Trauma and recovery: The aftermath of violence, from domestic abuse to political terror*. Basic Books.

Hirschberger, G. (2018) Collective trauma and the social construction of meaning. *Frontiers in Psychology*, 9, Article 1441. https://doi.org/10.3389/fpsyg.2018.01441

Iffland, B., & Neuner, F. (2016). Trauma and memory. In G. Fink (Ed.), *Stress: Concepts, cognition, emotion, and behavior* (pp. 161–167). Academic Press. https://doi.org/10.1016/B978-0-12-800951-2.00019-4

Klinic Community Health Centre. (2013). *Trauma-informed: The trauma toolkit* (2nd ed.). www.ctctbay.org/application/files/3615/4160/0382/The_Trauma-Informed_Toolkit_Second_Edition.pdf

Lebow, H. I. (2021, June 10). *How childhood trauma may affect adult relationships.* PsychCentral. https://psychcentral.com/blog/how-childhood-trauma-affects-adult-relationships

Levine, P. A. (2015). *Trauma and memory: Brain and body in a search for the living past: A practical guide for understanding and working with traumatic memory.* North Atlantic Books.

MacNair, R. (2002). The effects of violence on perpetrators. *Peace Review*, 14(1), 67–72. https://doi.org/10.1080/10402650220118224

MacNair, R. (2015). Causing trauma as a form of trauma. *Peace and Conflict: Journal of Peace Psychology*, 21(3), 313–321.

Maté, G. (2022, September 17). *All of us store trauma in our bodies.* Maria Shriver's Sunday Paper. www.mariashriversundaypaper.com/dr-gabor-mate

McAdam, E. (2022, April 14). *How trauma and PTSD change the brain.* [Video]. YouTube. www.youtube.com/watch?v=wdUR69J2u6c

National Child Traumatic Stress Network (NCTSN). (2003). *Complex Trauma in Children and Adolescents.* White paper. National Child Traumatic Stress Network.

National Institute for the Clinical Application of Behavioral Medicine (NICABM). (2017). *How trauma can impact four different types of memory.* www.nicabm.com/trauma-how-trauma-can-impact-4-types-of-memory-infographic

Rape Crisis England and Wales. (2022). *The 5 Fs: Fight, flight, freeze, flop and friend.* https://rapecrisis.org.uk/get-help/tools-for-victims-and-survivors/understanding-your-response/fight-or-flight

Richter-Levin, G., & Sandi, C. (2021). Labels matter: Is it stress or is it trauma? *Translational Psychiatry*, 11, Article 385. https://doi.org/10.1038/s41398-021-01514-4

Rousseau, D. (2023). *The effect of trauma on the brain.* Boston University. https://sites.bu.edu/daniellerousseau/2023/12/13/the-effect-of-trauma-on-the-brain

Sheng, J. A., Bales, N. J., Myers, S. A., Bautista, A. I., Roueinfar, M., Hale, T. M., & Handa, R. J. (2021). The hypothalamic-pituitary-adrenal axis: Development, programming actions of hormones, and maternal-fetal interactions. *Frontiers in Behavioral Neuroscience*, 14, Article 601939. https://doi.org/10.3389/fnbeh.2020.601939

Substance Abuse and Mental Health Services Administration (SAMHSA). (2014). *Trauma-informed care in behavioral health services. TIP 57.* www.ncbi.nlm.nih.gov/books/NBK207201/pdf/Bookshelf_NBK207201.pdf

Van der Kolk, B. (2000). Posttraumatic stress disorder and the nature of trauma. *Dialogues in Clinical Neuroscience*, 2(1), 7–22. https://doi.org/10.31887/DCNS.2000.2.1/bvdkolk

Van der Kolk, B. (2014). *The body keeps the score: Mind, brain and body in the transformation of trauma.* Penguin Books.

Veerman, A. L., & Ganzevoort, R. R. (2001). Communities coping with collective trauma. *Psychiatry*, 101, 141–148.

Walecki, N. (2022, October 26). *Special report: The hellish new trauma of living through multiple mass tragedies at once.* Cosmopolitan. www.cosmopolitan.com/lifestyle/a41428491/mass-tragedy-trauma

Index

Page numbers in *italics* denote figures, those in **bold** denote tables.

For Product Safety Concerns and Information please contact our
EU representative GPSR@taylorandfrancis.com Taylor & Francis
Verlag GmbH, Kaufingerstraße 24, 80331 München, Germany